MW01671304

Financial Instruments and Services

Financial Instruments and Services

Nalini Prava Tripathy

Reader
Postgraduate Department of Business Administration
Regional College of Management
Bhubaneswar

Prentice-Hall of India Private Limited
New Delhi - 110 001
2007

Rs. 175.00

FINANCIAL INSTRUMENTS AND SERVICES
Nalini Prava Tripathy

© 2004 by Prentice-Hall of India Private Limited, New Delhi. All rights reserved. No part of this book may be reproduced in any form, by mimeograph or any other means, without permission in writing from the publisher.

ISBN-978-81-203-2651-4

The export rights of this book are vested solely with the publisher.

Second Printing ... ... February, 2007

Published by Asoke K. Ghosh, Prentice-Hall of India Private Limited, M-97, Connaught Circus, New Delhi-110001 and Printed by Mudrak, 30-A, Patparganj, Delhi-110091.

Dedicated to my Dearest Friend who Bestowed on me the Inspiration and Strength to take up this work.

—Nalini Prava Tripathy

Contents

Chapter 13 Foreign Direct Investment in India 174–185

Preface

The last decade witnessed sea changes in the economic and financial services environment all over the world. With the liberalization sweeping over general and financial sector in particular, the financial service sector is set for a spectacular transformation. Financial sector has become more customer-friendly, offering a wide range of products through multiple delivery channels. The new and versatile financial instruments have given an impetus to the growth of financial innovations. The boom in the financial services companies is no doubt a welcome development. But at the same time, they require special skills to run financial services efficiently.

The prime objective of the book is to provide executives and management students an insight into the principles, operational policies, and practices of the financial services sector to meet the growing needs of the economy. The text has been divided into 13 chapters. All the chapters are organized fairly independent of each other and any chapter can be picked to gain knowledge about one particular topic without disrupting the continuity. Chapter 1 provides an overview of the financial market. It discusses and analyzes in brief, the first and second phases of reforms. The chapter outlines the emerging challenges in the second phase of reforms. The topics discussed delineate the operation and functioning of Indian capital market for an accelerated economic growth and overall development of the polity, society, and economy.

Chapter 2 deals precisely with the working of SEBI, which is the development agency of capital market and stock exchanges in India. Chapter 3 discusses stock exchanges which act as the barometer of general economic progress in a country. It treats stock exchanges as exerting a powerful influence and significant impact as a depressant or stimulant of business transactions and activities, as the case may be. Chapter 4 narrates about India's first unlisted security market which gave a new dimension to the financial sector with the objective of providing an opportunity to small companies to acquire public fund at low cost. Chapter 5 highlights that mutual funds came into existence to cater to the needs of vast Indian population by assuring a reasonable capital appreciation on the investment and also to provide a regular dividend at periodic intervals. Chapter 6 speaks of merchant banking as a service function which is engaged in providing a wide spectrum of financial and related services to their customers.

Chapter 7 discusses the concept of venture capital and how its purview is limited by high technology as well as adoption of risky ideas and practices which are usually confined to small scale enterprises operating with new ideas and technologies. It also substantiates that in the rapidly changing economic environment, quick industrialization and promotion of entrepreneurship roster the deepening of venture capital services. Chapter 8 encompasses credit rating which provides value-added information to the Indian economy, capital markets, industry and companies through various products and services. Credit rating spurs impetus to investors to channalize the inflow of savings into capital market activities which result in productive use of funds. Chapter 9 adumbrates factoring, which provides a new a venue of finance that is of immense benefit to industries inter alia helping in systematizing trade credit in India. Chapter 10 highlights that forfeiting business is accelerating mainly with a view to boosting export trade.

Chapter 11 covers the topic of lease financing leading to recognization as an attractive alternative to debt financing in India with the ever-increasing use of leasing by industrial units for the purpose of acquisition of fixed assets. The chapter details how "lease versus buy" decision making strongly favours lease. Chapter 12 explains that securitization is facilitating the transfer of capital from non-performing and idle assets to performing more efficient assets which help the economy to develop at a faster rate. The last chapter is devoted to FDI in India and abroad. It points out to the fact that some structural issues need to be addressed to avail the full potential of this dominant kind of investment.

In the book, all the relevant issues and their implications have been put in perspective as to the financial innovation in terms of products and instruments. The text proceeds to streamline the regulatory framework with latest sophisticated developments in their respective fields. The text is presented in a lucid manner and simple language to meet the specific needs of the academic community as well as corporate world. The text certainly acts as a catalyst, motivator, and facilitator thereby leading the students to pursue a well deserved career in today's dynamic and innovative financial system for desired economic growth.

I hope this book will definitely go a long way to create sustained interest and curiosity in the minds of the readers and students in particular as it would supplement and enrich the corpus of existing literature on the subject—financial services.

I have great pleasure and pride to acclaim my profuse thanks and good wishes to Prentice-Hall of India for bringing out the book in a record time. Last but not least, I have to keep in record that I am solely responsible for any inconsistencies or errors/omissions that have crept inadvertently in the publication. At the same time, I look forward to constructive suggestions and opinions from readers to improve the text.

Nalini Prava Tripathy

Chapter 1

Financial Market in India

1.1 INTRODUCTION

Financial deregulation and innovations have changed the whole structure and functioning of financial markets of many industrialized countries since the beginning of 1970s. This trend also influenced the growth of financial systems of several countries in the Asia–Pacific region during 1980s. Indian financial market has been going through a fascinating phase and it throws open excellent business opportunities to the financial service sectors. Financial system in India has made commendable progress in extending its geographical spread and functional reach.

1.2 FINANCIAL SECTOR REFORMS

The growth and evolution of financial market in India since the 1950s can be viewed in three broad phases. The first two decades of the 1950s and 1960s constitute a *phase of transition*. The period from 1969 to 1985, a span of a decade and a half, can be called the *period of expansion and diversification*. The subsequent period after 1985 has been marked by *consolidation, innovation, and liberalization*. The first of these three phases witnessed strengthening of the banking system by a process of amalgamation of weak, small banks as also through development of major term lending institutions, with active intervention by the Reserve Bank of India, in consonance with its developmental role. Special efforts were also made during this period to strengthen the cooperative financial structure. With the 'big push' provided by the nationalization of banks and introduction of the Lead Bank scheme, the fifteen year period from 1969 through to 1985 saw an unprecedented geographical expansion and functional diversification of the commercial banking system. This period also marked not only a very rapid expansion of branch network of banks, but also a complete re-orientation of their lending operations, seeking to combine socio-economic national aspirations with banking and at the same time, an increasing role in funding the public sector. In the present phase of growth of the financial market which started from 1985, the stress on efficiency and competitiveness has been conducive to relaxations in the control mechanism and allowing for innovation, diversification, and healthy competition among banks and other financial institutions. A series of policy changes which are under implementation, have been introduced, encompassing several sectors of the financial system. This is in consonance with the economic liberalization measures adopted with regard to industry, external trade, and technology.

In the evolution of economic institutions, development of corporate form of organization marks the turning point in triggering rapid industrialization and economic growth. This organization has flourished on account of several positive features such as limited liability, separation of ownership and management, and easy transferability of ownership interest. The growth of capital market, where the ownership interest is initially sold and later traded is, therefore an essential prerequisite for faster industrial growth.

The Government of India implemented the economic reforms, including financial sector reforms, with the object of improving efficiency and effectiveness of the financial system. It was also aimed at conceding operational freedom for flexibility to the financial system through prudential regulation and supervision in a free financial environment. The last two decades have seen a phenomenal expansion in the geographical coverage and financial spread of our financial system. The development of the financial sector is a major achievement and has contributed significantly to the increase in our savings rate, especially of the household sector. A financial system essentially comprises the financial institutions, instruments, and the market that together provide the necessary framework for mobilization and allocation of savings. A vibrant, efficient, and innovative financial system is the key to the rapid and sustained growth of the economy. Financial service is a segment of the financial system as shown in Fig. 1.1.

The financial system consists of organized sector and unorganized sector. Unorganized financial system comprises money lenders, indigenous bankers, lending pawn brokers, land lords, traders etc. This part of the financial system is not directly under the control of Reserve Bank of India. On the other hand, the organized financial system comprises money market, capital market, new

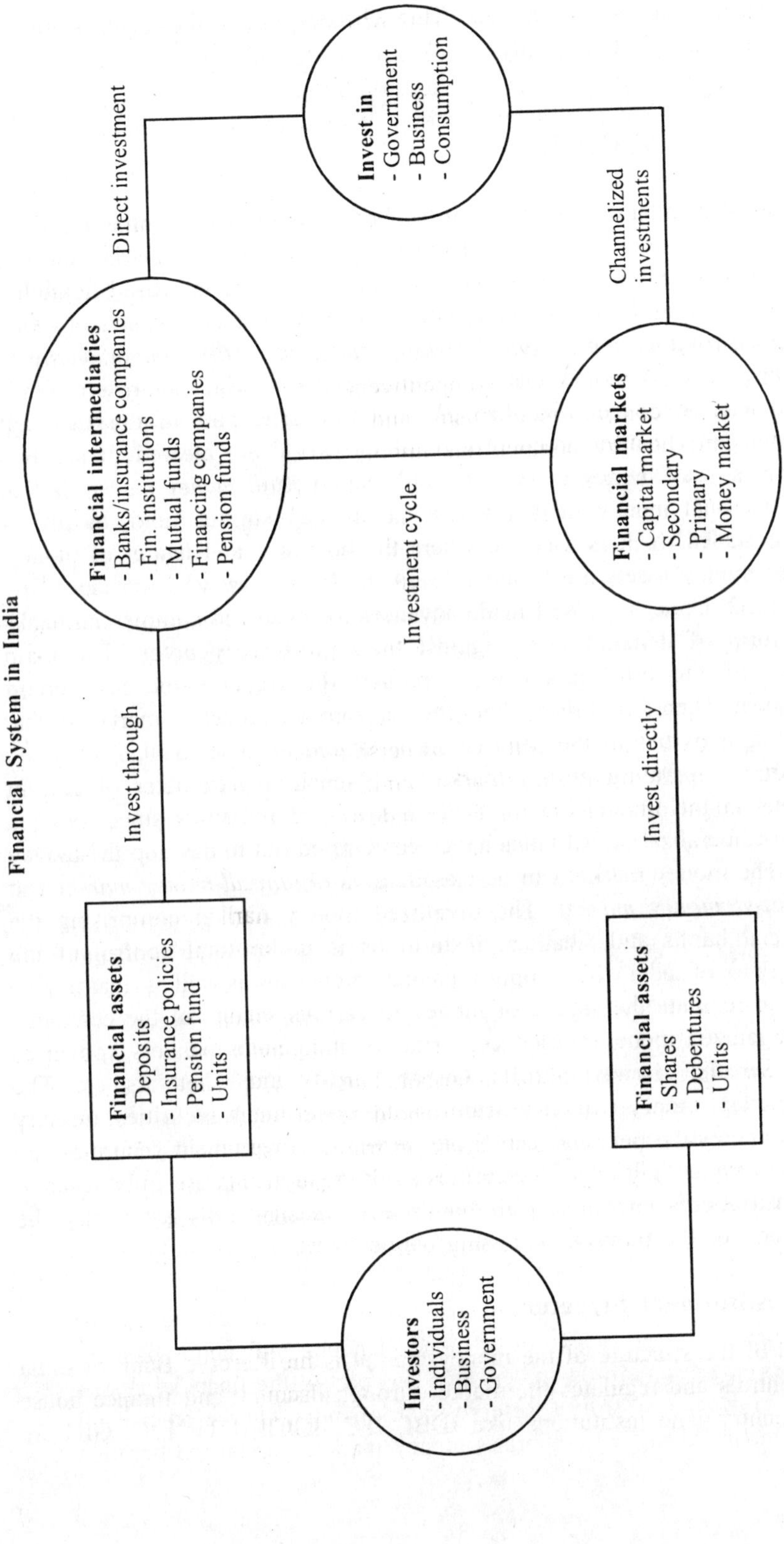

Source: Mutual Funds Management & Working Book, 1996, p. 3.

Fig. 1.1 Financial system in India.

issue market, and stock market. This chapter limits the discussions to organized financial system only.

1.3 MONEY MARKET

The position of money markets in our economy system has become important with the recent liberalization of monetary policies. Money market ensures efficient functioning of the financial system and provides increased flexibility in banks operation. J.S.G. Wilson defined money market as a "*centre in which financial institutions congregate for the purpose of dealing impersonally in monetary assets*". A money market is a mechanism in which short-term funds are lent and borrowed, and through which a large part of the financial transactions of a particular country or of the world are cleared. It has two components—call money market and bill market. *Call money market* is that part of national money market where day to day surplus fund, mostly of banks, is traded in. It is a centre where the borrower and lender of money, and near money assets are brought together. *Bill market* was introduced by RBI in 1952. Under this, RBI made advances to scheduled commercial banks in the form of demand loans against their promissory notes. The main objective of the bill market is to reduce the reliance on cash credit arrangement. Therefore, bill market scheme promotes an active market so that the lending activities of the bank could be shared by other banks.

A freely operating money market is a sensitive barometer of current conditions in the financial markets. In a series of measures since 1987, a number of liberalization activities have been carried out to develop the money market. The money market can be classified as *organized money market* and *unorganized money market*. The organized money market comprising the commercial banks and financial institutions is under total control of the Reserve Bank of India which applies qualitative controls as well as quantitative controls to regulate the supply of money to various sectors of the economy. The unorganized money market comprises of indigenous bankers known as Multani Shroffs, Marwari Shroffs, Gujrati Shroffs, and Chetbiars, etc. The most important money market instruments are government securities, treasury bills, commercial paper, and certificate deposits. Government securities are usually known as "gilt-edged" securities as the repayments are fully secured. These instruments encompass all bonds and treasury bills issued by the government for the purpose of raising public loans.

1.3.1 Institutional Structure

The head of the structure of the money market is the Reserve Bank of India which controls and regulates the market through discount and finance house of the country. The institutions like IDBI, IFC, ICICI, UTI, LIC, GIC are operating in these markets. In April 1991, RBI allowed the entry of any entity with bulk lendable resources of Rs. 20 crores and also money market mutual fund to enter the call money market.

Characteristics of money market

The following are the characteristics of money market:

(i) It is a market for short-term funds for not exceeding a period of one year.
(ii) It deals with those assets which can be converted into cash immediately.
(iii) There is no formal place for money market and transactions generally take place over telephone or fax messages.
(iv) Transactions are made without the help of brokers.
(v) The commercial bank plays generally a dominant role in this market.
(vi) It establishes the link between the RBI and banks.
(vii) The inter-bank markets match the deficits and surplus of banks.

1.3.2 Money Market Instruments

(a) Treasury bill: Treasury bill represents short-term borrowings of the government. Treasury bill market refers to the market where treasury bills are bought and sold. Treasury bills may be classified into four categories:

14-*day treasury bill:* It was introduced on May 20, 1997. The auction of 14-day treasury bills are held on a weekly basis. The amount outstanding as at end March 2000, stood at Rs. 325 crores. The 14-day intermediate treasury bills introduced on April, 1997. It was introduced to cater to the needs of investing the surplus funds of state government, foreign central bank, etc. The amount outstanding was Rs. 2383 crores as at end March 2000 of which the share of state government was 96.18%.

91-*day treasury bills:* There are two types of 91-day treasury bills, namely, (i) ordinary treasury bills and (ii) ad hoc treasury bills. 'Ordinary' treasury bills are issued to the public and other financial institutions for meeting the short-term financial requirements of the central government. These bills are freely marketable; can be bought and sold at any time; and have a secondary market.

'Ad hoc' treasury bill is always issued in favour of the RBI. These are not sold through tender or auction. The ad hoc treasury bills are purchased by the RBI on tap and RBI is authorized to issue currency notes against them. The holder of these bills can always sell them back to the RBI. The 91-day treasury bills for the country outstanding at the end of 2000–01 was Rs. 1501 crores.

182-*day treasury bills:* These are introduced by RBI and initially issued by RBI on monthly basis. RBI does not purchase the treasury bills before the maturity period but they can be sold by the investors in the secondary market through Discount and Finance House of India (DFHI). The DFHI makes advances getting the financial support from RBI. The outstanding amount for the 182 treasury bills was Rs. 1590 crores according to the Indian central budget 2000–01.

364-*day treasury bills*: It was introduced in at the end of April 1992. These are sold through auction which is conducted once in a fortnight. The 364-day treasury bills have become popular due to their higher yield with liquidity and safety. These bills are not rediscountable with the Reserve Bank of India. The outstanding amount was placed Rs. 12,996 crores during 1999–2000.

(b) Commercial bills: Banks make advances to the customers against commercial bills. In the needs of fund by bankers it can be rediscounted in the money market to get ready money. This rediscount period is 90 days but it can be rediscounted earlier in the secondary market.

(c) Inter bank call money: The inter bank call money market is the core of the formal money market. Banks borrow from the call money market in order to meet sudden demand for funds for payments and to obtain funds to meet any likely shortfalls in their cash reserves to meet the Cash Reserve Ratio (CRR) stipulation. In India, inter bank call money market is the single most important source for banks for getting overnight and short-term funds.

(d) Commercial paper: Commercial paper is a short-term unsecured instrument issued by a company in the form of promissory notes with fixed maturities. The maturity period ranges from 15 days to less than 1 year. Since it is a short-term debt, the issuing company is required to meet dealers fees, rating agency fees, and any other relevant charges. Commercial Paper (CP) has gained popularity all over the world because it provides funds at a relatively lower cost. Another important feature of CP is that through this instrument the firm may raise large amount of funds which is not possible through a single bank.

Eligibility for issue of commercial paper: In India, the emergence of CP has added a new dimension to the money market. Hence, the RBI has relaxed the initial guidelines which were laid down for the issue of CPs. The following are the guidelines governing the issue of commercial paper:

(i) The CP has to be issued at discount in the forms of promissory note where interest is always front-ended and maturity value is always equal to face value.

(ii) The issuing firm must have a net worth of at least Rs. 4 crores and the company should have fund based working capital limit of Rs. 4 crores.

(iii) The current ratio should be 1.33:1 and debt-equity ratio not more than 1.5:1.

(iv) It must have a credit rating of P2/A2 or higher from the CRISIL/ICRA of not less than two months old at the time of issue of CP but this condition has become optional since the latter part of 1994.

(v) The RBI has made mandatory for banks, consortia, and syndicates to restrict the cash credit component to 75 per cent of the maximum permissible bank finance and the overall capacity of each borrower to issue CPs is 56 per cent of a borrower's maximum permissible bank finance.

(vi) The company must be listed on one or more stock exchanges but the Government companies are exempted from this stipulation.

(vii) The issue of a CP also bears the expenses of stamp duty and requires to obtain the approval of the Reserve Bank for each issue of the commercial paper.

(viii) Now the RBI has abolished the facility of stand by arrangement as a result, it is no longer mandatory for banks to automatically restore the cash credit limits of corporate bodies.

(ix) CP can be issued to any person or corporate bodies registered or incorporated in India (including banks), as well as non-incorporated bodies.

(x) The issuing company is required to appoint a bank or leader of the consortium bank to verify the signature of the issuing company who have signed in the CP.

(xi) The issuing company is required to appoint a dealer who would arrange the investor for the commerical paper.

(xii) CP is generally issued at a discount and is freely transferable by endorsement. Its delivery is not subject to tax deducted at source.

(xiii) The face value of a single commerical paper should not be less than Rs. 25 lakh and in multiples of Rs. 5 lakh thereafter.

(xiv) The comercial paper shall be issued for a minimum maturity period of 15 days to one year.

(xv) The minimum size of an issue is Rs. 1 crore and the minimum unit of subscription is Rs. 25 lakh.

Advantage of commercial papers: The advantage of CPs lies in the simplicity they offer, as large amounts can be raised without having any underlying transaction. Secondly, CPs provide flexibility to the company to raise funds in the money market wherever it is favourable. Thirdly, CPs can raise fund from the inter-corporate market which is not under the control of any monetary authority. Also CPs provide cheaper finance to the borrowers and at the same time offer good rate of return to the investors.

(e) Certificate of deposit (CD): This is a bearer certificate and is negotiated in the market. CDs can be issued by scheduled commercial banks at a discount on face value and the discount rates are determined by the market. CDs were introduced in June 1989. The minimum denomination of CD was reduced to Rs.1 lakh in June 2002, and new and outstanding CDs were converted to demat form by October 2002. It should be noted that maturity periods and interest rates are no longer controlled by RBI and the instrument has now become a market determined instrument. The RBI guidelines for the issue of CDs can be listed as follows:

RBI guidelines

(i) The denomination of CDs should be in multiples of Rs. 5 lakh subject to the condition that minimum size of an issue to a single investor is Rs. 25 lakh.

(ii) CDs can be issued to individuals, corporations, companies, trust funds, associations, etc. Non Resident Indians can also subscribe to CDs but only on non-repatriation basis.

(iii) The maturity period of CDs should not be less than 3 months and not more than a year. The minimum lock-in-period for CDs is 15 days.

(iv) Banks have to maintain CRR and SLR on the price of issue of CDs.

(v) CDs are freely transferable by endorsement and delivery but only after 45 days of the date of issue to the primary investor.

(vi) CDs are issued in the form of usual promissory notes payable on a fixed date without any grace period. CDs are subject to the payment of stamp duty.

(vii) Banks cannot grant loans against CDs and neither can they buy back their own CDs before maturity.

(f) Repurchase option: The major development in the government securities market is the introduction of a repurchase facility. This instrument of Repurchase Agreement (REPOs) between the RBI and commercial banks started in December 1992. REPO includes the acquisition of funds through sale of agreed securities and is simultaneously committed to repurchase the same at a predetermined price, generally within a period of 14 days to one year. REPO is thus a collateral borrowing and represents a liability to the seller at the purchase price, and reflects the conceptual obligations to transfer funds to the banks on the date of maturity of agreement. To improve the transmission mechanism of monetary policy and further develop the money and debt markets in the light of the recommendations made by the 'Narasimhan Committee', it has been decided to develop the REPOs market with appropriate regulatory safeguards. These safeguards include delivery versus payment, uniform accounting, valuation and disclosure norms, and restricting REPOs to instruments held in dematerialized form with a depository. These prudential safeguards have been designed to ensure transparency and accountability as also at the same time increasing liquidity and depth in the securities market. Accordingly, it has been decided to allow UTI, LIC, IDBI, and other non-bank participants in the money market to access short-term liquidity through REPOs thereby facilitating their cash management and gradual move out of the call money market.

(g) Money market mutual funds: In order to create an additional short-term avenue for investment and to bring money market instrument within the reach of individuals and smaller bodies, the Reserve Bank of India set up money market mutual funds (MMMFs) in April 1991. The MMMFs invariably and excessively invest their investing resources in very high quality money market instruments. Recently, some liquid schemes of private sector mutual funds have started offering 'cheque writing' facility. Such facility provides more liquidity to unit holders and hence has been advocated in the interest of the savers investors.

RBI guidelines for setting up MMMFs: The RBI announced norms for setting money market mutual funds on April 21, 1992. The following are the guidelines for setting up MMMFs:

1. *Eligibility:* Scheduled commercial banks and public financial institutions can set up MMMFs under section 4A of the Companies Act, 1956 or through their existing mutual funds/subsidiaries engaged in funds management.

2. *Structure:* MMMFs can be set up departmentally in the form of a division/department of the bank i.e. "in house" MMMFs wherein the assets and liabilities of such MMMFs would form a part of the banks' balance sheet or a separate entity i.e. a "trust".

(i) MMMFs can be operated either as money market deposit accounts or MMMFs. Money market deposit accounts scheme can be operated either by issuing a deposit receipt or through the issue of passbook without cheque book facilities. The MMMFs can float both open-ended and close-ended schemes. According to the RBI's credit policy announced on October 29, 1999 MMMFs can be set up only as trusts for operational convenience.

(ii) When MMMFs are set up as a trust, the sponsoring bank should appoint a board of trustees to manage it.

(iii) The day-to-day management of the schemes under the fund, as may be delegated by the board of trustees where the fund is set up as a trust, should be looked after by a full time executive trustee or a separate fund manager if set up as division of a bank or a financial institution.

(iv) The banks and public financial institutions are free to formulate special schemes as per their requirements, subject to the guidelines stipulated by the RBI. The MMMFs have to foreward the details of the scheme together with the copies of the offer letter, application form and so on to the RBI, at least one month before announcing the launch of any scheme.

3. *Size of MMMFs:* There is no restriction on the minimum size of MMMFs. There are also no ceilings for raising resources under various schemes by MMMFs.

4. *Subscribers:* MMMFs can be issued only to individuals. Individuals, inclusive of Non Resident Indians (NRIs), may also subscribe to shares/units of MMMFs on a repairable basis.

5. *Minimum size of investment:* MMMFs are free to determine the minimum size of investment by a single investor. The investor cannot be guaranteed a minimum rate of return on investment while announcing any scheme.

6. *Minimum period:* The minimum lock-in-period is 15 days.

7. *Investments:* The resources mobilized are invested exclusively in various money market instruments like treasury bills, call/notice money, commercial paper, and certificates of deposits.

8. *Resource requirements:* Resource requirements do not apply to MMMFs.

9. *Stamp duty:* The shares/units issued by MMMFs are a subject to stamp duty.

10. *Insurance cover:* The funds invested in a MMMFs do not come under the insurance cover from the deposits insurance and Credit Guarantee Corporation of India. This aspect must be clearly stated in the offer document of the MMMFs.

11. *Delivery of instrument:* MMMFs should invariably take delivery of the money market instruments purchased and must give delivery of the instrument sold.

12. *Format of certificates of MMMFs:* The units of MMMFs should be issued in the form of a certificate indicating the number of units purchased by the investor.

13. *Application form:* MMMFs may devise suitable application form for subscribing to their schemes.

14. *Security aspect:* Since the units are freely transferable, due care must be exercised by the MMMFs in the matters of printing or ensuring safe custody of the instruments. They should be signed by two or more authorized signatories.

15. *Regulatory authority:* The setting up of MMMFs requires prior authorization of Reserve Bank of India. MMMFs started by a financial institution are required to comply with the guidelines that may be issued by RBI from time to time.

16. *Accounting:* The accounts of the MMMFs are to be kept distinct and separate from those of their parent institutions. In the case of "in house" MMMFs, it is to be ensured that there is no conflict of interest between the MMMFs and their parent organization. The transfer of assets between the MMMFs and the sponsoring institutions has to be at the market rates and is subject to the approval of the Sponsoring Institution Board.

17. *Statement of accounts and disclosures:* The MMMFs have to maintain a separate account of each scheme launched by it, segregating the assets under each scheme. They have to prepare an annual statement of accounts which contain, inter alia, statement of the assets and liabilities, and the income and expenditure account duly audited by qualified auditors, other than the auditors of the parent organization. An abridged version of the annual accounts together with the reports of the auditors has to be published for the information of the subscriber to the concerned schemes.

18. *Management of MMMFs:* "In house" MMMFs have to take adequate measures to ensure that the management, accounting, and custody of their assets are kept distinct and separate from those relating the sponsoring institutions.

19. *Net asset value:* The MMMFs have to calculate the NAV of each scheme and disclose it periodically for the benefit of the investor. To start with, NAV can be determined and disclosed once a week.

20. *Expenses:* The total expenses of the fund including pre-issue expenses, trusteeship fees/management fees, etc. are to be kept at reasonable levels and disclosed fully in the fund's annual reports or balance sheets.

21. *Furnishing report to Reserve Bank of India:* The sponsor banks and the financial institutions should furnish to Reserve Bank of India, in duplicate, the following reports on a regular basis:

(i) The quarterly report indicating the performance of the MMMF as a whole and each scheme thereof.

(ii) The audited annual statement of accounts, together with the reports of the auditors.

(iii) Scheme-wise details of the investment portfolio of the funds, value of such investment changes in portfolio since the annual report and asset-wise exposure.

1.3.3 Discount and Finance House of India (DFHI)

The Discount and Finance House of India (DFHI) was set up in April 1988 in pursuance of the recommendations of the working group on money market under the chairmanship of Mr. N. Vaghul. The DFHI was set up jointly by the Reserve Bank of India, public sector banks, and financial institutions to deal in short-term money market instruments. The paid-up capital of Rs. 100 crores was contributed jointly by the RBI (Rs. 51 crores), public sector banks (Rs. 33 crores), and financial institutions (Rs.16 crores). The main objectives of DFHI are to:

- provide liquidity to money market instruments.
- provide safe and risk free short-term investments avenues to institutions.
- facilitate money market transactions of small- and medium-sized institutions that are not regular participants in the market.

The main functions of DFHI are as follows:

(1) To discount, rediscount, purchase and sell treasury bills, trade bills, bills of exchange, commercial bills and commercial papers.

(2) To play an important role as a lender, borrower, or broker in the inter-bank call money market.

(3) To promote and support company funds, trusts and other organizations for the development of short-term money market.

(4) To advise governments, banks, and financial institutions in evolving schemes for growth and development of money market.

The DFHI participates in the call, notice and term markets as a borrower and as a lender.

1.4 CAPITAL MARKET

Capital market is generally understood as the market for long-term funds. This market supplies funds for financing the fixed capital requirement of trade and commerce as well as the long-term requirements of the Government. The long-term funds are made available through various instruments such as debentures, preference shares, and common shares. The capital market can be local, regional, national, or international. The capital market is classified into two categories, namely, (i) primary market or new issue market, and (ii) secondary market or stock exchange. As a rule, only when a country's primary market is alone, it is possible to ensure a good degree of activity in the secondary market because it is the primary market which ensures a continuous flow of securities to the secondary market. On the contrary, if secondary market is only active but not transparent and disciplined, it becomes difficult to develop and sustain the cult of equity and related investment in the primary market. This is because the liquidity which the secondary market imparts to such investments in the hands of the investors is adversely affected.

1.4.1 Importance of Capital Market

Capital markets are markets where productive capital is raised and made available for industrial purposes. It provides an avenue for investors and household sector to invest in financial assets which are more productive than physical assets. A developed capital market can solve the problem of paucity of funds. It facilitates increase in production and productivity in the economy and hence enhances the economic welfare of the society. Indian capital market acts as an intermediary to mobilize savings and to channelize the same for productive use consistent with national priorities. The industrial securities issued through the primary market are traded in the secondary market which provides liquidity and short-term as well as long-term yields. An efficient primary market prepares base for effective and cost efficient mobilization of resources by bringing together the users and investors of funds. Thus, both the primary and secondary markets help each other and make the capital market efficient, healthy, and strong. The number of stock exchanges record a steep rise followed by sharp increase in the number of listed companies and the investors. Table 1.1 shows the upsurge of market capitalization, trading volume, and number of listed companies for the years 1990–2003.

Table 1.1 Growth in the Indian capital market

(Rs. in crores)

At the end of financial year	No. of stock exchange	No. of brokers	No. of Listed companies	Market capitaliza-tion	Turnover	SGL turnover	Derivatives turnover
1990–91	20	—	6229	1,10,279	—	—	—
1991–92	20	—	6480	3,54,106	—	—	—
1992–93	22	—	6925	2,28,780	—	—	—
1993–94	23	—	7811	4,00,077	2,03,703	—	—
1994–95	23	6711	9077	4,73,349	1,62,905	50,569	—
1995–96	23	8476	9100	5,72,257	2,27,368	1,27,179	—
1996–97	23	8867	9890	4,88,332	6,46,116	1,22,941	—
1997–98	23	9005	9833	5,89,816	9,08,681	1,85,708	—
1998–99	23	9069	9877	5,74,064	10,23,382	2,27,228	—
1999–00	23	9192	9871	11,92,630	20,67,031	5,39,232	—
2000–01	23	9782	9954	7,68,863	28,80,990	6,98,121	4038
2001–02	23	9687	9644	7,49,248	8,95,817	15,55,653	1,03,847
2002-03	23	9519	9413	6,31,921	9,86,908	19,55,731	4,42,343

Source: Chartered Secretary, April, 2004

The growth in the Indian capital market is presented in the Table 1.1. The number of stock exchanges increased from 9 in 1980 to 23 today. All the exchanges are fully computerized and offer 100% online trading. Some 9,413 companies were available for trading on stock exchanges at the end of March 2003. The market capitalization grew ten fold between 1990–91 and 1999–2000. All India market capitalization is estimated at Rs. 6,31,921 crores at the end of March 2003. The trading volumes on exchanges have been witnessing phenomenal growth during 1990s. The average daily turnover grew from about Rs. 150 crores in 1990 to Rs. 12,000 crores in 2000, peaking at over Rs. 20,000 crores. However it declined substantially to Rs. 9,86,908 crores in 2002–03.

The resource mobilization from the primary market is depicted in the Table 1.2. Average annual capital mobilization by non-government public companies from the primary market increased manifold during the 1980s, with the amount raised in 1990–91 being Rs. 4312 crores. Again the capital raised by these companies rising sharply to Rs. 26,417 crores in 1994–95. However it decreased to 1,878 crores in 2002–03. The market appears to have dried up since 1995–96 due to interplay of demand and supply side forces.

Indian market is getting integrated with the global market though in a limited way through Euro issues. Since 1992, Indian companies have raised over Rs. 40,000 crores through ADRs/GDRs. By the end of December 2003, 517 FIIs were registered with SEBI. They had net cumulative investments of over US$ 23 billion by the end of December 2003.

The investment in the new issues became attractive following nearly double appreciation in the price of new issues just on listing in 1994.

In the total amount raised through the public offerings, share of equity in relation to debentures and bonds has increased significantly over the years which is shown in the Tables 1.3.

It is evident that Indian capital market has become an even more important place of activity in the newly unveiled economic regime. Thus the growth of capital market has posed new challenges to economic and financial stability. As a result, a number of new innovative financial instruments have surfaced in recent years as an offshoot of the wide ranging developments taking place in the financial sector throughout the world. We now discuss some innovative instruments in detail.

1.4.2 Financial Instruments

Euro convertible bond: Euro convertible bond is an unsecured security which can be converted into depository receipts or local shares. It offers the investors an option to convert the bond into equity at a fixed price after a minimum lock-in-period. Thus call option allows the company to force conversion if the market price exceeds the particular percentage of the conversion price. Indian companies prefer to issue GDRs whereas foreign investors favour convertible bonds.

Fully convertible cumulative preference shares (Equipref): Equipref is a very recent introduction in the market. The shares have to be listed on one or more stock exchanges in the country. It has two parts. The first part is convertible into equity shares automatically and second part is converted into equity shares after a lock-in-period at the request of the investors. Conversion into equity shares after the lock-in-period takes place at a price which is 30%

Table 1.2 Resource mobilization from the primary market

(Rs. in crores)

Issues \ Year	90–91	91–92	92–93	93–94	94–95	95–96	96–97	97–98	98–99	99–00	2000–01	2001–02	2002–03
Corporate Securities	**14,219**	**16,366**	**23,537**	**44,498**	**48,084**	**36,689**	**37,147**	**42,125**	**60,192**	**72,450**	**78,396**	**74,330**	**70,039**
Domestic Issues	14,219	16,366	23,286	37,044	41,974	36,193	33,872	37,738	59,044	68,963	74,199	71,988	66,613
Non-Govt.													
Public Co.	4,312	6,193	19,803	19,330	26,417	16,075	10,410	3,138	5,013	5,153	4,890	5,692	1,878
PSU Bonds	5,663	5,710	1,062	5,586	3,070	2,292	3,394	2,982	—	—	—	—	—
Govt. Companies	—	—	430	819	888	1,000	650	43	—	—	—	350	—
Banks & FIs	—	—	356	3,843	425	3,465	4,352	1,476	4,352	2,551	1,472	1,070	2,989
Private Placement	4,244	4,463	1,635	7,466	11,174	13,361	15,066	30,099	49,679	61,259	67,836	64,876	61,746
Euro Issues	—	—	702	7,898	6,743	1,297	5,594	4,009	1,148	3,487	4,197	2,343	3,426
Government Securities	**11,558**	**12,284**	**17,690**	**54,533**	**43,231**	**46,783**	**42,688**	**67,386**	**106,067**	**113,336**	**128,483**	**152,508**	**181,979**
Central Government	8,989	8,919	13,885	50,388	38,108	40,509	36,152	59,637	93,953	99,630	115,183	133,801	151,126
State Governments	2,569	3,364	3,805	4,145	5,123	6,274	6,536	7,749	12,114	13,706	13,300	18,707	30,853
Total	**25,777**	**28,650**	**41,227**	**99,031**	**91,315**	**83,472**	**79,835**	**109,511**	**166,259**	**185,786**	**206,879**	**226,838**	**252,018**
Mutual Funds	**7508**	**11,253**	**13,021**	**11,244**	**12,274**	**–5,833**	**–2,036**	**4,064**	**3,611**	**19,953**	**11,135**	**7,137**	**4,580**

Source: Chartered Secretary, April, 2004

Table 1.3 New capital issues by non-government public limited companies

(Rs. in crores)

Security & types of issue	2001–02 (April-March) No. of issues	2001–02 (April-March) Amount	2002–03 (April-March) No. of issues	2002–03 (April-March) Amount	2002–03 (April-January) No. of issues	2002–03 (April-January) Amount	2003–04 (April-January) No. of issues	2003–04 (April-January) Amount
1	**2**	**3**	**4**	**5**	**6**	**7**	**8**	**9**
(1) Equity shares (a+b)	6	860.4	5	460.2	3	431.6	8	674.6
	(3)	(654.3)	(5)	(391.2)	(3)	(366.6)	(5)	(565.3)
(a) Prospectus	4	852.7	3	206.7	1	178.1	6	577.9
	(2)	(653.7)	(3)	(201.0)	(1)	(176.4)	(4)	(539.3)
(b) Rights	2	7.7	2	253.5	2	253.5	2	96.7
	(1)	(0.6)	(2)	(190.2)	(2)	(190.2)	(1)	(26.0)
(2) Preference shares (a+b)	—	—	—	—	—	—	—	—
(a) Prospectus	—	—	—	—	—	—	—	—
(b) Rights	—	—	—	—	—	—	—	—
(3) Debentures (a+b)	4	774.0	1	217.5	1	217.5	—	—
(a) Prospectus	1	69.5	—	—	—	—	—	—
(b) Rights	3	704.5	1	217.5	1	217.5	—	—
of which:								
(i) Convertible (a+b)	3	518.1	1	217.5	1	217.5	—	—
(a) Prospectus	1	69.5	—	—	—	—	—	—
(b) Rights	2	448.6	1	217.5	1	217.5	—	—
(ii) Non-convertible(a+b)	1	255.9	—	—	—	—	—	—
(a) Prospectus	—	—	—	—	—	—	—	—
(b) Rights	1	255.9	—	—	—	—	—	—
(4) Bonds (a+b)	9	4,058.0	3	1,200.0	1	400.0	3	1,250.9
(a) Prospectus	9	4,058.0	3	1,200.0	1	400.0	3	1,250.9
(b) Rights	—	—	—	—	—	—	—	—
(5) **Total (1+2+3+4)**	**19**	**5,692.4**	**9**	**1,877.7**	**5**	**1,049.1**	**11**	**1,925.5**
(a) Prospectus	14	4,980.2	6	1,406.7	2	578.1	9	1,828.8
(b) Right	5	712.2	3	471.0	3	471.0	2	96.7

Source: Reserve Bank of India Bulletin, April, 2004

lower than the average market price. The dividend on fully convertible cumulative preference shares is fixed and shall be given only for the portion that represents second part shares. Only a few companies have tried this instrument. Equiprefs are presently being offered largely to the financial institutions like the UTI. Uniworth International Ltd. was the first company to issue these shares and succeeded in mopping up to Rs. 16 crores. UIL's equipref shares were a combination of equity and preference shares.

Triple option convertible debentures: Every debenture holder has an opportunity to acquire two equity shares at par for each debenture. As regards the non-convertible portion which had warrants attached to them, investors were given three options. They can retain the non-convertible portion and sell the warrants and get equity shares in return or retain non-convertible portion, surrounding the warrants and apply for equity shares.

Warrants: A warrant is an option, issued by a company, granting the buyer the right to purchase a number of shares of its equity share capital at a given exercise price during a given period. An equity warrant increases the marketability of debentures and reduces the need for the efforts of brokers/sub-brokers by way of private placement. Thus, it provides an effective tool for lesser dependence on financial institution and mutual funds for subscribing to the security. Many companies including Deepak Fertilizers, Essar Gujarat, Reliance Industries, CEAT Tyres, Ranbaxy Laboratories, Bharat Forge, Proctor & Gamble, ITC Agro-Tech, and Tata Steel have issued warrants. In a situation, where the market is lukewarm in its response to new issues, equity warrants can be an added attraction for investors to apply for the issues offering equity warrants with their securities.

Secured premium notes (SPNs): SPN is issued along with a detachable warrant, and is redeemable after a notified period with features of medium to long-term notes. Each SPN has a warrant attached to it which gives the holder the right to apply for, or seek allotment of one equity share, provided the SPN is fully paid. The conversion of detachable warrant into equity shares is done within the time limit notified by the company. There is a lock-in-period for SPN during which no interest is paid for the invested amount. In July 1992, Tata Iron and Steel Co. Ltd. (TISCO) was the first company to issue SPNs to the public alongwith the right issue. The main objective of this issue was to raise money for its modernization programme without expanding its equity excessively in the next few years. The SPN was issued with a face value of Rs. 300 to be repaid in four equal annual instalments of Rs. 75 each from the end of the fourth year together, with an equal amount of Rs. 75 with each instalment which will consist of a mix of interest and premium on redemption. This instrument has a low borrowing cost and is beneficial for capital intensive projects.

Zero interest convertibles: Also known as *zero coupon bonds*, the zero interest convertibles refer to those convertibles which are sold at discount from their eventual maturing value and have zero interest rate. One advantage from the investors point of view is that it eliminates reinvestment risk. From the companies point of view, it is attractive to issue these convertibles as there is no immediate interest commitment. The companies like Mahindra & Mahindra, and HB Leasing and Finance have adopted this scheme.

Deep discount bonds: Deep discount bonds pay a coupon rate which is substantially lower than the market rate at the time of issue. One of the advantages of DDB is the elimination of investment risk. It helps the companies which take time to stabilize their operations and which have initial small cash flow rising steadily to a high level to take care of the redemption. The investors also gain the benefit of capital gains taxation.

Floating rate bonds (FRB): Floating rate bonds made their first appearance in the Indian capital market in 1993 when State Bank of India adopted a reference rate of the highest rate of interest on fixed deposit receipt of the bank, providing floor rate for minimum interest payable at 12% p.a. and call option to the bank after 5 years to redeem the bonds earlier than the maturity period of 10 years at certain premium. The floating rates are set equal to the treasury bill rate plus a predetermined spread.

Securitization: Securitization is a synthetic technique of conversion of assets into securities, securities into liquidity and subsequently into assets, on an ongoing basis. This increases the turnover of business and profit while providing for flexibility in yield, pricing pattern, issue, risk and marketability of instruments used to the advantage of both borrowers and lenders. In securitization, generally a financial institution holds a pool of individual loans and receivables, creates securities against them, get them rated and sell them to investors at large. The most suitable assets for securitization for the banks are housing loans, auto loans, lease rentals, corporates trade receivables etc. Indian financial market is still at an infancy stage. So securitization is emerging to be a very innovative technique enabling finance companies to retail market their liabilities in order to lower their cost of funds besides increasing the liquidity. The initial headway has already been made by Citi Bank in association with ICICI.

Layered premium issue: The layered premium issue was introduced by Merchant Bankers to overcome the inherent dangers of fixing premia for issues. A floor rate is fixed with the consensus of the shareholders. The underwriters will also be given the option of underwriting from the highest premia to the lowest. The issue is then auctioned to the investors. This innovation will provide tremendous flexibility to the issue.

Repurchase of shares: Repurchase of shares by companies is a part of the capitalization process. The company repurchases the shares to reduce the share capital by two methods. As per the first method, the shares are purchased from the floor of the stock exchanges. The second method asks for purchasing the shares directly from the shareholders. Repurchase of shares is an alternative to cash dividend.

Derivatives: Financial intermediaries abroad have created new varieties of instruments and transaction called derivatives and to create risk managements tools such as options, futures and swaps are used to transform one or more properties of an asset or liability. Financial liberalization has brought inherent risk, and as a result, corporate and institutional investors are looking towards derivatives for hedging the risks. Since the volume of international trade and capital flows are rising, more and more banks are exposed to various currencies and the emerging derivatives in foreign countries are increasingly used by banks to bring variations in the sensitivity of their funds and also the underlying portfolio. So it is high time for the Forex dealers in India to familiarize with the complexity of the instruments and acquire skills to handle them.

Options: Options are basically derivatives in the nature of legal contracts. They are derived from underlying assets which could be stocks, bonds, or currencies. An option contract gives the holder the right to buy or sell the underlying stock at a price on a future date. This price is referred to as the *strike price*. Depending on whether the holder is a buyer or a seller, the options are termed put and call. A *call option* conveys the right of the holder to buy a specified quantity of the stock while a *put option* conveys the right of the holder to sell. The buyer or the holder gets the right as laid down in the option, while the writer is the one who has the obligation to honour the terms when the option is exercised. Option trading has a good market in India since there is enough scope for speculation.

Futures: A *future contract* is essentially a series of forward contracts. There are two types of people who deal in futures—speculators and hedgers. Speculators buy and sell futures for the sole purpose of marketing a profit by selling them at a price that is higher than their buying price. Such people neither produce nor use the asset in the ordinary course of business. In contrast, hedgers buy and sell futures to offset an otherwise risky position in the spot market. In the ordinary course of business, they either produce or use the asset. In a forward contract, the trader who promises to buy is said to be in 'Long position' and the one who promises to sell is said to be in 'Short position' in future. The long position in a future contract is the agreement to take delivery and short position in a future contract is the legally binding agreement to deliver.

Swaps: A *swap deal* is a transaction in which the bank buys and sells the specified foreign currency simultaneously for different maturity dates which would help banks to eliminate exposure risk. It can also be used as a tool to enter arbitrary operations that led the economy to be fully opened up.

Non-voting shares: Non-voting shares enable a company to raise capital without diluting the promoter's holding. The finance ministry guidelines say that non-voting shares should not exceed 25% of the total paid-up capital of the company. Shareholders buying these shares gain through a dividend which is 20% higher than on voting shares. If a company fails to pay dividend, non-voting shareholders on a prorata basis until the company resumes paying dividend.

A major indicator of the level of development of an economy is the sophistication of its capital market. Since liberalization has begun, the response measures for handling the capital market has been enormous. It is visible with the creation of SEBI, NSE, regulated BSE, floating of mutual funds, financing institutions, and credit rating system.

SUMMARY

Four and half decades of Indian economic planning and subsequent liberalization had led the country to an ecstatic phase of development. The development through disintermediation, deregulation, globalization, and emergence of vibrant capital market has contributed to the expansion of opportunities. As a result, capital market has emerged as the major contributor to the growth of foreign exchange reserves of the country. Infact, in the emerging world market, India has beaten several developing countries. In the post liberalization era, the finance sector has witnessed a complete metamorphosis. The recent economic reforms encompassed a series of measures to promote investors protection and encourage the growth of capital market. Free entry into capital market for new issues by companies and free pricing of shares for new issues has been ensured. Different financial institutions and markets compete for a limited pool of savings by offering different instruments. Money and capital markets increase competition between suppliers. Capital market enables contractual savings and collective investment institutions to play a more active role in the financial system.

REVIEW QUESTIONS

1. What is a money market? Discuss the various money market instruments and list their features.
2. What is a commercial paper? What steps have been taken in recent years to make commercial paper market a developed one?
3. State the functions of the Discount and Finance House of India.
4. Distinguish between money market and capital market.
5. Explain the various new instruments introduced in the capital market.
6. Write short notes on
   (a) Money market mutual fund
   (b) Euro convertible bonds
   (c) Warrants

QUIZ

1. The component of money market is:
(a) Government securities market
(b) Bill market
(c) Primary market

2. The Capital market instruments among the following is
(a) Share certificate
(b) Secured premium notes
(c) Inter-bank call money

3. The major player in the Indian money market is:
(a) Indigenous banks
(b) Reserve Bank of India
(c) State Bank of India

State whether the following are true or false.

4. Companies raise capital in new issue market only through public issues. (T/F)

5. Commercial paper can be issued only by commercial banks. (T/F)

6. Capital market supplies fund for financing working capital requirement. (T/F)

Fill up the blanks.

7. The Government securities are known as ....

8. The commercial paper is issued for a minimum maturity period of ....

9. The CDs are short-term deposit instruments with maturity period ranging from .... to ....

10. The DFHI commenced its operation on ....

REFERENCES

Agarwal, Sanjiv, "The Indian Money Market", Facts for You, Jan. 1994, p. 39.

Chartered Financial Analyst, March, 1994.

Chugh, Anup Kumar, "Capital Market Instruments", *State Bank of India Monthly Review*, Vol. XXXIV, April, 1995, p. 176.

Goiporia, M.N., "An Overview of the Financial Markets", *Vichar*, Vol. 5, April, 1992, p. 3.

Madden, J.T. and M. Nadler, *The International Money Market*, 1935, p. 108.

Reserve Bank of India, "Report on Currency and Finance", 1998–1999; "Report on Trend and Progress of Banking in India", 1998–99 and 1999–2000 and *Bulletin*, April, 2000.

Reserve Bank of India, Bulletin, May 1999, pp. 713–714.

Singh, K.P., and A.K. Sinha, "Primary Market and Spread of Equity Culture in India", *The Indian Journal of Commerce*, Vol. XLVIII, No. 184, Sept. 1995, p. 1.

Tripathy, Nalini Prava, "Capital Market—A Better Environment for Better Tomorrow", *International Conference on Accounting in Changing Perspectives*, Jan. 4–5, 1997, Calcutta.

Verma, Sanjeev, "Innovations in Financial Products", *ICFAI National Convention*, 1994, Hyderabad, p. 4.

Chapter 2

Securities and Exchange Board of India (SEBI)

2.1 INTRODUCTION

The Securities and Exchange Board of India was constituted as a regulatory authority over various constituents of the capital market in the year 1988. Though legally SEBI came into existence in 1988, it was made operational and effective from 1992 when it was empowered to secure an autonomous position.

2.2 OBJECTIVES

SEBI is vested with powers concerning various aspects of the capital market such as regulating the stock exchanges, various intermediaries and mutual funds, as also promoting investors' education and training of intermediaries and the establishment of self-regulating organizations (SROs). These powers also require SEBI to take steps to prohibit fraudulent and unfair trade practices as also insider trading in the securities markets. The objectives of SEBI are depicted in Fig. 2.1.

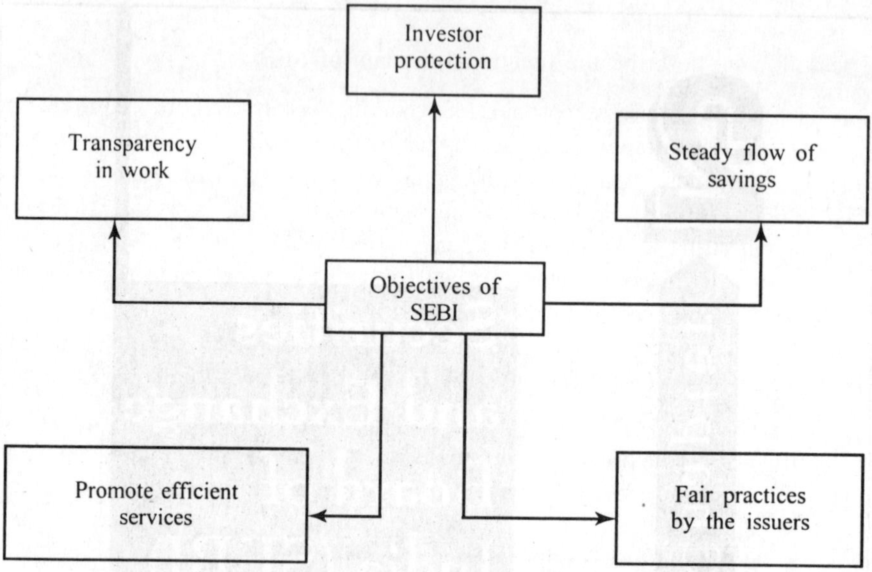

Fig. 2.1 Objectives of SEBI.

SEBI's efforts were always to create an effective surveillance mechanism for the securities market, and encourage responsible and accountable autonomy on the part of all players in the market, who should discipline themselves and observe the rules of the game.

The organization

The board consists of the following members:

(a) Chairman.

(b) Two members from the officials of the ministries of Central Government dealing with finance and law.

(c) One member from amongst the officials of the Reserve Bank of India.

(d) Two or three members appointed by Central Government.

The activities of the SEBI can be divided into four operational departments. These are: primary market department, issue management and intermediaries department, secondary market department, and institutional department. These departments are headed by an executive director. In addition to this, there are two other departments, namely, legal department and investigation department. These are also headed by the officers of the rank of executive directors. SEBI also has two advisory committees—one for primary and the other for secondary markets. The committees are constituted from amongst the market players, investors, and eminent persons associated with capital market. However, these committees are non-statutory in nature.

Job entrusted to SEBI

The following describe the functional domain of SEBI:

(i) SEBI creates a proper and conducive atmosphere required for raising money from the capital market. The atmosphere comprises the rules, regulations, trade practices, customs, and relations among institutions, brokers, investors and companies. It works to restore the trust of investors and particularly to safeguard the interest of the small investors. This can be achieved by meeting the needs of the persons connected with the security market and establishing proper coordination among the three main groups directly connected with its operations, namely, (a) investors, (b) corporate sectors, and (c) intermediaries.

(ii) SEBI educates investors and makes them aware of their rights in clear and specific terms. It provides investors with information and makes sure that the market maintains liquidity, safety, and profitability of the securities which are crucial for any investment.

(iii) SEBI creates a proper investment climate and enables the corporate sector to raise industrial securities easily, efficiently, and at affordable minimum cost.

(iv) SEBI develops a proper infrastructure so that the market automatically facilitates expansion and growth of business to middlemen like brokers, jobbers, commercial banks, merchant bankers, mutual funds, etc. Thus, it ensures that they provide efficient service to their constituents, namely, investors and the corporate sector at a competitive price.

(v) SEBI makes the law more effective in the existing status as far as they relate to the industrial securities, mutual funds, investments in units, LIC savings plan, chitfund companies, and securities issued by housing/industrial societies and corporations with the purpose of investing in housing/industrial projects.

(vi) SEBI creates the framework for more open, orderly, and unprejudiced conduct in relation to takeover and mergers in the corporate sector to ensure fair and equal treatment to all the security holders, and to facilitate such takeovers and mergers in the interest of efficiency by prescribing a mechanism for more orderly conduct.

To achieve its objectives, the board plays a dual role by working both as a controlling authority and a development institution. This can be described as follows:

(i) SEBI devises laws with a unified set of objectives, single administrative authority, and an integrated framework to deal with all the aspects of the securities market.

(ii) It shall also play an active role in interaction with the Institute of Chartered Accountants of India in upgrading and making the accounting and auditing standards more effective. It tries to bring discipline in management in financial reporting and acts firmly with cases where window dressing and accounting tricks are employed to the detriment of the interest of users of such financial statements.

(iii) It introduces a system of two-stage disclosure at the time of initial issue and makes compulsory for the companies to provide detailed information to all the stock exchanges, journalists, and investors on demand.

(iv) It examines the feasibility of introducing a dealers' network by which securities can be bought or sold over the counter as in a retail shop. This is done to smoothen liquidity and investment opportunities.

(v) It works as an authoritative institution to see that the intermediaries are financially sound and equipped with professional and competent manpower.

(vi) It makes law-making and observance flexible enough to suit the prevailing market conditions and circumstances. It ensures that the rules are versatile and non-rigid to provide automatic and self-regulatory growth.

Functions

The main functions of SEBI are as follows:

(i) Subject to the provision of this ordinance, it is the duty of the board to protect the interest of investors in securities and to promote the development of, and to regulate the securities market by such measures it thinks fit.

(ii) Regulating the business in stock exchanges and any other securities markets.

(iii) Registering and regulating the working of stock brokers, sub-brokers, share transfer agents, bankers to an issue, trustees of trust deed, registrars to an issue, merchant bankers, underwriters, portfolio managers, investment advisers, and other such intermediaries who may be associated with securities markets in any manner.

(iv) Registering and regulating the working of collective investment schemes including mutual funds.

(v) Promoting and regulating self-regulatory organizations.

(vi) Prohibiting fraudulent and unfair trade practices relating to securities markets.

(vii) Promoting investor education and training of intermediaries of securities market.

(viii) Prohibiting insider trading in securities.

(ix) Regulating substantial acquisition of shares and takeover of companies.

(x) Calling for information form, undertaking inspection, conducting inquiries and audits of the stock exchanges and intermediaries, and self-regulatory organization in the securities market.

(xi) Levying fees or other charges for carrying out the purposes of this section.

(xii) Conducting research for the above purposes.

(xiii) Performing other such functions as may be prescribed.

(xiv) Promoting fair practices and code of conduct for all SROs.

Powers with SEBI

The SEBI has the power to call periodical returns from recognized stock exchanges. Also it may call any information or explanation from recognized stock exchanges. It can direct enquiries to be made in relation to affairs of stock exchanges. The bye-laws are to be granted by the SEBI for all recognized stock exchanges. It can also amend bye-laws of recognized stock exchanges. The public companies are compelled by SEBI for listing of securities. It can grant registration to market intermediaries. It can levy fees and other charges for carrying out the purpose of regulation. It can penalize members of stock exchanges for violating securities law. It can make rules about the manipulative practices. The SEBI Act was amended in October 2002. This entrusted SEBI with wide powers including seizure of books and accounts, impose penalty limit to Rs. 25 crores on insider trading, slap a penalty of Rs.1 lakh a day and up to Rs. 1 crore in cases where investors are cheated. SEBI has also been given power to suspend the governors of the stock exchanges.

SEBI goals

In the year 2000, SEBI set for itself the tasks of speeding up the following measures:

(i) Pursuit of healthy corporate governance regulations,

(ii) Introduction of derivative trading,

(iii) Internet trading practices by brokers, and

(iv) Promotion of trading debt market.

SUMMARY

The control of SEBI on all players in the capital market and stock market, including merchant bankers, mutual funds, registers, brokers, sub-brokers, and portfolio managers is strengthened and made effective. SEBI has prepared comprehensive rules and regulations for controlling the stock-market and intermediaries with a view to improving trading practices, and rules for disclosures and other measures of investor protection.

REVIEW QUESTIONS

1. What are the jobs entrusted to SEBI?
2. Explain the functions and powers of SEBI.

QUIZ

State whether the following are true or false.

1. Training to intermediaries is given by SEBI. (T/F)
2. The new company can issue shares only at par. (T/F)

Fill up the blanks.

3. .... prohibits insider trading in the securities markets.
4. SEBI came into existence in ....
5. .... protection is the major responsibility of SEBI.

REFERENCES

Avadhani, V.A., "*Investment Management*", Himalaya Publishing House, New Delhi, 1996, p. 206.

Desai, Vasant, "*The Indian Financial System*", Himalaya Publishing House, New Delhi.

Government of India, *Report of the High Powered Committee on Stock Exchanges*, 1985.

Gemarat, Sanjeev, "Insider Trading" *The Chartered Accountant*, July 1993.

Pandya, V.H., "Emerging Scenario in the Capital Market and SEBI's Role", *Forum of Free Enterprise*, 1994, p. 5.

Roa, Mohana P., "*Working of Mutual Fund Organizations in India*", Kaniska Publishers, New Delhi, 1998, pp. 172–173.

Chapter 3

Stock Exchanges

3.1 INTRODUCTION

The National Stock Exchange (NSE) was set up by IDBI and other all India Financial Institutions in Bombay in November 1992 with a paid-up equity of Rs. 25 crores. It was set up to strengthen the move towards professionalization of the capital market as also to provide nationwide securities trading facilities to investors. Another important stock exchange is the Bombay Stock Exchange (BSE). The Bombay Stock Exchange of India has during the last few years taken various measures to improve the quality of secondary market in India and to make India an attractive destination for both domestic and foreign investors. Bombay Stock Exchange has been constantly innovative in its operation so as to provide better services to its elements be it brokers/investors or listed companies.

3.2 OBJECTIVES OF NSE

The objectives of NSE can be listed as:

(1) To establish a nationwide trading facility for equities, debt instruments, and hybrids.

(2) To ensure equal access to investors all over the country through an appropriate communication network.

(3) To provide a fair, efficient, and transparent securities market to investors using electronic systems.

(4) To enable shortening settlement cycles and book entry settlement system.

(5) To meet the current international standards of securities market.

The Pherwani committee recommended the setting up of the national market system based on the new stock exchange which was already set up in Bombay. To make the national market system effective, the committee recommended several support agencies to provide high quality trading, and settlement and depository services. It has recommended that there should be three tiers namely, stock exchanges at Mumbai, Kolkata, Delhi, Chennai, and Ahmedabad; regional stock exchanges like these in major stock capitals; and additional trading floors, sponsored or managed by the Principal or a Regional Stock Exchange. The structure would be as:

- Regular stock markets which are 23 in number at present.
- National market system with separate set of licensed brokers all over the country.
- Retail broking through a series of registered sub-brokers.
- Additional Trading Floor licensed for trading in securities on the basis of a regional stock exchange quotations.
- OTCEI for risky and venture some small companies.

NSE is setting up its own satellite communication system which will eventually be extended to most of the places in the country where significant investor population exists. With its nationwide telecom network, NSE will truly be able to provide equal access for buying or selling securities anywhere in the country.

Listing of securities

All medium and large size companies with paid-up equity of Rs. 10 crores are eligible to be listed on regular stock exchange can be listed on NSE.

3.2.1 Operational Highlights

Of the total trading turnover of Rs. 9,08,691 crores by the 22 stock exchanges in 1997–98 the trading turnover of NSE was the highest which accounted for about 45% of the total trading volume during 2000. NSE witnessed a turnover of Rs. 1,00,032 crores during 2000–2001 and 6,17,989 crores during 2002–03. The operational highlight is presented in Table 3.1.

At the end of March 2000, NSE had 991 trading members of whom 861 were corporate members. The NSE has adopted a fully automated screen-based trading system which allows trading members to trade from their

Table 3.1 Operation of National Stock Exchange

(Rs. in crores)

Year	2000–01	2001–02	2002–03
Turnover	1,00,032	5,13,167	6,17,989
Number of listed companies	5869	793	673
Market capitalization	5,71,553	6,36,861	5,37,133

Source: RBI Annual Report 2002–03.

offices through communications network. The exchange has allowed for trading 1300 securities of medium and large companies with nationwide investor base.

3.3 BOMBAY STOCK EXCHANGE (BSE)—A DYNAMIC BODY

Table 3.2 gives the operational highlights of BSE.

Table 3.2 Operation of Bombay Stock Exchange

(Rs. in crores)

	2000–01	2001–02	2002–03
Listed companies	5869	5782	5650
Turnover	10,00,032	3,07,292	3,14,073
Market capitalization	5,71,553	6,36,861	5,37,133

Source: RBI Annual Report 2002–03.

3.3.1 Book-Building Transaction

Book-building is a novel and budding concept in India. Book-building is a process of fixing the price for a share on the basis of feedback from potential investors. Accordingly allocation is made by the company on the highest price bid by the investors. The trading commences from the next day. The steps involved in the book-building process are (also shown in Fig. 3.1):

Step 1: The company appoints merchant bankers as book-runner or book-running lead manager who files a draft prospectus with SEBI. The draft prospectus is circulated to eligible investors with a price-band. Price-band is arrived at by the book-runner in consultation with the issuer.

Step 2: Book-runner forms a syndicate of about 100 to 130 members along with joint lead managers. The syndicate members procure subscription from the investors including members of the public. These members collect orders from their clients on the amount of securities required by them. The book-runner obtains order from these members and builds up line trading.

Step 3: Book-runner conducts awareness campaigns which include advertising, road shows, and holding conferences.

Step 4: Syndicate members create demand and feedback for the book-runner.

Step 5: Book-runner builds up "Book" after receiving the orders from the members of the syndicate.

Step 6: Book-runner is required to close the "Book" in consultation with the issuing company and determine the size of the placement portion.

Step 7: Book-runner finalizes the allocation to syndicate members and enters into a procurement agreement with them. Procurement agreement is signed between the issuer and syndicate members for the "placement portion".

Step 8: Final prospectus is filed with Registrar of Companies (RoC) along with procurement agreements within two days of the determination of the offer price and receipt of acknowledge card from SEBI.

Step 9: The placement portion closes a day before the opening of the public portion. Book-runner is required to collect application money one day prior to opening of the issue from the subscribers to the placement portion.

Step 10: Allotment and listing of public portion is made on the 11th day after closure of issue. Allotment of net offer to public is made as per the existing statutory requirements within 30 days.

3.3.2 BOLT Transaction

In the last couple of years, the nature of competition has changed. It is a competition of offering better services and lower costs to attract business. The exchange took a big leap in May 1995, when it introduced order-cum-quote driven electronic trading for all the listed securities. [BOLT refers to BSE on bid to pick up the shares. Thus, it is somewhat similar to an auction.] The steps involved in book-building process are shown in Fig. 3.1.

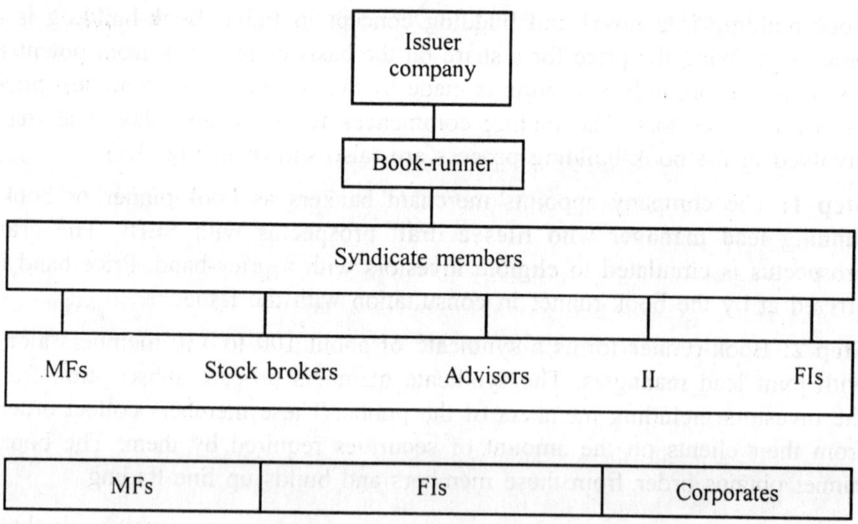

Fig. 3.1 Book-building process.

The BOLT system was set up to achieve the following goals:

(a) Increase in market transparency.

(b) Enhancement in market quality through improved liquidity, by increasing quote continuity, and market depth.

(c) Reduction in settlement risk due to open traders, by elimination of mismatches, and improvement in information availability by catering to broad-based information requirements.

(d) Betterment of MIS systems, and

(e) Introduction of flexibility in systems, so as to handle growing volumes easily, to incorporate changes in business rules, and to support geographical dispersion of market activity.

To facilitate the small investors, SEBI has reduced the individual minimum subscription limit for primary issues from Rs. 5,000 to Rs. 2,000. From this point of view SEBI, is working more as developer of capital market rather than just being a regulator. Bombay Stock Exchange had a turnover of Rs. 3,14,073 crores and a market capitalization of Rs. 5,37,133 crores in 2002–03. The increase in volumes was facilitated by an increase in the number of cities covered by BOLT network to over 275 in March 2000 and an increase in the number of trade work stations to 3803.

3.3.3 Trade Guarantee Fund (TGF)

One of the most important achievements of the BSE has been the establishment of Trade Guarantee Fund. The TGF has been operating from May 12, 1997. It is the first and only scheme of this kind approved by the SEBI. The introduction of TGF affirms commitment of the exchange to be the most transparent stock exchange in India. The main objectives for setting up of TGF are:

(1) To guarantee settlement of bonafide transactions of members of the exchange inter se which form part of the stock exchange settlement system so as to ensure timely completion of settlements of contracts and thereby protect the interest of investors and the members of the exchange.

(2) To inculcate confidence in the minds of secondary market operations in general and global/foreign institutional investors in particular, to attract large number of domestic and international players in the capital market.

(3) To protect the interest of investors, promote the development and regulate the secondary market.

The BSE through the introduction of the TGF displayed its commitment towards investors by making itself one of the safest stock exchanges in India.

3.4 SECURITIES TRADING CORPORATION OF INDIA (STCI)

STCI has been promoted and set up by the Reserve Bank of India in May 1994 with an authorized capital of Rs. 500 crores to activate secondary market trading in government securities. It plays a vital role in market matters by providing two-way quotas for a government securities and public sector bonds. The improved liquidity through this institution would make holding of government securities more attractive.

3.5 STOCK HOLDING CORPORATION OF INDIA (SHCIL)

The SHCIL was set up in October, 1987 by seven all India financial institutions, namely, IDBI, IFCI, ICICI, LIC, GIC, UTI, and IRBI. It had a paid-up capital of Rs. 7 crores subscribed by the sponsoring financial. It provides infrastructural facilities for post-trading services, such as clearing, depository and other support services. Its services were extended to banks and mutual funds. It provides clearing house facilities to promote speedier transfer of securities. This corporation acts as a central clearing agency for registering the transfer of securities and reduce the time lag in effecting transfers. SCHIL has floated two companies—National Depository Corporation of India Ltd. (NDCIL) and Indian Securities Depository Nominee Company Ltd. (ISDNCL) —to execute the introduction of a scripless trading system when the depository legislation is passed.

SUMMARY

National Stock Exchange was set up to serve as a model exchange providing nationwide screen-based trading and electronic clearing and settlement systems. Stock Holding Corporation of India was incorporated in 1987 to act as a central securities depository in the country offering post-trading and custodial services to institutional investors.

REVIEW QUESTIONS

1. Discuss the salient features of NSE in the capital market.
2. Make a comparison between BSE and NSE.
3. What do you mean by book-building transaction?

QUIZ

State whether the following are true or false.

1. The companies with paid-up equity capital Rs.10 crores are eligible to be listed in NSE. (T/F)
2. The NSE has been established with the object of meeting international standards of securities market. (T/F)
3. The BOLT system was set up to achieve increase in market transparency. (T/F)

Fill up the blanks.

4. Trade Guarantee Fund has been in operation since ....
5. The SHCIL was set up in ....

REFERENCES

Bombay Stock Exchange Annual Reports, 1996–97 and 1999–2000.

Rastogi, A.B., "Reforms at the Stock Exchange, Mumbai", 1997, Corporate Planning Group, the Stock Exchange, Mumbai".

Rastogi, A.B., "*Trade Guarantee Fund*".

Reserve Bank of India, Bulletin 1996–97, 2000–2002.

Chapter 4

Over the Counter Exchange of India (OTCEI)

4.1 INTRODUCTION

India enjoys the privilege of having the tradition of trading in securities. The stock market activities in India were relatively low key activities till the beginning of 80s. The Indian stock market grew so fast in the 80s that the decade itself has been christened, inter alia as the 'decade of the capital market'. All the investors and entrepreneurs during that period flocked to the stock market and as a result the trading and settlement systems were not able to keep pace with the increased load. The burgeoning growth of the stock market has inevitably resulted in problems of ill-liquidity transparency, and listing and trading of smaller and medium companies. The listing requirements are also too stringent to be followed.

A company with a paid-up capital of then Rs. 3 crores could not be listed on stock exchange. So small companies were denied to avail the opportunity for raising funds from the public, thus limiting their growth. There has to be a change for the better. Therefore OTCEI was set up to deal with the problems of both investors and small- and medium-sized companies.

4.2 OVER THE COUNTER EXCHANGE OF INDIA (OTCEI)

Over the counter exchange of India (OTCEI), a different kind of stock exchange was launched in 1992 under section 25 of the Companies Act 1956 with the objective of providing an opportunity to small companies to assess public funds at low cost. It is also recognized as a stock exchange under section 4 of the Securities Contracts Act, 1956 enabling the listed companies to be treated as companies in which the public is substantially interested. OTCEI was promoted by UTI (Rs.160 lakhs), ICICI (160 lakhs), IDBI (136 lakhs), IFCI (64 lakhs), LIC (64 lakhs), GIC and its subsidiaries (64 lakhs), SBI Capital Market Ltd. (88 lakhs) Canara Bank Financial Service Ltd. (64 lakhs). It is registered with an authorized capital of Rs. 8 crores. OTCEI is ringless, electronic and national stock exchange designed for investor convenience. Equity shares, preference shares, debentures, bonds, warrants and exim scrips are traded in OTCEI. The minimum issued capital of companies designing to be listed on stock exchange is Rs. 30 lakhs. Companies listed on the OTCEI enjoy the same status as available to other companies listed on any other stock exchange in the country except that they cannot be listed or traded on any other stock exchange in India.

4.2.1 Promoters

OTCEI has been promoted by all India financial institutions such as, UTI, ICICI, IDBI, IFCI, LIC, GIC, SBI capital markets, and Canara Bank Financial Services Ltd. The number of shares held and the share holding pattern of the promoters is shown in Table 4.1.

Table 4.1 Share of promoters in OTCEI

Institution	No. of shares held	Share holding pattern (%)
UTI	20,00,000	20
ICICI	20,00,000	20
IFCI	8,00,000	8
LIC	8,00,000	8
IDBI	17,00,000	17
GIC	1,60,000	1.6
SBI Capital Ltd.	11,00,000	11
Canara Bank Financial Services Ltd.	8,00,000	8
New India Insurance	1,60,000	1.6
Oriental Insurance	1,60,000	1.6
United India Insurance	1,60,000	1.6
National Insurance	1,60,000	1.6

The top executives of the promoters are on the Board of Directors of the OTCEI. The operations of OTC are supervised by SEBI and Government of India.

Primary market operations

In the primary market when a new issue is opened for subscription, the application forms along with the prospectus will be available with brokers, agents, and stock exchanges. Investors can apply, deliver the cheques, and collect receipt from the banker for the issue at the end of the subscription period. Cheques are collected and application is forwarded to the registrars for the issue. OTCEI approves the allotment and takes it for listing. Companies can go public in OTCEI in two ways (i) the issue may either be a 'direct primary issue', or (ii) it can be done through the mechanism of a 'brought out deal'. *Direct primary issue* offers the shares directly to the public. In *brought out deal*, companies may offload shares to the sponsor at an earlier date. The sponsor then makes the offer of sale of these shares at a latter date to the public at possibly a higher price, to make up for the cost of holding the shares till the time shares are offered to the public. In case of indirect offer, the pricing of the issue is decided by the sponsor as per the relaxation announced by SEBI.

Secondary market operation

The trading system in OTC secondary market is such that the prices quoted for either sale or purchase of share can be seen on the computer terminal by investors and dealers. It provides 24 hours trading facilities. Figure 4.1 presents a bird's eye view of the OTCEI.

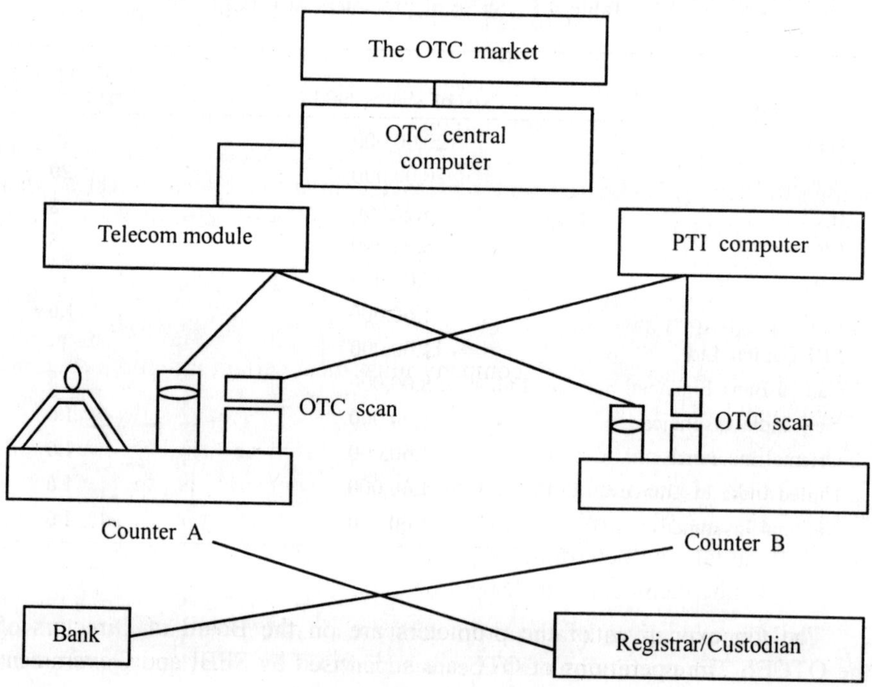

Fig. 4.1 The OTC market.

The secondary market operation is briefly described in Fig. 4.2.

Investor can walk up to OTCEI counter

↓

View the price on OTCEI scan

↓

Decide to buy or sell

↓

Purchase	Sell
Pays cheque for purchase	Gives CR and TD (Transfer Deed to counter)
↓	
Receives temporary CR (Counter Receipt)	Receives SCSS (Sale Confirmation Slips)
↓	
Returns when cheque is cleared and collects final CR	Returns when CR and TD are cleared and collects final cheque

Fig. 4.2 Secondary market operation.

Like all other stock exchanges, the transactions in the secondary market are not settled by auction, which a jobber normally does in a regular exchange. The shares are displayed by the counters and the investors can approach as many counters as possible and negotiate the rates for striking deals. Though the share certificate is not traded in the OTCEI but CR is traded. CR is a tradable document containing (a) name of the investor, name of the company, number of shares, address of the registrars, (b) price, commission, date and time of transaction, (c) investor's signature, investor's name of the bank, and account number, and (d) name and signature of the issuing counter. Four copies of CR are prepared and sent to the investor, counter, OTCEI, and registrar. Anybody who wants a share certificate has to deposit the CR with the registrar and collect the share certificate.

4.2.2 Listing Criteria

To be listed on the OTCEI, a company must meet certain minimum specified requirements. These are:

(a) The company desirous of being to get listed on OTCEI must appoint one of the members of OTCEI as its sponsor. The sponsor has to appraise the project, analyze its financial worth, manage its issue of capital, and determine the price at which the shares are offered to the public/members and dealers of OTCEI.

(b) Companies with a paid-up equity capital between Rs. 30 lakhs to 25 crores are eligible to be listed on OTCEI. These companies must be 'sponsored' by a member of the OTC exchange.

(c) The size of the issue should be a minimum of Rs. 20 lakhs or 25% of the paid-up capital, whichever is higher.

(d) Companies engaged in leasing, hire/purchase, finance, investment, amusement parks, etc. cannot be listed on OTCEI.

(e) Companies covered under MRTP/FERA may be listed on OTCEI if they satisfy listing guidelines on any other recognized stock exchange.

(f) The companies under OTCEI must have four centres from the northern, eastern, southern, and western, regions of the country for collection of application forms regarding issue of securities.

(g) OTCEI permits listing only when an issue is fully subscribed. In the event of the issue not being fully subscribed, the sponsor undertakes the responsibility for subscribing to the unsubscribed portion.

(h) The company has to pay one time listing fee of Rs. 6000 and annual listing fee of 0.05% of their paid-up capital in case of equity shares and 0.05% of the gross amount issued in case of any other security.

4.3 ADVANTAGES

OTCEI is a ringless–scripless electronic market that brings together traders around the nation. Besides single window access, it offers the investors total safety, transparency, and liquidity. The following are some of the benefits available to the investors:

(1) **Ringless trading:** OTCEI has appointed members and dealers who would open counter at various places where investors can buy or sell the listed securities.

(2) **Authorized dealers:** All members and dealers are authorized and approved by the OTCEI.

(3) **Safety:** Every investor on the OTCEI is provided an Invest OTC card that comes free of cost. This card can be availed when a person is allotted shares for OTC issue. This card can be used for all transactions and application for OTC issues. It provides the safety and security of investment.

(4) **Liquidity:** Every scrip has a compulsory market-maker at any time to offer buy and sell quotes for the scrip, thus offering an entry and exit by any investor for any scrip listed on the OTC exchange.

(5) **Transparency:** PTI–OTC scan display the best prices at which market-makers are willing to buy and sell their scrips. The exact price

at which the investor makes the transaction is printed on the trading documents for the confirmation. So investors' interests are safe and disputes are minimized.

(6) **Sponsorships:** Every scrip listed on OTCEI has a sponsor from among the OTC members. The sponsor appraises the scrip for investor worthiness thus providing quality of investment.

(7) **Transfer of security:** Shares are transferred to the investor's name within 7 days of submitting application. This is done by submitting transfer deeds to any of the OTCEI counters, if the investor's consolidated holding does not exceed 0.5% of the issued capital of the company.

(8) **Access:** Every OTC counter acts as a single window to the entire OTC exchange nationwide. So the investor could buy or sell at the nearest counter.

(9) **Low cost of issue:** The members of the OTCEI act as a wholesaler of securities by buying the entire issue from the company at a negotiated price and selling it to the public for relieving the company from all burdens relating to issue of securities.

(10) **Allotment:** The investors do not wait for long as the allotment of shares is expected to be completed in every aspect in 35 days and the trading begins immediately thereafter.

(11) **Quick settlements:** Purchase of shares and payment are completed within a week of OTCEI transaction.

OTCEI is not only advantageous to the investors, it is also beneficial to the companies. Following are some advantages that OTCEI offers to the companies:

(1) Small- and medium-sized companies can raise required capital through OTCEI.

(2) The cost of public issue is low.

(3) The companies listed on OTC are subjected to low income tax.

(4) The liquidity of the shares is ensured so that it further induces investment in this market.

(5) Companies which require listing on OTCEI have to offer 10% of the share capital for listing, as against 60% being offered to the public in other stock exchanges.

(6) There is no trading ring in case of OTCEI. Its counters can be dispersed all over the country to reach national stock exchange integrated by an electronic communication network.

4.4 PLAYERS IN THE OTCEI MARKET

Companies, investors, members, and dealers are the players in the OTCEI market. *Companies* refer to those whose securities are traded on OTCEI and *investors* are the ones who deal through the OTCEI centres. Both *members* and *dealers* can perform broking, trading, and becoming voluntary market makers. The member can be a public financial institution, mutual funds, banking subsidiaries, merchant banks, and venture capital funds approved by SEBI and other non-banking finance companies having the standing and status, and sufficient financial resources to carry out the activities of sponsorship and trading. The member must act as sponsor, market maker, broker, investor and minimum networth of 2.5 crores. On the other hand, dealers can be any individual, corporate body, or partnership firms having a net worth of Rs. 5 lakhs and at least 40% of the share capital of such corporate bodies should be held by the promoters. Dealers must have the knowledge of trading, stock evaluation, share transfer rules, and laws and must have financial strength to be able to carry on the trading and market making function.

4.4.1 International Players

In America, the OTC represented by U.S. NASDAQ (National Association of Securities' Dealers-Automated Quations) was born in 1971 as a ringless electronic security trading system is the fourth largest market in the world, next only in turnover to the New York, Tokyo, and Korean stock exchanges. In US, more than 90% of the corporate bands are traded on the OTC market and most of them listed on the New York Stock Exchange (NYSE). Of the over 4000 companies listed on NASDAQ, about 600 fulfill the NYSE's listing requirements but have preferred to be in NASDAQ. The Japanese OTC market is rapidly becoming a major emerging market in the far east and the introduction of a computerized online trading system (JASDAQ) will ensure the continued rapid expansion of this market. So far, OTC exchange in India has met with resounding success while markets abroad are getting saturated.

4.5 TRADING MECHANISM

Every investor who trades on the OTC exchange has to be registered with the exchange. He has to get himself registered by giving the investor registration form duly filled in by any one of the OTC counters. Investor registration is required to be done once only and valued for trading on any OTC counters. The main objective of investor registration is to facilitate computerized trading and provide safety of operations to the investors. An investor can buy and sell any listed scrip at any OTC counter and can also apply for a service like transfer of shares, splitting and consolidation of shares, registering power of attorney, and change of holders' names, etc. OTC exchange has designed its electronic computerized trading system in such a way that it makes trading quicker, transparent and disciplined, and settlements faster and efficient. The listing company in OTCEI ensuring investment worthiness and the listing criteria of the OTC exchange allows entry into the capital market for small companies which are otherwise denied access on other exchanges. The trading in OTCEI is not in the traditional ring but it is screen based. The OTC quotes are displayed on the PTI-OTC, scanned and allowed to all investors coming to them to trade during market hours. All the counters are connected by a telecom (computer) network to the OTC's central computer system.

The scrips listed on the OTC exchange is 'sponsored' by its members. As sponsors, members compulsorily make market in that scrip, which ensures liquidity. This compulsory market-making provides for availability of both buy and sell quotes for the scrip, from the sponsor of the scrip. OTC trading also provides for transfer of shares by registrars up to a certain percentage of issued capital portfolio. Its nationwide presence provides investors with easy access to the national market and the market-making concept ensures liquidity in the scrip. In this way, the OTC exchange boosts investors' confidence in trading over its system.

4.6 PRESENT SCENARIO

The OTCEI index registered a 172% growth from 188 OTCEI points in March 1994 to 324 points in March 1995. Three years since its inception, barely 44 scrips are listed on OTCEI against upwards of 7500 scrips listed at Dalal Street and 490 scrips listed at the new entrant National Stock Exchange (NSE). Further at the OTCEI, the turnover per day is a meagre Rs. 1 crore for the listed scrips and another Rs. 50 lakhs for permitted securities. In comparision, the turnover volume at the Bombay Stock Exchange (BSE) is Rs. 250 crores and at the NSE is Rs. 75 crores. The allotment of the first two issues in OTCEI was completed in record 28 days and the presence of a number of market-makers promotes healthy competition and maximization of return to the investors. Still OTCEI is in its infancy stage. It is now operating in 54 cities in 19 states. The OTCEI is moving towards setting higher standards for the benefit of the corporates and the investing community in India. The turnover in OTCEI during 2000–2001 was Rs. 126 crores and it slashed down to 4 crores in 2001–2002. Further it reported nil turnover during the year 2002–03.

4.7 FUTURE OUTLOOK

The major problem behind the OTCEI is the lack of investor interest and awareness. Secondly, the OTCEI should not be vested with the sole authority of licensing dealers throughout India. Once it becomes monopolistic in nature, it is likely to become bureaucratic in operations and autocratic in its dealings. Also OTCEI should function exclusively for small companies and provide much needed finance to the small- and medium-sized companies. Therefore, counter these problems, SEBI has also put on its thinking cap to relax certain restrictions in the eligibility criteria for improving the listing in OTCEI. So they are now allowing the leasing, hire/purchase, and amusement parks companies to be listed in the OTCEI. In addition to these three types of companies, ones which are covered under FERA/MRTP act are now allowed to be listed under OTCEI. OTCEI also plans to bring down issued capital from 40% to 25%. All this would lead to a flood of OTC issues. OTCEI is also taking necessary steps to make itself more popular among investors.

SUMMARY

OTCEI is being set up to provide liquidity to shares of smaller, closely held companies. OTCEI is the first exchange to set up market-makers to provide two-way quote for each scrip for both buying and selling. So the capital market acts as a catalyst for economic development. The objective is a vibrant, internationally competitive, efficient, and transparent capital market which is equally important to the needs of India's economic and social development.

REVIEW QUESTIONS

1. State the salient features of OTCEI.
2. Discuss the advantages of OTCEI to investors and the companies.
3. Discuss the trading mechanism of OTCEI.

QUIZ

State whether the following statements are true or false.

1. OTCEI was set up to deal with the problems of both investors, and small- and medium-sized comapnies. (T/F)
2. Companies engaged in leasing, hire/purchase finance, and investments can be listed on OTCEI. (T/F)
3. Every investor who trades on the OTC exchange has to be registered with the exchange. (T/F)

Fill up the blanks.

4. .... are the players in the OTCEI market.
5. Small- and medium-sized companies with a paid-up capital of Rs. .... may be enlisted on the OTCEI.

REFERENCES

Chandra, Prasanna, "*The Investment GAME*", Tata McGraw-Hill, New Delhi, 1993.

Chartered Financial Analyst, October, 1994.

Chartered Financial Analyst, April–March, 1995.

Dedhia, Manish V "OTCEI—A New Dimension in the Capital Market in India", *Management Accountant*, June, 1992.

Economic Times, February 1992.

Hariharasubramaniam, R., "OTCEI—A New World of Investment", *Financial Express.*

Shirali, Jaideep "OTC Exchange of India", *Chartered Secretary*, July, 1993.

Thakkar, Mahesh, "*A New Era—Keeping you in Touch with the Happenings on OTCEI*".

Chapter 5

Mutual Funds in India: An Overview

5.1 INTRODUCTION

A mutual fund is a single, large professionally managed investment organization that combines the funds of many individual investors having similar investment objectives. It designs its schemes to meet the needs of different types of investors in terms of nature of investments, dividend distribution, and liquidity, etc. The entire income/profits are distributed among the investors in proportion to their investments. However, expenses for managing the fund are charged to the fund. Mutual fund activity has come to play an important role in our development efforts.

5.2 HISTORY

The concept of mutual fund is not new. At the very dawn of commercial history, Egyptians and Phoenicians were selling shares in vessels and caravans in order to spread the risk of these perilous ventures. Much later, in 1822, Societe General de Belgique was formed, which embodied the modern concept of sharing risk. The Foreign and Colonial Government Trust of London formed in 1968 was the real pioneer to propose modern day concept of mutual funds. Later in 1873, the Scottish American Trust was established by Robert Flemming at Dundee. In England, the early institutions were created under legal form, known as the Old English Trust. The persons who had acquired experience in large trust estates were appointed as trustee, and capital was entrusted to them for purchasing securities. British investment trusts are successful and presently they are popular with unit trusts.

Although many nineteenth century British investment trusts invested in American stocks, the first American investment trust was the closed-end Boston Personal Property Trust created in 1893. It was not until the 1920s that the U.S. experienced a boom in closed-end investment trusts. The great bull markets of the 1920s and 1980s provided fertile soil for mutual funds. In their first incarnation and heyday, mutual funds played a central role in the robust stock market of the 1920s. The first mutual fund, the Massachusetts Investor Trust, was launched in Boston in 1924. After the 1929 stock market crash, these closed-end investment trusts were characterized as the "evil trusts" that manipulated the stock market, and had a hand in causing the Great Crash of 1929. These changes added to the flourishing of securities regulation initiated in the 1930s, which caused the creation of the Securities and Exchange Commission (SEC). The SEC recommended the passage of legislation which materialized in 1940. The Investment Companies Act of 1940 gives the rules and regulations for the establishment and management of mutual funds.

Since 1940, the growth of open-ended mutual funds has been dramatic. The growth of closed-end mutual funds has been slower and more erratic but they continue to exist. However, as can be seen in Fig. 5.1, from 1984 to 1990 there has been a rebirth in the popularity of closed-end funds. Although Fig. 5.1 shows that mutual fund growth from 1940 was positive, it did not

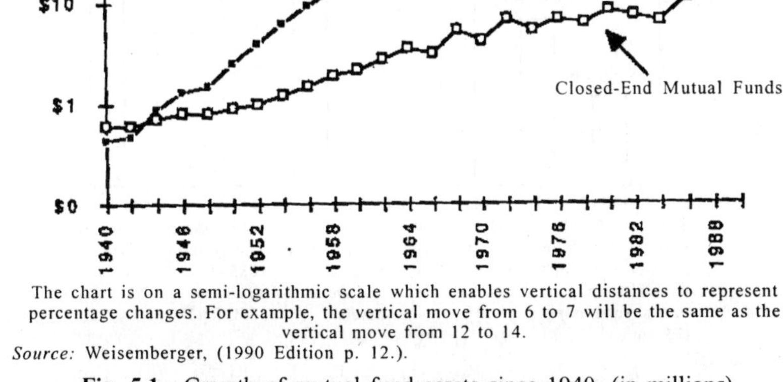

The chart is on a semi-logarithmic scale which enables vertical distances to represent percentage changes. For example, the vertical move from 6 to 7 will be the same as the vertical move from 12 to 14.

Source: Weisemberger, (1990 Edition p. 12.).

Fig. 5.1 Growth of mutual fund assets since 1940. (in millions)

take off until the mid 1970s. As people's enthusiasm was soon snuffed out because the market collapsed in 1969–70 and again in 1973–74. The number of mutual funds grew from 68 funds in 1940 to more than 3000 funds by 1990 is shown in Table 5.1.

Table 5.1 Number of mutual funds

Year	Number
1940	68
1945	73
1950	103
1960	161
1970	361
1975	426
1980	564
1981	665
1982	857
1983	1,026
1984	1,247
1985	1,531
1986	1,843
1987	2,323
1988	2,718
1989	2,918
1990	>3,000

Source: Mutual Fund Fact Book, 1990, p. 22.

A chart showing the growth of mutual funds during the last 50 years (1940–1990) is given in Fig. 5.2. In the year 1965, there were only 2–3% of

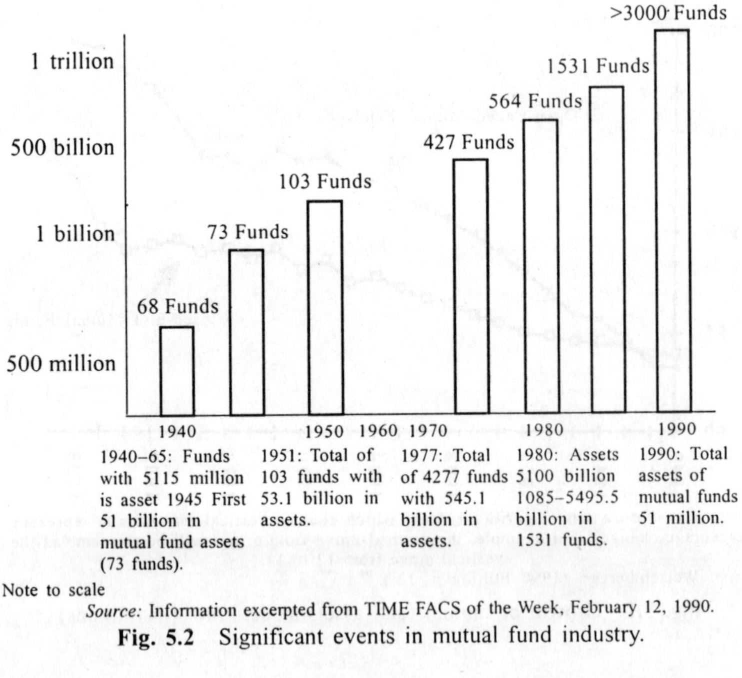

**Note*: Note to scale

Source: Information excerpted from TIME FACS of the Week, February 12, 1990.

Fig. 5.2 Significant events in mutual fund industry.

U.S. households that owned fund shares. Today one-fourth of all U.S. household invest in mutual funds. In a recent study done in U.S., mutual funds have been labelled as the bank deposits of 1990s. Assets of worldwide mutual funds stood at $11.2 trillion at the end of the first quarter of 2003, down slightly from the level at the end of 2002. The statistics included 38 countries which is depicted in Fig. 5.3.

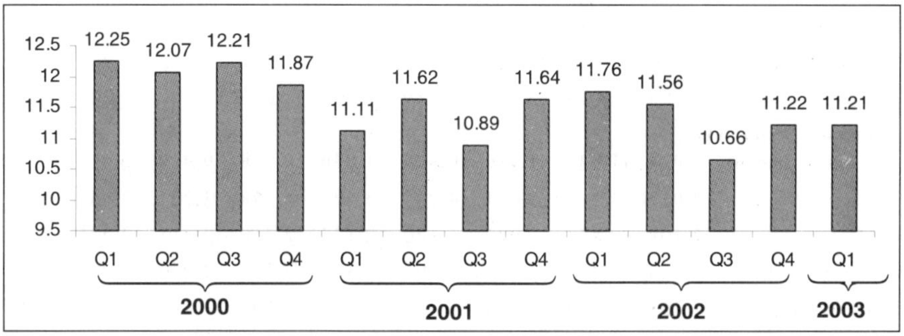

Fig. 5.3 Assets of worldwide mutual funds (trillions of U.S. dollars, end of quarter).

Mutual fund assets in the United States fell 2.0% in the first quarter, while assets of other countries rose collectively by 2.5%. The strength in fund assets outside United States reflected weakness in the U.S. dollar, which moved lower against most currencies. Measured in local currencies, fund assets have been found to have declined over the first quarter in the majority of countries, including nine of the ten largest countries.

Worldwide equity fund assets, measured in U.S. dollars, dropped by 4.2% in the first quarter and most stock markets came under selling pressure during the quarter, with many European and several Asia-Pacific exchanges posing double-digit losses. In contrast, bond fund assets rose 5.7%, paced by strength in Europe and the Americas. Money market fund assets rose slightly, as sizable gains in Europe offset declines in the United States and the Asia-Pacific region. Balanced/mixed funds recorded a small decline in assets. It is presented in Fig. 5.4 and Table 5.2.

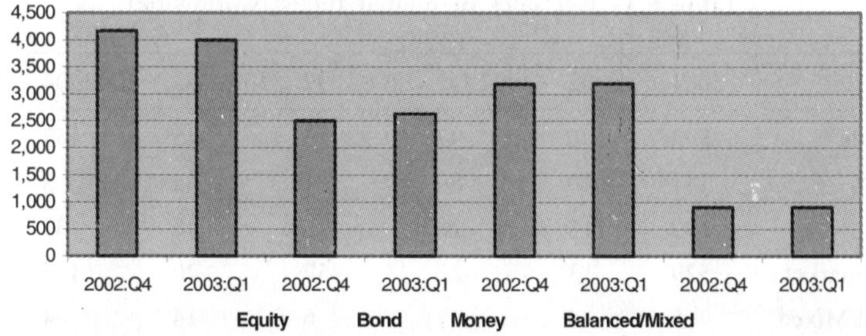

Fig. 5.4 Worldwide assets of equity, bond, money market and balanced/mixed fund (billions of U.S. dollars, end of quarters).

Table 5.2 Status of mutual funds at different times

	1998	1999	2000	2001	2002:Q1	2002:Q2	2002:Q3	2002:Q4	2003:Q1
All reporting countries	**9,299**	**11,391**	**11,867**	**11,635**	**11,763**	**11,559**	**10,663**	**11,217**	**11,210**
Equity	4,137	5,878	5,962	5,132	5,240	4,814	3,971	4,173	3,999
Bond	2,173	2,104	2,077	2,203	2,201	2,336	2,395	2,499	2,642
Money market	2,071	2,287	2,480	2,982	2,973	3,027	3,025	3,185	3,197
Balanced/Mixed	810	971	1,022	938	944	951	855	907	903
Others	58	55	190	189	195	205	190	202	213
Countries reporting in every period	**9,024**	**11,023**	**11,110**	**10,865**	**11,030**	**10,778**	**9,910**	**10,412**	**10,378**
Equity	4,017	5,713	5,697	4,885	5,027	4,598	3,772	3,965	3,791
Bond	2,108	20,428	1,982	2,120	2,136	2,259	2,317	2,422	2,562
Money market	2,066	2,282	2,402	2,901	2,886	2,933	2,929	3,080	3,083
Balanced/Mixed	781	939	965	888	904	908	815	862	859
Others	51	47	64	71	77	80	76	82	84

Source: National Mutual Fund Associations.

Table 5.3 reveals that net sales of mutual funds were $13 billion in the first quarter of 2003, down from $153 billion in the fourth quarter of 2002. The decline largely resulted from a net outflow of $56 billion from money market funds, which reversed a $117 billion net inflow in the previous quarter. In the low-interest rate environment in the United States, the net outflow from U.S. money market funds was $69 billion. Several Asia-Pacific countries also experienced net outflows from money market funds, while European countries collectively saw strong net inflows. Equity funds posted a small outflow of $14 billion in the first quarter, with weakness evident in the United States, Canada, and most European countries. In contrast, Asia-Pacific countries eked out a small net inflow. On the other hand balanced/mixed funds experienced a small net outflow.

Table 5.3 Net sales of mutual funds (worldwide)

	2001	2002	2002:Q1	2002:Q2	2002:Q3	2002:Q4	2003:Q1
All Funds	892	190	97	–15	–45	153	13
Equity	151	40	80	21	–64	3	–14
Bond	199	118	28	9	48	32	87
Money market	529	13	–27	–57	–20	117	–56
Balanced/Mixed	5	–4	7	6	–14	–4	–4
Others	9	23	9	5	4	5	0

Net sales at bond funds were a robust $87 billion in the first quarter of 2003 and represented 3.6% of assets of those 27 countries that reported net flow data. The first quarter pace, if maintained for a full year, would far outstrip net sales in 2001, a year of strong inflows. The strength in net sales was widespread, with 22 countries experiencing inflows to bond funds.

At the end of first quarter of 2003, assets of equity funds represented 36% of all worldwide mutual fund assets. The asset share of money market funds was 29%, while that of bond funds was 24% as exhibited in the pie chart shown in Fig. 5.5.

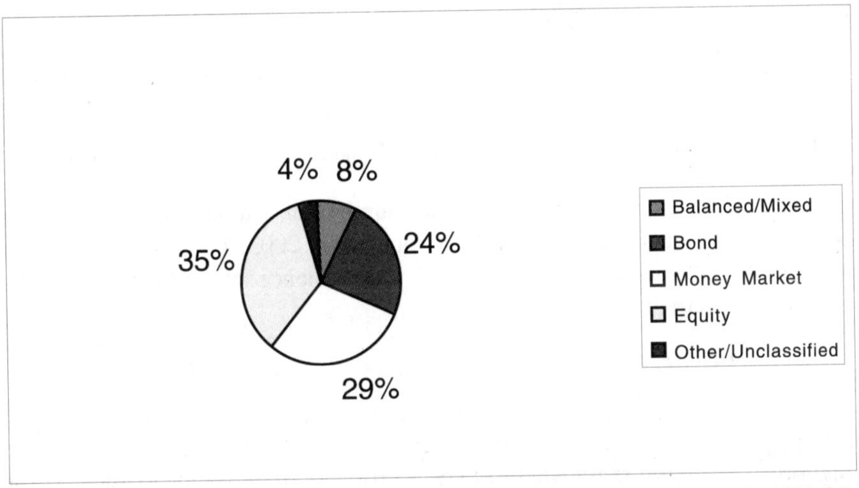

Fig. 5.5 Composition of worldwide mutual fund assets by type of fund, 2003:Q1.

Figure 5.6 reveals that 59% of worldwide mutual find assets were in the Americas at the end of the first quarter of 2003, 31% were in Europe, and remaining 10% in Africa and Asia-Pacific region. Figure 5.7, on the other hand, depicts the composition of worldwide mutual funds by type of fund, for Ist quarter of the year 2003 in America.

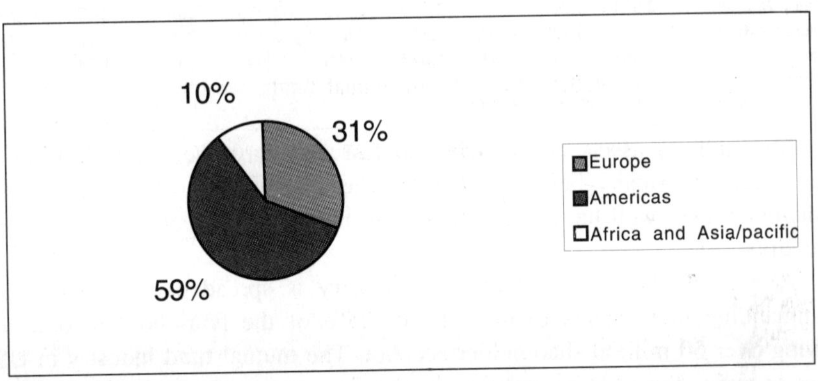

Fig. 5.6 Composition of worldwide mutual fund assets by region, 2003:Q1.

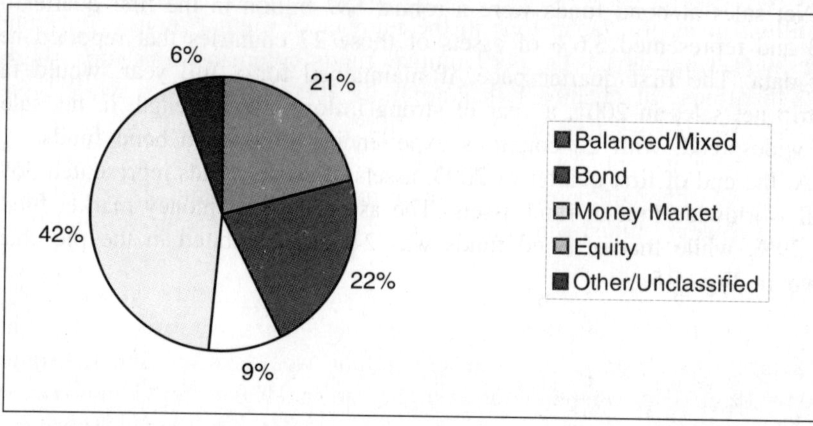

Fig 5.7 Composition of worldwide mutual funds by type of fund, 2003:Q1.

It is evident from Table 5.4 that the number of mutual funds worldwide stood at 53,150 at the end of the first quarter of 2003. Of these, 43% were equity funds, 22% were bond funds, 21% were balanced/mixed funds, and 9% were money market funds.

Table 5.4 Number of funds, 1998–2003:Q1 (end of period)

	1998	1999	2000	2001	2002:Q1	2002:Q2	2002:Q3	2002:Q4	2003:Q1
All reporting countries	**50,365**	**52,767**	**51,557**	**52,589**	**53,105**	**52,413**	**52,979**	**53,040**	**53,150**
Equity	15,465	22,463	20,337	22,329	22,748	22,847	22,969	22,845	22,617
Bond	11,261	15,491	13,113	12,012	12,006	11,573	11,646	11,503	11,554
Money market	3,050	6,739	4,648	4,188	4,207	4,108	4,226	4,346	4,521
Balanced/Mixed	5,754	6,375	11,110	11,110	11,283	11,032	11,266	11,183	11,180
Others	514	612	968	1,259	1,160	1,117	1,099	1,258	1,329
Countries reporting in every period	**34,337**	**35,989**	**39,367**	**41,866**	**42,045**	**42,297**	**42,602**	**42,405**	**42,162**
Equity	14,463	15,666	18,637	20,740	20,963	21,003	21,099	20,817	20,603
Bond	10,867	10,884	10,176	9,843	9,850	9,904	9,957	9,947	9,907
Money Market	2,921	2,701	2,786	2,729	2,715	2,683	2,686	2,674	2,666
Balanced/Mixed	5,593	6,149	6,926	7,514	7,532	7,710	7,775	7,725	7,681
Other	493	589	842	1,040	985	997	1,085	1,242	1,305

Source: National Mutual Fund Associations.

Mutual fund assets are growing so fast and consumer bank deposits so slow that Americans believed that by the turn of the 21st Century that individuals may well have more money in mutual funds than in savings bank accounts.

At present the U.S. mutual fund industry is spread over 30,000 funds, commanding investments to the tune of 25% of the household income and having over 50 million shareholder account. The mutual fund industry in USA now occupies the premier position in the financial sector while banking and insurance companies lag behind. The mutual fund industry serves about

50 million investors. Japan tops in the number of mutual funds with around 5400 funds whereas USA's 3400 mutual funds command four times higher assets than those of Japan. UK has around 1,400 mutual funds, while France ranks second in asset formation, with 1000 mutual funds only next to USA.

The growing popularity of mutual funds in USA is basically due to the good returns when compared to the stock market returns and low-risk factors. Returns of many mutual funds are much higher than the returns of S&P 500 index.

During 1920s in Canada, many closed-end investment companies were born. These are generally known as investment trusts. The first mutual fund in Canada to issue its share to general public was the Canadian Investment Fund in 1932. The two other funds organized in 1930 were: Commonwealth International Corporation Limited and Corporate Investors Limited. These three funds are now amongst the giants of mutual funds in Canada. Subsequently, hundreds of mutual funds both open and closed-end have been developed and expanded in many countries in Europe, the far east, and Latin America.

Mutual funds/unit trusts are popular financial intermediaries in many countries. In the U.S., mutual funds are the second largest financial institutions after the banking sector whose assets were worth $2161.4 billion at the end of 1994. In December 1995, the European community issued a directive to coordinate laws, regulations, and the administrative provisions relating to mutual funds. This is popularly known as Undertakings for Collective Investment in Transferable Securities. The directive establishes a common regulatory scheme for investment policies, public disclosure, structure, and control. These policy changes encouraged the growth of mutual funds all over the globe. Countries in the Asia-Pacific region that include Hong Kong, Thailand, Singapore, and Korea have also entered this field with a big bang.

5.3 MUTUAL FUND INDUSTRY IN INDIA

The concept of mutual funds is not very old in India. It only showed up in sixties, after a century old history elsewhere in the world. Reacting to the needs for a more active mobilization of household savings to provide investible resources to industry, the idea of first mutual fund in India was born out of the far-sighted vision of Sri T. Krishnamachari, the then finance minister. He wrote to the then Prime Minister Pandit Jawahar Lal Nehru outlining the need for an institution which would serve as the conduit for these resources to the Indian capital market and RBI was entrusted to create this special institution. The idea of mutual fund began to take shape in India in 1963 with the set-up and enactment of Unit Trust of India (UTI) when the UTI Act, 1963 was framed to operate both as a financial institute and an investment trust. In 1964, the board of trustees formulated an open-ended scheme and launched it with scale of units being open in the month of July 1964 at the nominal value of Rs.10 each. Thus, the UTI came out with its first open-ended scheme in 1964. During the initial phase of the developments of mutual funds between 1964 and 1987, UTI alone managed the show with five open-ended funds. The second phase between 1987 and 1992 witnessed the broadening of the base of the industry by the entry of mutual funds sponsored by commercial banks and public sector financial institutions. Followed by the government's decision to permit nationalized banks to set up mutual funds, the State Bank of India (1987), Life Insurance Corporation (1989), General Insurance Corporation (1991), Canara Bank (1987), Indian Bank (1990), Bank of India (1990), and Punjab National Bank (1990) sponsored by public sector banks have also joined the race. Beginning with an asset base of Rs. 25 crores in 1964, the industry has grown at a compounded average growth rate of 27% to its current size of Rs. 90,000 crores. The period 1986–1993 can be termed as the period of Public Sector Mutual Funds (PMFs). From one player in 1985, the number increased to eight in 1993. The public sector as a whole enjoyed monopoly in the industry till 1992 when private players were allowed in the mutual fund industry. The year 1992–93 marked a turning point in the history of mutual funds in India. Series of measures were launched as a prelude to economic liberalization and reforms process. The mutual fund industry was opened to the private domestic and foreign players. The first private sector mutual fund, Kothari Pioneer, was launched in 1993. The euphoria created later on by Morgan Stanley Fund (September, 1994) is all history now. The other players like Jardine Fleming, George Soros, and Capital International along with the host of domestic players joined the party. But for the equity funds, the period of 1994–96 was one of the worst in the history of Indian mutual funds.

1999—Year of funds

Mutual funds have been around for a long period of time (to be precise, for 36 years) but the year 1999 witnessed immense potential and developments in this sector. This year signalled the year of resurgence of mutual funds and saw the regaining of investor confidence in these mutual funds. During this time, all the participants were busy carrying out the revival of the funds—the AMCs, the unit holders, and the other related parties. However, the sole factor that gave major lift to the revival of the funds was the then union budget. The budget brought about a large number of changes in one stroke. An insight of the union budget on mutual funds taxation benefits is provided later in the text. It made mutual funds more attractive and provided acceptability among the investors. The union budget exempted mutual fund dividend given out by equity-oriented schemes from tax, both at the hands of the investors as well as the mutual funds. Now that the industry is moving from infancy to adolescence, it is maturing and the investor and funds are frankly and openly discussing difficulties, opportunities, and compulsions.

What is mutual fund?

With the growth of the economy and the capital market in India, the size of investors has also increased rapidly. In fact, small investors in India have regularly invested in public issues to finance big and small green-field projects of known and unknown promoters. They have been benefited out of such investments in the past. As the stock market crumbled later on and new issues flopped, small investors again started to look for a good opportunity. In this situation, mutual funds proved that they are able to deliver the goods. The concept of mutual funds was conceived to mobilize savings from the people and invest them in a mix of corporate and government securities. The mutual fund operators actively manage this portfolio of securities and earn income through dividend, interest and capital gains which is eventually passed on to mutual fund shareholders. So mutual funds are financial intermediaries as illustrated through the Fig. 5.8.

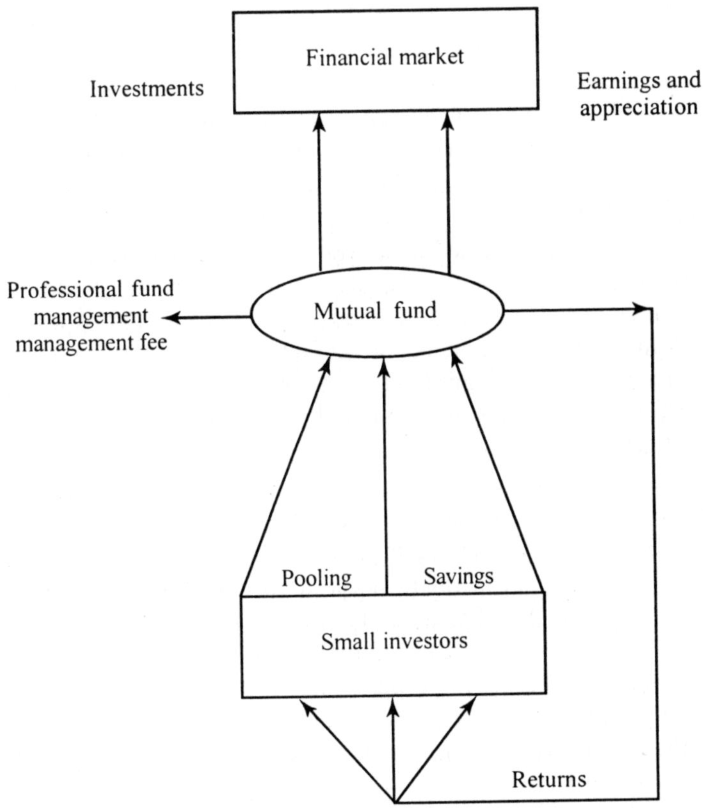

Soucre: Mutual Funds: Management and Working book, 1996.

Fig. 5.8 Mutual funds as financial intermediaries.

People define mutual funds in different ways. According to James L. Pierce, it is a non-depository or non-banking financial intermediary which acts as an "important vehicle for bringing wealth holders and deficit units together indirectly". Weston J. Fred and Eugene F. Brigham, in their book *Essentials of Managerial Finance*, state that "mutual funds are corporations which accept dollars to buy stocks, long-term bonds, and short-term debt instruments issued by business or government units. These corporations pool funds and thus reduce risk by diversification". As per mutual fund fact book (published by the investment company institute in the U.S.), "a mutual fund is a financial service organization that receives money from shareholders, invests it, earns returns on it, attempts to make it grow, and agrees to pay the shareholders cash-on-demand for the current value of his investment". Encyclopaedia Britannica offers another definition: "mutual fund, also called unit trust or open-ended trust is a company that invests the fund of its subscribers in diversified securities and in turn issues units representing shares in those holdings. They make continuous offering of new shares at the net asset value and redeem the shares on demand at net asset value determined daily by the market value of the securities they hold". Frank Reilly defines mutual funds as "financial intermediaries which bring a wide variety of securities within the reach of the most modest of investors". In the words of Joel Ross, "mutual fund means 'taking the pool' of money and investing it in the securities of a wide range of companies. Managers of mutual funds decide when to buy, sell, or hold in order to achieve the objective of the fund ··· policy removes the risk associated with putting all your eggs in one basket, as the typical small investors tend to do". The VNR dictionary of business and finance says mutual fund is "an investment fund that pools the invested funds of others and invests these funds on their behalf, usually in a specific kind of investment, such as money market instruments, municipal bonds, or common stock". Thomson dictionary of banking defines a unit trust as "a method of investment by which money subscribed by many people is pooled in a fund, the investment and management of which is subject to the strict legal provision of a trust deed. The fund is invested in securities on behalf of subscribers by a management company. The management company and the trustee who must be independent of each other are parties to the trust deed which defines their respective responsibilities towards the subscribers to the trust fund and details the rules for the operation of the trust". Merriman in his work on unit trusts defined unit trust as follows: "the unit trust is a trust similar to a will or marriage settlement to which there are three parties—the management company, which operates as a distinct entity from the trust it conducts; the trustee, usually a well known bank or insurance company; and the unit holders, who occupy the position of beneficiaries under the trust deed. The essential principle of the unit trust is the deposit of a block of stock exchange securities with the trustee and the sale to the public of ownership fractions units or subunits of this largers block. The management company (with the trustee's cooperation to a lesser or greater degree according to the responsibility undertaken in the trust deed) retains the administration of the securities, but not their custody, which vests in the trustees". Prevention of Fraud (Investment) Act, 1958 of England defines a unit trust scheme as "any arrangement made for the purpose, or having the effect of providing facilities for the participation by persons as beneficiaries under a trust, in profits or income arising from the acquisition, holding, management or disposal of securities or any other property whatsoever". According to SEBI (mutual funds) regulations 1993, mutual fund means "a fund established in the form of a trust by a sponsor to raise money by the trustee through the sale of units to the public under one or more schemes for investing insecurities in accordance with these regulations".

To sum up, mutual fund, an investment company, is a financial intermediary concerned with gathering savings of the individuals. Institutions channelize these savings essentially in corporate securities in such a manner as to ensure its investors a triple benefit of steady return and capital appreciation along with low risk. In a mutual fund, there are three entities operating. They are: (i) an agency which mobilizes savings and gets a commission, (ii) an investment agency which gets a prescribed rate of commission, and (iii) a trustee institution which is normally a bank which holds the stock of securities of the mutual fund. In India, the investment trusts are established according to the provisions of the Indian companies act. The difference between mutual funds and investment company are tabulated in Table 5.5.

Table 5.5 Mutual funds vs. investment companies

	Mutual funds/Unit trusts	Investment companies
Objective	Mobilization of savings from the investors, mostly household	Mobilization of savings of the investors of household and corporate sector. Highest belongs to the promoters of the company
Organization	Organized and managed according to SEBI regulations 1993 and UTI act 1963 in case of Unit Trust of India	Incorporated under the Companies Act, 1956 and manage according to the provisions of the act.
Capital structure	Initial capital would be provided by the sponsor. Scheme-wise capital is decided based on the nature of the scheme. Units are offered out of the scheme capital. No debt capital.	Capital structure shall be at par with any other industrial company. No scheme-wise capital shares are offered out of the company's equity capital. Capital may be debt capital also and has the advantage of gearing.
Name of the schemes	Either open-ended or closed-end, with a wide variety of investment objectives	Neither open-ended nor closed-end
Liquidity	Closed-end scheme units are traded on the organized stock exchanges. Open-ended schemes offer repurchase facility and some closed-end schemes may also offer repurchase or premature encashment.	The company's shares are traded on the stock exchange. No repurchase of shares.

5.4 MUTUAL FUNDS' SUPERIORITY VIS-À-VIS OTHER INVESTMENT OPTIONS

(a) **Company fixed deposit:** It is common knowledge that the plethora of regulations concerning the fixed deposits of the companies have failed to check the malpractices indulged in by companies. Non-payment of interest, and delayed payment of interest and principal is frequent and even financially sound companies which declare dividends do not have a good track record when it comes to fixed deposits. Although in the amended companies act a grievance redressal machinery has been set up for deposits, the procedure is time consuming.

(b) **Bank time-deposits:** Bank time-deposits, though they are 100% risk-free up to a certain limit, do not earn a reasonable return in rhythm with the inflation rate which is often in double digits. Also the deposit does not carry any substantial tax benefit. The interest earned is only one category of income which can be claimed along with other categories for tax deduction under section 80L of the Income Tax Act. There is also no scope for appreciation of its nominal value.

(c) **Investment in shares:** Share market is a very delicate and complicated area and though one would be in a position to make handsome gains when the market is in boom, there is also a likelihood of the investors losing their money when they fail to correctly forecast the company/market trend.

So there is every reason to think that there would be a shift from bank or company deposits to mutual funds.

5.5 IMPORTANCE OF MUTUAL FUNDS

Owing to the size, operating economics and ability to commit large sums of money for long periods, the mutual funds enjoy ample resources at their disposal by mobilizing resources of the investors. The mutual funds with the expert and experienced management cadre can secure large varieties of high yielding "Blue chip" securities and show better results to the investing public. Therefore, the investors now prefer investing their resources in various mutual fund schemes, than managing themselves. The following reasons can be stated for the rising popularity of mutual funds:

(1) With an emphasis on increase in domestic savings and improvement in deployment of investment through markets, the need and scope for mutual fund operation, has increased tremendously. The basic purpose

of reforms in the financial sector was to enhance the generation of domestic resources by reducing the dependence on outside funds. This calls for a market-based institution which can tap the vast potential of domestic savings and channelize them for profitable investments. Mutual funds are not only best suited for this purpose but also capable of meeting this challenge.

(2) An ordinary investor who applies for share in a public issue of any company is not assured of any firm allotment. But mutual funds, those subscribe to the capital issue made by companies get firm allotment of shares. Mutual funds, later sell these shares in the share market and to the promoters of the company at a much higher price. Hence mutual funds help develop confidence among the investors.

(3) The psyche of the typical Indian investor has been summed up by Mr. S.A. Dave, former chairman of UTI, in three words—yield, liquidity, and security. The mutual funds, being set up in the public sector, have given the impression of being as safe a conduit for investment as bank deposits. Besides, the assured returns promised by them have been great for the typical Indian investors.

(4) As mutual funds are managed by professionals, they are considered to have a better knowledge of market behaviour. Besides, they bring a certain competence to their job. They also maximize gains by proper selection and timing of investment.

(5) Another important thing is that the dividend and capital gains are reinvested automatically in mutual funds and hence are not fritted away. The automatic reinvestment nature of a mutual fund is a form of forced saving and can make a big difference in the long run.

(6) The mutual fund operations provide a reasonable protection to the investors. Besides, presently all schemes of mutual funds provide tax relief under section 80L of the Income Tax Act and in addition, some schemes provide tax relief under section 88 of the Income Tax Act which leads to the growth of mutual funds.

(7) Mutual fund creates awareness among urban and rural middle class people about the benefits of investment in capital market through profitable and safe avenues. Therefore, mutual fund could be able to mop up a large amount of the surplus funds available with these people.

(8) The mutual fund attracts foreign capital flow to the country and secures profitable investment avenues abroad for domestic savings through the opening of offshore funds in various foreign countries. In view of recent liberalized economic and industrial policies and concessions such as excise and customs given in recent budget for the growth of industrial sector, the capital market—both primary issue

market and secondary—have been witnessing unprecedented boom. Hence mutual funds have been able to speed their wings by spreading their funds in various industrial sectors.

(9) Risk of loss due to ill-informed and misinformed purchase/sales is reduced as the managers of mutual funds have better access to information. Many investors have fell prey to misleading and motivated "headline" leads and lips. This risk is reduced by diversification of portfolio in terms of companies and industries. Even a small investor in mutual fund can get the benefit of diversification.

(10) Lastly, another notable thing is that mutual funds are controlled and regulated by SEBI and hence are considered safe. Due to all the benefits, the importance of mutual funds has been increasing.

5.6 CLASSIFICATION OF MUTUAL FUNDS

Mutual funds can be classified under four different categories:

(1) Operational classification
(2) Portfolio classification
(3) Geographical classification
(4) Structural classification.

5.6.1 Operational Classification

Mutual Funds are broadly categorized into three types, namely, (a) open-ended mutual funds, (b) closed-end mutual funds, and (c) interval funds.

Open-ended mutual funds

SEBI regulations defines open-ended schemes as "a scheme of a mutual fund which is offering units for sale or has outstanding any redeemable units and which does not specify any duration for redemption or repurchase of units". Open-ended mutual funds are open throughout the year for investment and redemption. The units are bought and sold directly by the fund. Therefore there is more certainty and transparency. The corpus are gradually increased to allow proper investment and redeemable at that day's NAV and money returned immediately. Each open-ended scheme of a mutual fund is required to raise at least Rs. 50 crores as its minimum corpus funds. If the minimum amount or Rs. 50 crores or 60% of the targetted amount, whichever is higher not raised, then the entire subscription has to be refunded to the investors. First 45 days of the subscription period should be considered for determining the target figure or minimum size of the scheme. When an individual investor redeems, open-ended funds offer a fair price related to the fund's net asset value (NAV) or the true worth of fund, thereby largely eliminating the speculative element. Open-ended funds are offering overnight processing whenever an investor wants to put in or take out their money. By offering systematic investment and withdrawal plans as well as dividend reinvestment options, open-ended funds have been able to offer tailored solutions to meet the requirements of a wide cross-section of investors. For the large number of mutual fund investors in India, open-ended funds have really come as a big boon.

Closed-end mutual fund

Closed-end mutual funds have a definite period after which their shares/units are redeemed. The units are offered to the investors through the public issues and after the date of closure, the entry to the investor is closed. Closed-end mutual fund schemes are generally trades among the investors in the secondary market since they are to be quoted on stock exchanges. Their price is determined on the basis of the demand and supply in the market. Each closed-end scheme is required to raise at least Rs. 20 crores as its corpus fund. If the minimum amount of Rs. 20 crores or 60% of the targetted amount, whichever is higher, is not raised for closed-end scheme the entire subscription is refunded to the investors. The closed-end schemes are permitted to be kept open for subscription for more than 45 days. Generally the redemption period of the closed-end scheme would be five to ten years, the fund may also provide premature encashment by offering repurchase after two to three years of commencement of the scheme. The closed-end mutual funds have been popular till 1994 but now open-ended mutual funds are very popular due to distinctive feature of regular sale and purchase of securities.

Interval funds

Interval funds combine the features of open-ended and closed-end schemes. They are open for sale or redemption during predetermined intervals at NAV related prices.

5.6.2 Portfolio Classification

Mutual funds differ with reference to their instruments. Therefore, different mutual funds are designed to meet the needs of the investors. This section discusses the types of mutual funds classified on the basis of their portfolios.

Growth-oriented funds or equity-oriented funds

The objective of such a fund is to provide capital appreciation to its investors and accordingly a substantial portion of the corpus is invested in high growth equity shares and other equity-related instruments. The scheme may or may not declare dividends. This is a high-risk investment fund with high capital gain potential and low current income assurance. This fund is ideal for investors having a long-term outlook seeking growth over a period of time.

Income-oriented funds

The main objective of this fund is to provide regular income to the investors in the form of dividends. The dividends may be cumulative or non-cumulative on a quarterly, half yearly, or yearly basis. The corpus of the scheme is invested in fixed income securities like debentures, bonds, etc. and a relatively lower percentage in shares. These funds are ideal for capital stability and regular income.

Balanced funds or income- and growth-oriented funds

These funds aim at distributing both income and capital appreciation to the investors.Technically the corpus of this scheme is invested equally in high growth equity shares and in fixed income earning debentures. But after the Budget 1999, these funds have begun investing more than 51% in equity and the rest in debt to make the returns tax-free in the hands of the investors.

Bond funds

Bond funds are more liquid, diversified, and conservative investments with modest capital gains. These are expected to be very secure with a steady income and have a very low risk. Bond funds provide fixed return for those who desire safety.

Stock funds

Such funds are established for those who are willing to accept significant risks in the hope of very high returns. These are called common stock funds. The assets held in the fund are entirely the common stocks of diversified list of industrial corporation. It is best suited for risk takers who are interested in capital growth rather than regular income.

Index funds

These funds invest only in those shares which are included in the market indices and in exactly the same proportion. Whenever the market index goes up, the value of such index funds also goes up. Conversely when the market index comes down, the value of such index funds also goes down.

Industry funds

The industry funds invest its resources in a particular foreseeing growth potential industries like cement, steel, jute, power real estate, etc. These funds carry high risks and gains as the performance of these funds is directly exposed to a specific sector.

Tax relief fund

This is popularly known as equity-linked saving schemes. These are essentially closed-end schemes. The investment would be high in equity share. The investor can claim deduction or rebate in the income tax to the extent of his investment in the fund, subject to the provisions of the Income Tax Act 1961. They are listed on stock exchanges. There would be a minimum lock-in-period of three years and the scheme shall not provide any type of liquidity during this period.

Leveraged funds

Leveraged funds or borrowed funds are used in order to increase the size of the value of the portfolio and benefit the shareholders by gains exceeding the cost of the borrowed funds. Funds are generally unused in speculative and risky investments.

Real estate funds

Real estate funds are closed-end type funds. The fund is so named because of primary investment in real estate ventures. Such funds are of various types depending upon real estate transaction.

Money market mutual funds

These funds are generally invested in money market instruments such as treasury bills, certificate of deposits, commercial papers, bills discounting, etc. These are regulated on the basis of specified guidelines laid down by the Reserve Bank of India.

Asset management mutual funds

These are also called Asset Management Companies (AMCs). These funds have special characteristics of dealing with assets other than securities. These funds can acquire various assets and give them on lease basis to needy lessees.

Liquid funds

These funds invest in short-term debt securities with high liquidity. In these type of funds, profitability plays second fiddle, while liquidity assumes priority.

5.6.3 Geographical Classification

On the basis of geographical limits, mutual funds schemes can be classified as domestic mutual funds and offshore mutual funds.

Domestic mutual funds

Domestic mutual fund schemes mobilize the savings of the citizens of the country. However the NRIs and foreign investors can invest in these schemes. All the schemes in vogue in the country are the domestic mutual fund schemes.

Offshore mutual funds

These funds enable the NRIs and international investors to participate in Indian capital market. Further these funds are governed by the rules and procedures laid down for the purpose of approving and monitoring their performance by the Department of Economic Affairs, Ministry of Finance and the directions of RBI. The UTI was the first institution to launch offshore mutual fund—India Fund, in London in 1986 and mobilized 7.5 crores pounds. It launched another fund, namely, India Growth Fund in 1987 in the USA and succeeded in mobilizing U.S. $ 6 crores. Similarly, State Bank of India collected as high as U.S. $ 15.7 crores in 1988 through its India Magnum Fund. The Citi Bank also launched an offshore mutual fund for NRI investors in 1989–90. All offshore funds have received overwhelming response from the foreign investors. They keep up the expectation of the investors. To attract resources from outside, the Government of India reduced the tax rate on dividends payable to the offshore funds. Apart from tax concessions private sector has also been permitted to set up these mutual funds.

5.6.4 Structural Classification

From the point of view of financial market structure, mutual funds can be divided into two categories, namely, (a) capital market mutual fund, and (b) money market mutual fund. Mutual funds generally invest the pooled resources in capital market instruments whereas money market mutual funds invest in money market instruments.

5.7 ADVANTAGES OF INVESTING IN MUTUAL FUNDS

The mutual funds offer the following advantages to the investors:

(i) *Professional management:* The mutual fund institutions provide experienced and skilled professionals who have knowledge in security analysis and portfolio management and analyze the performance and prospects of companies. They also help to select suitable investments to achieve the objectives of the mutual fund schemes.

(ii) *Diversifications:* Mutual funds invest in a number of companies across a broad cross-section of industries and sectors. This diversification reduces the risk because seldom do all stocks decline at the same time and in the same proportion. Thus, the investor gets a proportion of the average market. This specific characteristic of mutual fund is not seen in case of any other type of alternative investment instrument.

(iii) *Convenience:* Investing in a mutual fund reduces paper work and helps to avoid many problems such as bad deliveries, delayed payments, and unnecessary follow-up with brokers and companies. Mutual funds save time and make investing easy and convenient.

(iv) *Return potential:* Over a medium to long-term, mutual funds have the potential to provide higher returns as they invest in a diversified basket of selected securities.

(v) *Low costs:* Mutual funds are a relatively less expensive way to invest compared to directly investing in the capital markets because their benefits of scale in brokerage, custodial and other fees translate into lower costs for investors.

(vi) *Liquidity:* The mutual funds provide easy liquidity to those who want to dispose of their units after a stipulated period of time. The open-ended mutual funds offer instantaneous liquidity through repurchase facility. Closed-end schemes also offer the facility of repurchase after a specified period in addition to listing on the stock exchanges.

(vii) *Transparency:* Mutual funds provide regular information on the value of their investment in addition to disclosure on the specific investment made by the scheme, the proportion invested in each type of security, and the fund manager's investment strategy and outlook.

(viii) *Flexibility:* Through features such as regular investment plans, regular withdrawal plans, and dividend reinvestment plans, investors can systematically invest or withdraw funds according to their needs and convenience.

(ix) *Choice of schemes:* Mutual funds offer a variety of schemes to enable investors to take advantage of opportunities not only in the equity, debt, and money markets but also in specific industries and sectors.

(x) *Tax benefits:* Many of the mutual funds offer the benefits of tax exemption to the investors. In India for equity-linked schemes of mutual funds under section 88, tax rebate up to 20% of investment is available. Under section 80L income from mutual funds dividends alongwith other specified incomes up to Rs. 15,000 is exempted from tax. But it is now no longer applicable in accordance to the annual budget of 1999. Dividend income from mutual funds is totally tax free.

(xi) *Government regulation:* All mutual funds are registered with SEBI, and they function within the provisions of strict regulations designed to protect the interests of investors. The operations of mutual funds are regularly monitored by SEBI.

(xii) *Shareholders services:* Mutual funds also offer many useful shareholder services. One important service is the automatic reinvestment of distributions for people who want it. Owners of individual stocks are often more inclined to take their cash dividends and spend them. Many funds have systematic withdrawal plans, which are handy for retired individuals. Other important services include automatic investment plans, retirement plans, and record keeping for tax purposes.

(xiii) *Safety from loss due to unethical practices:* The probability of loss stemming from fraud, scandal, or bankruptcy involving the fund's management company is very small. By transferring investment risk to shareholders, mutual fund companies side-step the problems that have been especially painful for people dealing with certain thrifts, banks, and insurance companies among others.

(xiv) *Product structure:* Mutual funds are now taking their customers very seriously. They have started designing products to suit the needs of the common investors. A good example is the Tata Children's Fund which helps plan the education expenses of a child.

In addition to this, the mutual fund managers are new in a better position to read the market and take superior investment decisions. Entry of foreign and private mutual funds has resulted in a shake out of weak players. There have been mergers and closures with only a few strong and committed players left in the industry. Technology and investment driven improvements in investment convenience are also playing a key role in attracting the investors. Changes in cheque writing facility allow writing cheques to third parties. Further strengthening of the economy, sectoral reforms, strength of sectors like software, pharma, and FMCG have resulted in improved asset prices which helps the mutual funds deliver superior results.

5.8 PERFORMANCE EVALUATION OF MUTUAL FUNDS

In view of the different practices that were being followed in presenting the balance sheet by mutual funds in India, Securities and Exchange Board of India has come out with a standard format of the balance sheet, as also minimum disclosure requirements. The mutual fund industry does not have a standard accounting policy and hence comparison of performance can only be done after reducing the performance to a common denominator.

Any meaningful evaluation of performance necessarily has to measure total return per unit of risk or the ability to earn superior returns for a given risk class. There are various statistical techniques to measure this factor. With better and standardized disclosure requiremnts, mutual fund performance can more professionally evaluated in due course. This is expected to generate increasing pressure on fund managers for superior performance.

Mutual funds sell their shares to public and redeem them at current net asset value (NAV) which is calculated as:

$$\text{NAV of MF} = \frac{(\text{Total market value of all MF holdings}) - (\text{All MF liabilities})}{(\text{No. of MF units or shares})}$$

The net asset value of a mutual fund scheme is basically the per unit market value of all the assets of the scheme. This is better illustrated with the following example.

Name of the scheme : XYZ
Size of the scheme : Rs. 50,00,00,000 (Rupees fifty crores)
Face value of units : Rs. 10
No. of units : 5,00,00,000

$$= \frac{\text{Scheme size}}{\text{Face value of units}}$$

Investments : In shares
Market value of shares : Rs. 75,00,00,000 (Rupees seventy five crores)

$$= \frac{\text{Market value of investments}}{\text{No. of units}}$$

$$= \frac{\text{Rs. } 75{,}00{,}00{,}000}{5{,}00{,}00{,}000}$$

= Rs. 15

Thus each unit of Rs. 10 is now worth Rs. 15.

Simply stated, NAV is the value of the assets of each unit of the scheme, or even simpler value of one unit of the scheme. Thus, if the NAV is more than the face value (Rs. 10), it means money has appreciated and vice versa.

NAV also includes dividends, interest accruals, and reduction of liabilities and expenses, besides market value of investments.

5.9 CHOOSING A MUTUAL FUND

Investors should note the following points while choosing a mutual fund:

(1) Investment objective

The schemes offered by mutual funds should be chosen based on investment objectives such as:

- Regular income
- Pure growth oriented
- Balanced fund
- Tax savings
- Period of scheme
- Liquidity/Open-ended schemes/listing.

(2) Past performance

The past performance of fund manager should be checked even though it does not assure about or indicate the future performance. The risks are however lower if the fund manager's capability is superior.

(3) Equity research

Equity research capability and other fund management techniques are important factors in deciding about a fund.

(4) Global linkages

The fund manager's understanding of Indian capital markets and the global linkages is critical to the process of investment decision making.

(5) Transparency in fund accounting

Choose a mutual fund which assures full transparency of the investments made and discloses NAV periodically to assist the investor in understanding the value of investment, and the area where investments have been/are to be made.

(6) Investor service

Funds which pay emphasis to investor servicing help in sorting out procedural grievances, if any.

Judged the efficiency

The test of efficiency of a good mutual fund shall comprise of evaluation of mutual fund on the basis of its:

(i) Stability	— Whether a mutual fund is stable or not so far as its schemes are concerned.
(ii) Liquidity	— Whether the schemes offer liquidity by way of their listing on stock exchange.
(iii) Growth	— Whether the mutual funds are offering increase in net asset value, and there is consistent growth in dividend and capital appreciation.
(iv) Credibility of issuer	— Previous track record of issuer should be checked.
(v) Returns	— Assured or otherwise
(vi) Management approach	— Risk taking, portfolio, diversification, return maximization, bonus, etc.

5.10 MUTUAL FUND GUIDELINES ON ADVERTISEMENTS

SEBI has prescribed an advertisement code for mutual funds, the important features of which are as follows:

(1) Advertisement should not be published unless approved by the designated person.

(2) Advertisement should be true, fair, and clear. It should not contain a statement, assurance, promise, or forecast which is false or misleading.

(3) The sale offer should contain only information, substance of which is included in the fund's current prospectus.

(4) The advertisement should not be so framed as to exploit the lack of experience or knowledge of the investors.

(5) It should not contain any information, the accuracy of which is dependent on an assumption.

(6) It should not compare on fund with another unless comparison is fair.

(7) The mutual funds, which advertise yield must use standardized computations such as tax/value, annual yield, etc.

(8) If the advertisement guarantees a minimum return, it should also indicate the resources available to back such guarantee.

(9) Mutual funds shall indicate in their advertisements—the settlers, trustees, managers, and financial advisors to the fund.

(10) Mutual funds which advertise past performance should state that these are not indicative of future returns.

5.11 SEBI REGULATIONS

The SEBI regulations for the establishment and issue of schemes by mutual funds are as follows:

- Mutual fund shall be established in the form of trusts under the Indian Trust Act and managed by separately formed asset management company.
- Money market mutual fund would be regulated by the RBI and other mutual funds would be regulated by SEBI.
- Fifty per cent members of the board of AMC must be independent directors and must have no connection with sponsoring organization.
- The directors should have at least 10 years experience in the field of portfolio management, financial administration, etc.
- The AMC should have a minimum net worth of Rs. 10 crores.
- The SEBI has the authority to withdraw the authorization of AMC if they fail to work for the interest of investors. This stipulation is not applicable to banks sponsoring mutual funds.
- An AMC cannot act as the AMC for another mutual fund.

- AMCs are also allowed to do other fund based businesses such as providing investment management services to offshore funds, other mutual funds, venture capital funds, and insurance companies.
- The minimum amount to be raised with each closed-end scheme should be Rs. 20 crores and for the open-ended scheme Rs. 50 crores.
- Each scheme of the mutual fund is registered with SEBI before it is floated in the market.
- Closed-end schemes should not be kept open for subscription for more than 45 days. For open-ended schemes, the first 45 days should be considered for determining the target figure.
- If the minimum amount or 60% of the target amount is not raised, the entire subscription has to be returned to the investors.
- For each scheme, there should be a separate and responsible fund manager.
- The SEBI guidelines (1999) restrict MFs to invest not more than 10% of NAV of a scheme in shares or share related instruments of a single company.
- SEBI increased the maximum investment limit for MFs in listed companies from 5 to 10% of NAV in respect of the open-ended funds.
- The initial issue expenses should not exceed 6% of the funds raised under each scheme.
- All mutual funds must distribute a minimum of 90% of their profits in any given year.
- Every mutual fund is required to send the audited annual statements of accounts and six months unaudited accounts of net assets for each of its schemes to the SEBI.
- The SEBI shall lay down a common advertising code for all mutual funds to comply with.
- The SEBI after due investigation may impose penalty on mutual funds for violating the guidelines.

5.12 GROWTH TRENDS

With liberalization, the Indian industrial sector wants cheaper funds to face global competition. Banking intermediaries today cannot afford to reduce their margins but the household sector demands better returns. All these factors have spawned the success of a new intermediary called mutual funds. The mutual fund industry in India, which is a little over three decade old, has undergone a sea change since the introduction of mutual fund regulations in

1993. It was in this year that private and foreign mutual funds started participating in the industry. Today, the Industry consists of the Unit Trust of India, mutual funds sponsored by public sector banks, insurance corporations, and those set up by private and foreign funds as depicted in the Table 5.6.

Table 5.6 Indian mutual funds industry

(Rs. in crores)

	Sales for latest quarter*	Sales for 98–99	Redemption latest quarter*	Redemption 98–99	Assets on March 99
Unit Trust of India	1569	11679	2185	13364	53320
Bank-sponsored MFs	217	420	161	772	5481
FI-floated MFs	410	1312	106	512	2811
Private sector — Indian joint ventures	346	2739	328	2636	1016
Joint ventures predominantly Indian	1266	3019	840	2290	3040
Joint ventures predominantly foreign	1001	2208	744	1458	2804
Total	4809	21377	4364	21032	68472

Source: AMFI Newsletter, *April–June 1999.

The entry of private sector mutual funds has imparted competitive efficiency in the industry, helped investors to choose from funds with different maturity periods, and offered different risk-return trade-offs. Table 5.7 shows the amount mobilized by different mutual funds for the period 1987–88 to 1999–2000.

Table 5.7 Gross mobilization by mutual funds

(Rs. in crores)

Year	UTI	Public sector mutual funds	Private sector mutual funds	Total
1987–88	1763.00	258.00	N/A	2021.00
1988–89	3483.00	301.00	N/A	3784.00
1989–90	5504.00	1204.00	N/A	6708.00
1990–91	3182.00	2967.00	N/A	6149.00
1991–92	8686.00	2580.00	N/A	11266.00
1992–93	11051.00	1978.00	N/A	13029.00
1993–94	9288.00	387.00	1548.00	11223.00
1994–95	8686.00	1333.00	1333.00	11352.00
1995–96	5891.00	301.00	301.00	6493.00
1996–97	9589.00	172.00	344.00	10105.00
1997–98	9116.00	344.00	1978.00	11395.00
1998–99	13201.00	1677.00	7826.00	22704.00
1999–2000	9159.00	1548.00	19178.00	29842.00

Source: The Economic Times, January 3, 2000.

Table 5.8 Changing fund preferences

Year	Percentage of assets			
	Equity funds	Debt funds	Mixed (Equity + Debt) funds	Money market/ Liquid funds
1990	21.19	54.17	27.7	0
1993	43.88	29.91	26.2	0
1996	18.02	39.67	39.91	0
1999	21.92	48.37	25.29	2.17

Source: The Economic Times, January 3, 2000.

Table 5.7 shows the growth trend of mutual funds for the period 1987–2000 while Table 5.8 depicts the changing fund preferences of mutual funds. It is evident that market preferences keep changing every few years. At present, the industry has grown over the years and there are 36 mutual funds registered with Securities Exchange Board of India (SEBI). In 1997–98, 37 good schemes were launched by mutual funds (including one conversion scheme)—17 were open-ended while 20 were closed-end. In 1998–99, another 52 new schemes (including 10 conversion schemes) were launched. Of these, 34 were open-ended, 16 closed-end, and two were interval funds. Out of these 52 schemes in the last financial year, 29 came from private sector mutual funds, while 13 came from the Unit Trust of India and 10 from the public sector.

As in July 2002, private sector mutual funds have outstripped their public sector counterparts, mobilizing Rs. 72,781.64 crores against a paltry Rs. 5378.64 crores for the latter. UTI is managed to mobilize a meagre Rs. 961.03 crores over the same period. The Table 5.9 reveals that Rs. 79121.31 crores had been mopped up by the domestic mutual fund industry. The net inflow stood at Rs. 1203.50 crores for the same period. The private sector mutual funds posted the biggest gain net inflow of Rs. 6601.89 crores.

Table 5.9 Funds mobilized, repurchase/redemption amount and the net inflow/outflow of funds for the period April 2002 to July 31 2002

(Rs. in crores)

	Private sector	Public sector	UTI	Total
Mobilization of funds	72,781.64	5,378.64	961.03	79,121.31
Repurchases amount	66,179.75	4,737.36	7,000.70	77,917.81
Net inflow/outflow of funds	6,601.89	641.28	–6,039.67	1,203.50
Cumulative position of net assets as on 31st July 2002	48,388.01	8,218.76	45,786.78	1,02,393.55

Source: SEBI.

The total assets under all mutual funds were Rs. 1,02,393.55 crores as on 31st July 2002 as against Rs. 98,969 crores for the corresponding period of last year. The share of UTI continues to be stagnant at 44.72% (Rs. 45,786.78 crores) while private players now command assets of Rs. 48,388.01 crores (47.26%) pubic sector funds are the last at 8.02% or Rs. 8,218.26 crores.

The primary new issue market continues to be in the doldrums with investors shunning share offerings, but mutual funds have become the flavour of the season. More and more small investors are now opting for safer investment avenues like mutual funds. Mutual funds are giving steady and good returns now. Nearly 45 open-ended funds have outperformed the S&P (Nifty index of the National Stock Exchange. One of the important features of mutual funds is that most of them are already in leasing and hire–purchase business. Another development in this area is the organization of mutual funds by the reputed industrial houses like Birla and Tatas. Both industrial houses are engaged in collaboration of foreign banks to tap non-resident investments. At present, the SEBI has permitted Indian mutual funds to invest in Global Depository Receipts/American Depository Receipts (GDRs/ADRs) of Indian companies subject to a minimum of $20 million and a maximum of $50 million per mutual fund, subject to a limit of 10% of the net assets managed by the funds. Presently mutual fund industry has done a commendable job of not only providing innovative products, but at the same time providing returns. The mobilization has shown a rise of 115% when compared to the last quarter (Jan.–March) of 1998–99. The corresponding growth for bank deposits was a mere 17%. It cannot be denied that at Rs. 7,000 billion, the banking sector is ten times the size of the mutual funds industry. But it is equally true that preference towards mutual funds is increasing. Since 1990–91, mutual fund collections have grown 25% annually against a bank deposits growth rate of 14%. The comparative advantage of mutual fund acceptability is presented in the Table 5.10.

Table 5.10 Banks versus mutual funds in a nutshell

Parameter	Banks	Mutual funds
Returns	Low	Better
Administrative expenses	High	Low
Risk	Low	Moderate
Safety	Comparatively high	High
Liquidity	At a cost	Better
Investment option	Less	More
Network	High penetration	Low but improving
Quality of assets	Not transparent	Transparent
Capital appreciation	Nil	High
Interest calculation	Minimum balance between 10th & 30th of every month	Everyday
Guarantee	Maximum Rs.1 lakh on deposits	None

There is no doubt that the performance of mutual fund schemes is equally good in comparison with banks. An investor who maintains large balance in savings account actually loses money when inflation is taken into account. Investor gets interest only in the minimum balance after 10th day of every month while in case of mutual funds, interest is credited from day one. As investors start realizing the importance of real returns, more and more banks might lose their depositors.

The mutual funds have undergone considerable quantitative as well as qualitative changes. The result of this changing trend can be seen in the growing popularity of mutual funds. Of the total 275 mutual fund schemes now in existence, 103 are income schemes, 94 are growth schemes, and the rest are hybrids. Of the total investments managed by mutual funds, equity schemes account for 58% of the total assets. UTI's market share in fund mobilization fell from 74% in 1997–98 to 54% in 1998–99. It fell further to 45% in the first quarter of 1999–2000. However cumulatively, UTI still accounts for 76% of the total resources mobilized by Indian mutual funds. The recent bull run on the stock markets boosted the net income of unit scheme 64, the largest mutual fund scheme in the country. US-64 generated a net income of Rs. 563 crores during the first quarter of the then current financial year that ended September 1999. According to Unit Trust of India (UTI), the US-64 scheme saw a net inflow of Rs. 714 crores during the period. US-64 still remaining the main contributor to UTI's sales, notched up Rs. 1,548 crores out of the total sales of Rs. 4,613 crores during the quarter. Equity investments in US-64 portfolio stood at 69%. UTI managed 28 equity schemes with unit capital of about Rs. 6,155 crores as on September 1999. The number of mutual fund houses went on increasing, with many foreign mutual funds setting up funds in India and also the industry witnessed several mergers and acquisitions. At the end of January 2003, there were 33 mutual funds with total assets of Rs. 1,21,805 crores. The Unit Trust of India with Rs. 44,541 crores of assets under management was way ahead of other mutual funds.

In February 2003, following the repeal of the Unit Trust of India Act 1963, UTI was bifurcated into two separate entities. One is the specified undertaking of the Unit Trust of India with assets under management of Rs. 29,835 crores as at the end of January 2003, representing broadly, the assets of US-64 scheme, assured return and certain other schemes. The specified undertaking of Unit Trust of India, functioning under an administrator and under the rules framed by Government of India and does not come under the purview of the mutual fund regulations.

The second entity is the UTI Mutual Fund Ltd., sponsored by SBI, PNB, BOB, and LIC. It is registered with SEBI and functions in accordance to the mutual fund regulations. With the bifurcation of the erstwhile UTI which had in March 2000 more than Rs. 76,000 crores of assets under management and with the setting up of a UTI Mutual Fund, conforming to the SEBI Mutual

Fund Regulations, and with recent mergers taking place among different private sector funds, the mutual fund industry has entered its current phase of consolidation and growth. On October 31, 2003, there were 31 funds, which managed assets of Rs. 1,26,726 crores under 386 schemes. The growth of assets are presented in the Fig. 5.9.

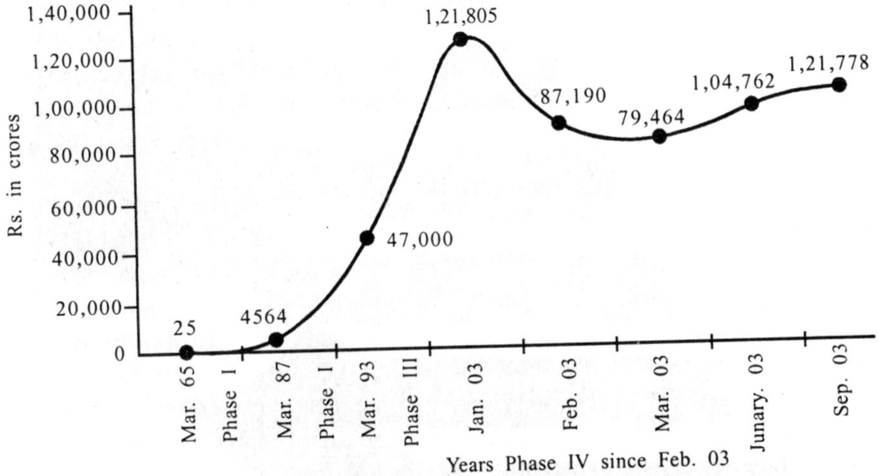

Fig. 5.9 Growth in assets under management.

Note: Erstwhile UTI was bifurcated into UTI Mutual Fund and the specified undertaking of the Unit Trust of India with effect from February 2003. The assets under management of the specified underking of the Unit Trust of India have therefore been excluded from the total assets of the industry as a whole from February 2003 onwards.

There is an increased sense of product differentiation by the investor community. The new breed of mutual funds has brought in quite a number of positive features like transparency, accounting standards, frequency of disclosure, context of disclosure, and manner of working. The new entrants have contributed enormously in all these areas. Despite the falling markets, mutual funds have been able to generate good returns for the investor. The mutual fund ladder is shown in the Fig. 5.10.

The mutual funds have also given opportunity to international investors to invest in Indian equities through the vehicle of offshore funds. Thus, India would remain as one of the most preferred places for international investment.

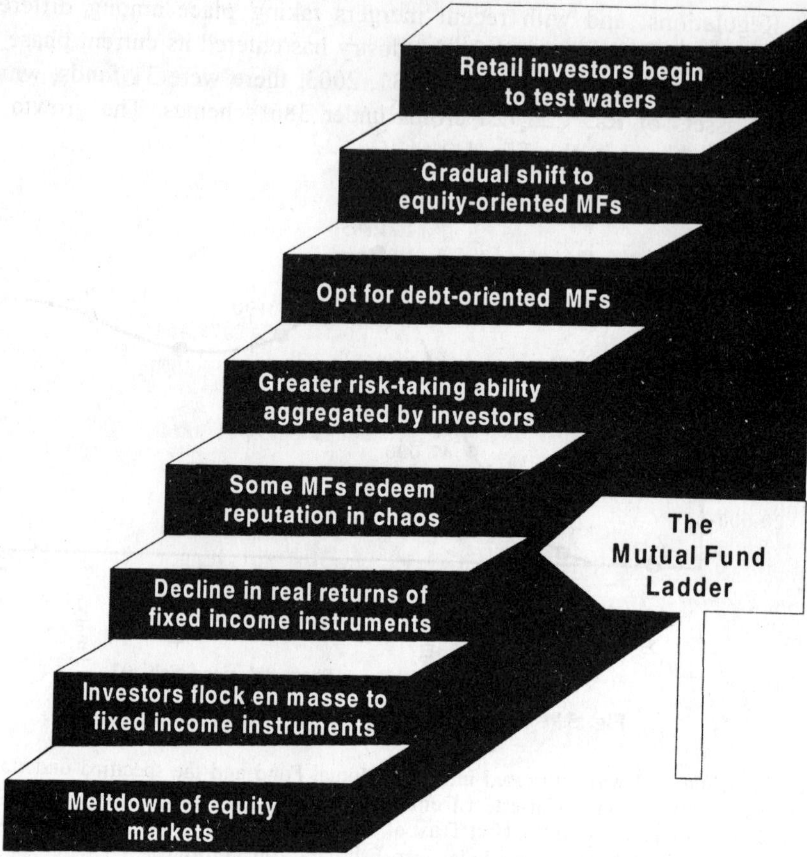

Fig. 5.10 The mutual fund ladder.

5.13 GLOBAL SCENARIO

Some basic facts

- The money market mutual fund segment has a total corpus of $1.48 trillion in the U.S. against a corpus of $ 100 million in India.
- Out of the top 10 mutual funds worldwide, eight are bank-sponsored. Only fidelity and capital are non-bank mutual funds in this group.
- In the U.S. the total number of schemes is higher than that of the listed companies while in India it is just 386 schemes.
- Internationally, mutual funds are allowed to go short. In India fund manager do not have such leeway.
- In the U.S. about 9.7 million households have been managing their assets online by the year 2003, such a facility is not yet available in India.

- Online trading is a great idea to reduce management expenses from the current 2% of total assets to about 0.75% of the total assets.
- 72% of the core customer base of mutual funds in the top 50 broking firms in the U.S. are to trade online by 2003.

Internationally, online investing continues its meteoric rise. Many have debated about the success of e-commerce and its breakthrough, but it is true that this aspect of technology could and will change the way financial sectors function. However, mutual funds cannot be left far behind. They have realized the potential of the Internet and are equipping themselves to perform better.

In fact, in advanced countries like the USA, mutual funds buy–sell transactions have already begun on the Internet, while in India the Internet is used as a source of information only.

Such changes could facilitate easy access, lower intermediation costs and better service for all. A research agency that specializes in Internet technology estimates that over the next four years mutual fund assets traded online will grow ten folds from $128 billion to $ 1,227 billion; whereas equity assets traded online will increase during the same period from $246 billion to $1,561 billion. This will increase the share of mutual funds from 34 to 40%.

5.14 SHORTCOMINGS IN OPERATION OF MUTUAL FUNDS

The mutual funds have been operating for the last twelve years in India. Thus, it is too early to evaluate their operation. However, one should not lose sight of the fact that in the formatory years of any institution, evaluation is very important as this raveals the real character of the systems. Following are some of the shortcomings in operation of mutual funds:

(1) The mutual funds are all externally managed. They do not have employees of their own. Also there is no specific law to supervise the mutual funds in India. There are multiple regulations while UTI is governed by its own regulations, the banks are supervised by Reserve Bank of India and the central government. The insurance company mutual funds are regulated under the central government regulations.

(2) Many of the investors are not willing to invest in mutual funds unless there is a promise of a minimum return.

(3) Unrestrained fund raising by schemes without adequate supply of scrips creates severe imbalance in the market.

(4) Many small companies did very well but mutual funds cannot reap their benefits because they are not allowed to invest in smaller companies. Not only this, mutual fund is allowed to hold only a fixed maximum percentage of shares in a particular industry.

(5) The mutual funds in India are formed as trusts. As there is no distinction made between sponsors, trustee and fund managers, the trustees play the role of fund managers.

(6) The increase in the number of mutual funds under various schemes has increased competition. As a result the funds lose their stabilizing factor in the markets.

(7) While UTI publishes details of accounts about their investments, mutual funds are still not publishing the profit and loss accounts and balance sheets after their operation.

(8) The mutual funds have eroded the financial clout of the institutions in the stock market for which cross transaction between mutual funds and financial institutions not only allow speculators to manipulate price but also provide cash leading to the distortion in the balanced growth of the market.

(9) Net asset value (NAV) is one of the important factors which decides the performances of a mutual fund scheme. Regulation 45 of SEBI states that every mutual fund shall follow a formula approved by the SEBI for computing the NAV for each of the schemes. But till date no regulation specifies the formula to be used for computation of NAV.

(10) India is a vast country with a comprehensive demographic profile. But mutual funds are only confined to urban and semi-urban markets. Moreover mutual funds till now, not have been able to introduce the schemes suitable to the needs of farmers, small entrepreneurs, and merchants to tap the rural savings.

(11) Investor relations play a vital role in mobilizing the resources. Most of the Indian companies and mutual funds have ignored this and failed to communicate to the investors about their organization and operation.

(12) Unlike banks, mutual funds do not have a strong distribution network. Apart from few, most MFs have to depend on the broker networks.

(13) Mutual funds have not yet developed product structuring to tap target customers.

(14) Most of the older schemes have been designed with complicated exit procedures. Further, investors are not adequately informed about the available exist options which creates a lot of confusion for the investors and they are compelled to liquidate their investments in the market at a highly discounted price.

(15) Fund managers invest in unlisted securities, sometimes in private limited companies to get better returns which leads to new risk profile.

(16) Long-term capital gains have been reduced from 20% with indexation benefits to 10% without indexation. But this is available only to securities under section 112 of the Income Tax Act. For mutual funds, it is an edge for the listed funds.

(17) There is a restriction on corporate investments up to a maximum of 60% of net worth of mutual funds. But there is no such stipulation for bank fixed deposits and gilt securities.

(18) There is a lack of access to call money market. As a result, redemption risk which is the second most important risk of open-ended schemes arises could not be mitigated.

(19) The cheque writing facility is available only to the money market mutual fund investors. So the mutual funds cannot issue cheques on behalf of another bank.

(20) The high cost of fruitless search for good buys or undervalued securities reduces the funds return to their shareholders to below what they could have expected if they had selected randomly. The cost factor is another problem facing the mutual fund industry.

(21) The development of mutual fund industry depends upon the maturity of the merchant banking industry. But unfortunately, the merchant banking industry in the Indian capital market is not sufficiently matured.

(22) There is a lack of product conceptualization and innovation in mutual fund industry.

(23) The most important aspect for success of a mutual fund is the ability to outsource certain critical activities. This concept is already prevalent manufacturing but has not been introduced in fund management.

(24) Lack of well-informed institutional market is the cause of market inefficiencies.

(25) Perhaps mutual funds are the most misunderstood financial products in India. Neither the investor nor the corporate finance manager perceives the product in a proper perspective. Further, mutual funds are not making efforts in investor awareness programme which is the need of the day.

(26) The lack of proper marketing and distribution system is another problem facing the mutual fund industry in India.

(27) Internet and thereby e-commerce which is inevitable now-a-days has not been introduced in mutual funds.

(28) The biggest problem the mutual funds face today in India is the lack of investors' confidence.

(29) Few mutual funds have already shown full portfolio disclosures but most mutual funds hesitate to declare their portfolios.

(30) The absence of proper benchmarks against which performance can be measured constitutes another big problem plaguing mutual fund research in India.

Possible causes for non-satisfactory performance of mutual funds

The following can be stated as the possible causes of the non-satisfactory performance of mutual funds:

(a) Excessive diversification of portfolio.

(b) Blue chip or hot securities do not result in more than average return.

(c) High turnover of portfolio may lead to huge payment of brokerage/commision.

(d) Poor investment planning.

(e) Poor use of forecasts such as income, profitability, and poor interpretation of government's policies, etc.

SUMMARY

Mutual funds started long back. Four decades later, in 1868, the mutual fund caravan reached England with the setting up of the foreign and colonial government trust. In the United States, the first mutual fund was launched in Boston in 1924. The take-off of mutual funds was however not spectacular. Two factors contributed to their slow growth. One, a number of closed-end mutual funds bombed in the market, and two, the great crash of 1929. These factors killed the public interest in the funds. It was only in 1940 that the formal attempt at regulating the functioning of mutual funds was made. But the public enthusiasm was soon snuffed out as the market collapsed in 1969–70. The number of mutual funds grew during 1940–1990.

Though the concept of mutual funds was first introduced in India as early as in 1964 with the setting up of the Unit Trust of India, it emerged popular in a big way only from 1987 onwards. As financial intermediaries, mutual funds mobilize savings from the masses and channelize them to productive investment avenues through capital market. Particularly they are very useful to small investors who do not have access to stock market. With the liberalization gaining momentum and with the opening up of the financial sector, monopoly of public sector mutual funds has come to an end. Many private sector mutual funds have now come to the picture. Kothari industries promoted the Kothari pioneer mutual fund in November 1993 followed by the foreign mutual funds led by Morgan Stanley which entered the Indian mutual funds industry in January 1994. The entry of private sector mutual funds then imparted competitive efficiency in the industry, and helped investors to choose from funds with different maturity periods, and offered different risk-return trade-offs.

Indian investors got attracted to invest their money in mutual funds for two reasons. First, they offer a better return than fixed deposits and second, the funds are being run by professionals with requisite infrastructure to monitor company workings and their outlook of stock markets, etc. There are also a good number of mutual funds operating various schemes tailored to meet the needs of their target customers. Basically they can be grouped under open-ended mutual funds and closed-end mutual funds. In addition to this, different mutual funds are designed to meet the objectives of different types of savers such as bond funds, income funds, money market funds, growth-oriented mutual funds, balanced funds, industry funds, tax relief funds, index funds, and offshore funds. However open-ended funds are more popular in India due to distinctive feature of regular sale and purchase of securities.

Despite all the advantages linked with mutual funds, people still prefer to invest their money independently. So far mutual funds have not been able to introduce the schemes which is suitable to the needs of farmers, small entrepreneurs, and merchants to tap the rural savings. Further mutual funds have not yet developed product structuring to tap target customers. There is a lack of product conceptualization and innovation. Weak distribution and marketing channels are another problem which the mutual fund industry are facing today. The merchant banking industry is not sufficiently matured and this has led to slow development of mutual fund industry. The interesting thing is that mutual funds are the most misunderstood financial products in India. Mutual fund industries are also not making efforts in investor awareness programmes which are the need of the day.

REVIEW QUESTIONS

1. Explain the origin and meaning of mutual funds.
2. Discuss the types of mutual funds.
3. Distinguish between open-ended and closed-end mutual funds.
4. Explain the importance of mutual funds.
5. Review the growth of mutual funds in India.
6. Discuss the problems faced by the mutual funds in India.

QUIZ

State whether the following statements are true or false.

1. Open-ended mutual funds are open for a limited period for investment and redemption. (T/F)
2. Each open-ended scheme of a mutual fund is required to raise at least Rs. 50 crores as its minimum corpus funds. (T/F)
3. Closed-end mutual funds have a definite period. (T/F)

4. The closed-end schemes are not permitted to be kept open for subscription more than 45 days. (T/F)
5. The growth-oriented mutual funds are more risk-oriented. (T/F)
6. Income-oriented funds are providing regular income to the investors. (T/F)
7. Risk is very low in bond funds. (T/F)
8. Index funds are invested in different securities. (T/F)
9. Tax relief funds are known as equity linked savings scheme. (T/F)
10. Liquid funds are invest in long-term securities.

Fill up the blanks.

11. Mutual funds are very popular in ....
12. .... regulates the function of mutual fund.
13. Mutual funds in India are formed as ....
14. .... is one of the important factors which decides the performance of a mutual fund schemes.
15. .... fund is best-suited for the business people.

REFERENCES

Ansari, M.N.A., "Mutual Funds in India: Emerging Trends", *The Chartered Accountant*, August 1993, p. 88.

Baur, M.M., S. Sundaram, and F.A. Smith, "Mutual Funds: The U.S. Experience", *Finance India*, Vol. IX, No. 4, Dec. 1995, p. 947.

Bansal, L.K., "*Mutual Funds: Management and Working*", Deep and Deep Publications, New Delhi, p. 42.

Business India, Sept. 20–Oct. 3, 1999, pp. 124–125.

Chartered Financial Analyst, February 2000, p. 52.

Dewan, Sonica, "Mutual Funds in India: A Review", *Business Analyst*, Vol. 19, No. 1, Jan.–June, 1998, p. 105.

Fortune India, March 31, 1999, p. 20.

Fredman, Albert J. and Russ Wiles, "*How Mutual Funds Work*", Prentice-Hall of India, New Delhi, 1997, pp. 10–11.

Goyal, Madan, "Mutual Funds in India, Here We Come", *The Journal of Indian Institute of Bankers*, Vol. 60, No. 4, Oct.–Dec. 1989, p. 238.

Gangadhar, V., "The Changing Pattern of Mutual Funds in India", *The Management Accountant*, Vol. 27, No. 12, December 1992, pp. 924–925.

Indro, D.C., C.X. Jiang, B.E. Patuwo, and G.P. Zhang, "Predicting Mutual Fund Performances using Artificial Neural Networks", *OMEGA, The International Journal of Management Science*, Sci. 27, 1999, p. 373.

"International Capital Markets Developments, Prospects and Policy Issues", IMF Publications, Washington D.C., September 1992, p. 4.

Jayadev, M., "*Investment Policy and Performance of Mutual Funds*", Kanishka Publishers, New Delhi, 1998, p. 52.

Jayakar, Roshini, "Rake in the Returns", *Business Today*, May 22, 1999, p.100.

Kumar, V.K., "In Search of Turnaround Strategies for Mutual Fund Industry", *The Management Accountant*, Vol. 24, No. 5, May, 1999, p. 337.

Kurup, N.P., "Mutual Funds", *PNB Monthly Review*, June, 1990.

"Mutual Funds", *Study Materials of XIMB*, p. 30.

"Mutual Funds: Future Stock", *Business India*, Oct. 24–Nov. 6, 1994, p. 54.

"Mutual Funds in USA-Growing in popularity", *Fortune India*, Oct. 16–31, 1993, p. 26.

"Mutual Fund Industry in India: A Historical Perspective", *Fortune India*, March 31, 1999, p. 23.

Mutual Fund Fact Book 1995, 35th ed., (Washington: Investment Company Institute, 1995), p. 65.

Merriman, C.O., "*Unit Trusts and How They work*", 2nd ed., London, 1959, pp. 11–12 quoted from L.C. Gupta, Readings in Industrial Finance, Delhi. Macmillan India, 1976, p. 340.

"Make Your Money Work Hard for You—The Easy Way," *Fortune India*, Oct. 1–15, 1994, p. 8.

Mathew, George, "Mutual Fund Mobilization Jumps 82 PC in Q1", *The New Indian Express*, August 7, 1999.

Nemivant, Tanuja R., "Unit Trust of India: On the Right Track", *Chartered Financial Analyst,* Vol. IV, XII, August 1999, p. 32.

Palande, Prabin and Madhus Suthanan, *The Financial Express*, Sept. 14, 1999, p. 6.

Pierce, James L., "*Monetary and Financial Economics*", John Wiley & Sons, 1984, p. 81.

Ravi, A.B., "*Indian Management*", Nov. 1994, p. 45.

Ram, Pattabhi, "*Chartered Financial Analyst*", Sept., 1997, p. 70.

Rao, P. Mohan, "*Working of Mutual Fund Organizations in India*", Kanishka Publishers Distributions, New Delhi, 1998, p. 5.

Rank, K. Reily, "*Investments*", New York: CBS College Publishing, 1982, p. 526.

Rajeshwer, Ch., "*Chartered Financial Analyst*", May 1999, p. 27–28.

Ross, Joel, "*Mutual Funds—Taking the Wrong of Out of Investing*", Prentice Hall, 1988, p. 8.

Santhanam, R., "Tax Incentives to Boost Capital Market", *Chartered Secretary*, April, 1999, p. 401.

Sec. 2 (m), SEBI (Mutual Fund) Regulations, 1993.

Sec. 2(a) SEBI (Mutual Funds) Regulations, 1993.

"*The New Encyclopedia Britannica*", Encyclopedia Britannica, Inc. 1994, Chicago, Vol. 8, p. 459.

"*The VNR Dictionary of Business and Finance*", van Nostrand, Rein Cold Company, New York, p. 183.

Tripathy, Nalini Prava, "Mutual Fund in India—A Financial Service in Capital Market," *Finance India*, Vol. No. 1, March, 1996, p. 85.

The Financial Express, November 19, 1999.

The Economic Times, Sept. 4, 1999.

The New Indian Express, Nov. 13, 1999.

The Financial Express, January 1, 2000.

The Financial Express, September, 1999.

Vijayakumar, A., "Mutual Fund—A Robust Galloping Indian Capital Market", *Indian Banking Today & Tomorrow*, June, 1996, p. 7.

Vidyashankar, S., "Mutual Funds—Emerging Trends in India", *Chartered Secretary*, August 1990, p. 639.

Verma, J.C., "*Guide to Mutual Funds and Investment Portfolio*", Bharat Publishing House, New Delhi, 1997, p. 3.

Weston, J. Fred and Eugene F. Brigham, "*Essentials of Managerial Finance*", 7th ed., Dryden Press, 1985, p. 36.

Yasaswy, N.J., "*Personal Investment and Tax Planning year book 93–94*", Vision Books, New Delhi, p. 234.

Chapter 6

Merchant Banking

6.1 INTRODUCTION

Merchant banking originated in the 13th century in the European countries. As far as the origin of this term is concerned, it is told that earlier merchants used to attend to extending of loans and arranging finance for trade purposes but as the time passed the subject of banking assumed more importance and the merchants switched over to banking activities, hence the term merchant banking. Rapid industrialization in India has led to the setting up of new industrial units and expansion, diversification, and modernization of existing units. The need for having expert advice and the guidance of specialists in the field has therefore become imperative. Only merchant banking can offer these services.

6.2 MEANING AND DEFINITION

Merchant banking is a non-banking financial activity similar to banking. Merchant banks are neither merchants nor are they necessarily banks. These are financial institutions providing valuable services like acceptance of bills of exchange, corporate finance, portfolio management, and other banking services. According to J.A.P. Herbert, "*Merchant banking is what merchant bankers do*". M.J. Rosenberg has defined merchant bank as "*an organization that underwrites securities for corporations, advices such clients on mergers, and is involved in the ownership of commercial ventures*". E. Reid in his presidential address to institute of bankers in London stated that "*these organizations are sometimes banks which are not merchants, and sometimes merchants who are not banks and sometimes houses which are neither merchants nor banks*. The notification of the ministry of finance, India defines a merchant banker as, "any person who is engaged in the business of issue management either by making arrangements regarding selling, buying or subscribing to the securities as manager; consultant adviser; or one rendering corporate advisory services in relation to such activities in the management".

6.3 ORIGIN OF MERCHANT BANKING

Merchant banking in Britain started in the 13th century when a few private firms engaged themselves in foreign trade and finance. The Dutch and Scottish traders made a beginning in merchant banking based on the model of British banks. In USA these banks were developed originally by the European merchant bankers. During 1960s and 1970s, Australian merchant banks came into existence with favourable economic environment. In West Germany, the merchant banks have developed a close link with the commercial banks with a well-established domestic network of branches offering a variety of services to customers. In 1972, commercial banks were made to acquire the merchant banks and to start their own subsidiaries to play the role of merchant banks in South Africa.

6.3.1 Indian Scenario

During the 19th century, the foreign merchant bankers operated in India through the popular agency house, East India House. In 1857, the Chartered Mercantile Bank of India came into existence. The National Grindlays Bank opened its branch in 1967. In 1970, the first National Citibank was started. The State Bank of India floated its merchant banking division in the year 1972. The commercial banks that followed State Bank of India were Central Bank of India, Bank of India, and Syndicate Bank in 1977; Bank of Baroda, Standard Chartered Bank, and Mercantile Bank in 1978; and United Bank of India, United Commercial Bank, Punjab National Bank, Canara Bank, and Indian Overseas Bank in late 1970s and early 1980s. ICICI also started merchant banking activities in 1973, followed by IFCI (1986) and IDBI (1991).

6.4 SERVICES OF MERCHANT BANKERS

The following are the broad range of activities rendered by merchant bankers:

(1) **Corporate counselling:** Corporate counselling is the beginning of the merchant banking services. Every industrial unit either new or existing needs it. The scope of corporate counselling is very vast. It covers a wide range of merchant banking activities and includes the services such as project counselling, project management, loan syndication, working capital management, capital restructuring, public issue management, fixed deposit, lease financing.

(2) **Project counselling:** This has originated from corporate counselling. It relates to project finance and includes preparation of project reports, cost of the project, and also arranging the financing pattern. The projects are appraised on the basis of the location, marketing, and technical and financial viability of the project.

(3) **Loan syndication:** It refers to a loan arranged by a bank for a borrower who is likely to be a large company, a local authority, or a government department. So the merchant banker first finalizes the cost of the project before approaching to financial institutions for term loans. After that the merchant banker designs the capital structure, determines the promoter's contribution, and decides the approximate amount to be raised. It also ensures that the project adheres to the guidelines for financing industrial projects. Merchant bankers render the comprehensive services of loan syndication to cover all types of arrangements.

(4) **Management of capital issues:** Management of capital issues involves selling of securities, namely, equity shares, preference shares, and debentures or bonds to the investors. The merchant bankers prepare the action plan and budget for the total expenses for the issues, drafting the prospectus getting the consent letter from SEBI, selecting the broker underwriters, selecting the advertising agency for pre-issue and post-issue publicity, coordinating with underwriters, brokers and bankers to the issue and stock exchanges. The merchant banker renders the advice to the issuer company regarding the type of security to be issued. For success of the issue, the merchant banker should keep close liaison and coordination with various agencies involved in public issue. It is the responsibility of the merchant banker to groom the issue to ensure full subscription.

(5) **Corporate advisory services:** Merchant bankers set up corporate advisory service branches to render exclusive services to their corporate customers. Also SEBI guidelines insist that all the issues should be managed by at least one authorized merchant banker. The success of the issue is dependent on the selection on the right type of security. So expert advice of merchant bankers is of immense importance to ensure success and security.

(6) **Portfolio management:** Portfolio management refers to minimizing the risk and maximizing the returns. Hence, the term portfolio management can be applied only to shares and debentures. Merchant bankers render portfolio management services to their customers and help the investors to choose right type of securities which is safe, and ensures liquidity and profitability. So merchant bankers need to keep regular market information and economic surveys.

(7) **Advisory services to mergers and takeovers:** The term merger means combination of two companies in a manner such that only one company survives and another goes out of existence. On the other hand, takeover refers to the purchase of a company by another company and in the process acquiring and controlling interest in the share capital of another existing company. Merchant banker act as a middleman between two companies by safeguarding the interest of both. He gets the approval from the financial institutions of the government or RBI.

(8) **Consultancy to sick industrial units:** A merchant banker guides the existing units for growth and diversification. He/she appraises their technology and process, assessing their requirements and restructuring their capital base and also chalks out the rehabilitation programme which can be accepted by the banks and other financial institutions. The merchant banker takes the responsibility to obtain the approval from Board of Industrial and Financial Reconstruction (BIFR) and sick industrial companies act 1985, for the financial reconstructing and technical rehabilitation of sick units.

(9) **Leasing:** In lease transaction, the merchant banker renders the services that include arrangement for lease finance facilities for leasing companies, advice on the optimal structuring of the transaction, legal documentation and tax counselling.

(10) **Issue management:** Management of public issue of shares/debentures has been the traditional service rendered by merchant bankers in India. The issue function may be broadly divided into pre-issue work management and post-issue work management.

Pre-issue work

(i) Appointment of underwriters, brokers, bankers, registrars, and advisors.

(ii) Preparation of the draft prospectus and obtaining clearance from stock exchange authorities.

(iii) Getting the prospectus signed by the Board of Directors, and filing it with stock exchanges.

(iv) Printing and distributing the prospectus all over the country and abroad.

Work during the issue

This comprises launching advertisement campaigns in print media, ratio and T.V., hoardings, posters, etc. Other activities carried out during the compaign are:

(i) Organizing investor conferences and broker conferences at leading centres.
(ii) Deciding on the opening and closing dates of the issue.
(iii) Obtaining collection reports.
(iv) Closing the issue.
(v) Organizing the necessary press releases.

Post-issue work

(i) If the issue is oversubscribed, the basis of allotment has to be finalized in consultation with the stock exchange authorities.
(ii) If the issue is undersubscribed, the underwriting liability of the underwriter has to be determined.
(iii) After allotment, share certificate has to be prepared and dispatched.
(iv) The listing agreement should be concluded with the stock exchanges and the shares should get listed.

6.5 QUALITIES OF MERCHANT BANKER

The merchant banker must possess certain qualities as described below:

(1) The merchant banker must have knowledge and information about the capital markets, trends in the stock exchange, psychology of the investing public, and technological and economical changes in the country.

(2) They must have ability to analyze and evaluate various technical, financial, and economical aspects concerning the formation of an industrial project.

(3) They must safeguard the interest of the investing public. So, the integrity and maintenance of high professional standards are necessary for the success of the merchant bankers.

(4) The merchant banker should realize the changing environment of capital market and keep cordial relationship with the investors.

(5) They must be able to develop innovative capital market instruments for satisfying the changing needs of investors.

(6) The merchant banker must be able to restrict the function to be performed, and concentrate and develop their strength to keep costs under control.

6.5.1 Problems Faced by Merchant Bankers

As per SEBI guidelines, merchant bankers are authorized to undertake only issue related activities, which restrict the scope of their activities.

The stipulation of net worth of Rs. 1 crore for authorization of merchant bankers creates problem for professional merchant bankers. In some cases, they need to close down their business.

The issuing companies do not cooperate in timely allotment of shares and refund of application money to the investor. This creates trouble for the merchant bankers.

6.6 GUIDELINES FOR MERCHANT BANKERS

SEBI guidelines as on April 1990

(1) All merchant bankers should have qualification in finance, law or business management.

(2) They should have adequate office space, equipment, and manpower.

(3) Two persons who have the experience to conduct business of merchant bankers should be appointed.

(4) A merchant banker should be fair in all transactions.

As per guidelines revised in 1992, merchant bankers are classified into four categories:

(a) Those authorized to act in the capacity of lead manager/ co-manager/advisor or consultant to an issue; or portfolio manager and underwriter to an issue having net worth of Rs. 5 crores.

(b) Those authorized to act in the capacity of co-manager or consultant to an issue; or portfolio manager having net worth of Rs. 50 lakhs.

(c) Those authorized to act only in the capacity of an advisor or consultant to an issue net worth Rs. 20 lakhs.

(d) Those authorized to act as an advisor or consultant to an issue having net worth nil.

(5) SEBI will supervise the activities of merchant bankers.

(6) The SEBI has laid the responsibility on merchant banks for the true disclosures and factual statements made on the prospects and the authenticity of such statements.

(7) SEBI has the power to suspend or cancel the authorization of merchant bankers in case of any violation of the guidelines.

(8) The merchant bankers are required to send quarterly reports on the public and right issues on hand, the names of companies, the size of the issue, and other details regarding these issues.

(9) The merchant bankers should abide by the code of conduct prescribed by the SEBI.

(10) For the issues over Rs. 100 crores, the number of lead manager may go up to a maximum of four/five.

(11) The merchant banker should make an agreement with corporate bodies about their mutual rights, liabilities, and obligations, etc.

6.7 FUTURE PROSPECTS OF MERCHANT BANKING IN INDIA

Merchant bankers play a very important role in supporting the entrepreneurs.

(1) Growth of primary market: If the primary market grows and number of issues increases, the scope for merchant banking will be enhanced.

(2) Entry of foreign investors: Now Indian capital market directly taps foreign capital through euro issues. FDI is increased in capital market. So merchant bankers are needed to advice them for their investment in India. The increasing number of joint ventures also require expert services of merchant bankers. If more and more NRIs participate in capital market, there will be great demand for merchant banker services.

(3) Changing policy of financial institutions: Now the lending policies of financial institutions are based on project orientation, so the merchant banker services will be needed by corporate enterprise to provide expert guidance.

(4) Development of debt market: If the debt market is enhanced, there will be tremendous scope. for merchant bankers. Now the NSE and OTCEI are planned to raise their fund through debt instruments.

(5) Corporate restructuring: Due to liberalization and globalization, the companies are facing lot of competition. In order to compete, they have to go for restructuring, merger, acquisitions, or disinvestments. This may offer good opportunity to merchant bankers.

SUMMARY

The merchant bankers provide valuable services like acceptance of bills of exchange, corporate finance, portfolio management, etc. They act as lead managers, co-managers, issue managers, financial advisors, etc. For the healthy growth of the market operation, the SEBI should enforce strict control on merchant banks and remove the weeds.

REVIEW QUESTIONS

1. Explain the origin and meaning of merchant banking.
2. Discuss the qualities required for a merchant banker.
3. What are the services rendered by merchant bankers?
4. Write a short note on "post-issue management".
5. Write short notes on
   (a) Corporate counselling
   (b) Project counselling
   (c) Issue management.

QUIZ

State whether the following are true or false.

1. Merchant bank deals with funds raised through money market and capital market. (T/F)
2. Punjab National Bank started the merchant banking division in 1972. (T/F)

Fill up the blanks.

3. ICICI started merchant banking activities in the year ....
4. SEBI guidelines insist that all the issues should be managed by at least .... authorized merchant banker.
5. All merchant bankers should have .... and .... as their educational qualifications.

REFERENCES

Baver, Hans Peter, "What is a Merchant Bank", *The Banker*, London, July 1976.

Francis, Jack Clark, *Management of Investments*", 2nd ed., McGraw Hill International.

Phadnis, Abhijit P., "Role of a Merchant Banker", *ICFAI Study Materials*.

Sivaloganathan, K., "Merchant Banking; Coming of the Age", *The Indian Journal of Commerce*.

Chapter 7

Venture Capital

7.1 INTRODUCTION

The Government of India implemented the economic reforms programme including financial sector reforms with the objective of improving the efficiency and effectiveness of the financial system conceding operational freedom for flexibility to it through prudential regulation and supervision in a free financial environment. And most of the financial sector reforms cover the capital market. The Indian capital market scenario has changed very fast over the past decade or so. It has emerged as major source of finance for the corporate sector. Savers have got attracted by the higher yield on new instrument. The banks have come under the pressure and have begun looking for new avenues of growth. Several new institutions and new instruments have appeared both in capital and money market. Mutual funds have established themselves as important financial intermediaries. Leasing hire/ purchase companies and factoring services have also entered into activities. New risky lines of business need support in the form of venture capital that has emerged to fill the particular need and carved out a good slice of the market.

7.2 VENTURE CAPITAL—ORIGIN AND CONCEPT

The origin of venture capital can be traced back to USA in 19th and 20th centuries. In 1946, the American Research and Development Organization was established as the first venture organization which financed over 100 companies and made over 35 times its investments. In 1989, the venture capital company provided Rs. 3,700 crores to 1500 companies. Banks also invested equivalent of over Rs. 1500 crores in 1988–89. Since then venture capital is one of the important contributors in the economic development of USA, UK, Europe, and Japan. The real development of venture capital took place in 1958 when the Business Administration Act was passed by the U.S. Congress. Venture capital was also successful in Britain due to government's business expansion scheme which permitted individuals to claim tax reliefs for investment in companies not listed on the stock exchanges. In UK, the concept became popular in the late 1960s. Japan got tempted by America to adopt the concept and is now experiencing an entrepreneurial and venture capital boom. In USA, venture capital created billion dollar product through digital equipment corporations, namely, Apple Computers and Silicon Valley. Observing the benefits reaped by western countries from the venture capital market, India has also initiated attempts to establish venture capital. Hence, the concept of venture capital is gradually coming into vogue and the financial institutions, public sector banks, and private sector have formed units to enter this field.

7.2.1 Concept

The term venture capital comprises of two words, namely, 'venture' and 'capital'. The term *venture* literally means a course or proceeding, the outcome of which is uncertain but which is attended by the risk of danger of 'loss'. On the other hand, the term *capital* refers to the resources to start the enterprise. However, the term venture capital can be understood in two ways. According to narrow sense, the capital which is available for financing the new business ventures is called venture capital. Generally, it involves lending finance to the growing companies. In the broad sense, venture capital is the investment of long-term equity finance where the venture capitalist earns his returns primarily in the form of capital gain. It is under the assumption that the entrepreneur and the venture capital would act as partners. It is a commitment of capital for the formation and setting up of small scale enterprises specializing in new ideas or new technologies. Venture capital does not deal in financing the enterprise which is engaged in trading, broking, investment or financial services, and agency or liaison work. It is generally considered as a high risk capital. Venture capital is not an injection of funds into new firm but also an input of the skills needed to set up the firm, design its marketing strategy, organize and then manage it.

7.3 DIMENSIONS OF VENTURE CAPITAL

Venture capital in India is available in four forms:

Equity participation: The venture capital finances up to 49% of the equity capital and the ownership remains with the entrepreneur.

Conventional loan: Under this, a lower fixed rate of interest is charged to the unit till its commercial operation. After normal rate of interest is paid, loan is to be repaid as per the agreement.

Conditional loan: A conditional loan is repayable in the form of royalty ranging between 2 and 15% after the venture is able to generate sales and no interest is paid on such loans.

Income notes: The income note combines the features of conventional and conditional loans in a way that the entrepreneur has to pay both interest and royalty on sales at low rates.

A distinct and peculiar practice adopted by venture capitalist is stage financing. Venture capitalist needs adequate financing of the four successive stages of establishment of his business, namely, development of an idea, start-up, fledging, and establishment to exploit the economies of scale and achieving stability. Through stage financing, venture capitalist minimizes his risk.

There are four successive stages for developing a project:

(i) **Seed capital:** In this first stage of project development, a small amount of capital is provided to the entrepreneurs for concept testing or translating an idea into business.

(ii) **Start-up finance:** The second stage sees the provision of start-up finance to the unit by the venture capitalists to manufacture a product.

(iii) **Additional finance:** In the third stage when the firm is not able to generate adequate funds to meet working capital needs, additional fund is needed to meet initial expenses.

(iv) **Establishment finance:** Funds are provided for major growth plans, generally used for capacity expansion, marketing and working capital.

7.4 VENTURE CAPITAL FINANCE IN INDIA

In the Indian context, the objective of venture capital assistance is to:

(a) Encourage the indigenous technology and its commercial applications.

(b) Adopt and modify the applications of imported technology in such a manner that it will be appropriate to the Indian environment.

(c) Setting up of pilot projects.

(d) Technological innovations and modernization.

(e) Developing appropriate technology.

(f) Meeting the cost of market surveys and market promotion programmes.

7.4.1 Importance

Venture capital is popular in different parts of the country as it plays a significant role in fostering industrial development by exploiting vast and untapped potentialities. The importance of venture capital is growing due to the following reasons:

(a) Even in the situation when entrepreneur having a good project idea but no previous entrepreneurial track record to leverage the firm, handles customers and bankers, venture capital can help the entrepreneurs in successful launch of their projects.

(b) Rapid growth of technology across the globe has led to the growth of technology in India but indigenous technology has been slack due to unwillingness of the people to take entrepreneurial risks. Thus, in this situation venture capital is considered to be significant as it provides strong impetus for entrepreneurs to develop the product with the new technology and commercialize them.

(c) Venture capital has gained importance as it solves the sickness of a company.

(d) As the venture capitalists are ready to lend their expertise and standing to the entrepreneur, the local groups and multinational companies can easily enter into joint ventures.

(e) Venture capitalists are also helpful to a large number of smaller units under which they are able to upgrade their technology to meet the demands of the major industrial units.

(f) Venture capitalists are also playing a significant role in tapping the potentiality of service sector. Thus, venture capital is booming to exploit the potential of Indian economy. All this will go a long way in broadening the industrial base, creation of jobs, flushing of exports and overall enrichment of the economy.

7.4.2 Advantages of Venture Capital

The advantages of venture capital can be listed as follows:

(a) Helps in the industrialization of the country.

(b) Helps in the technological development of the country.

(c) Generates employment.

(d) Helps in developing entrepreneurial skills.

(e) Benefits to the investor is that they are invited to invest only after the company starts earning profit. So the risk is less and healthy growth of capital market is entrusted.

(f) Profit to venture capital funds.

(g) Helps small and medium first generation entrepreneurs to translate their ideas into a reality.

(h) Promotes entrepreneurship and fosters entrepreneurism in the country.

7.5 REGULATORY STRUCTURE

The Securities Exchange Regulation Board of India by Act 1992, SEBI inter alia regulated venture capital industry. It announced the regulations for the venture capital funds in 1996, with the primary objective of protecting the interest of investors and providing enough flexibility to the fund managers to make suitable investment decisions. Venture capital funds appoint an asset management company to manage the portfolio of the fund. Any company proposing to undertake venture capital investments is required to obtain certificate of registration from SEBI. Venture capital fund can invest up to 40% of the paid-up capital of the invested company or up to of 20% of the corpus of the fund in one undertaking. At least 80% of funds raised by VCF shall be invested in equity shares or equity related securities issued by company whose shares are not listed on recognized stock exchange. Venture capital investments are required to be restricted to domestic companies engaged in business of software, information technology, biotechnology, agriculture, and allied sectors.

7.6 VENTURE CAPITAL INDUSTRY IN INDIA

In the era of economic liberalization in India which started in 1980s, new financial products and services were introduced to support the resulting growth in the industrial sector. Venture capital financing has come to assure significance to develop entrepreneurship and exploit technological potential in India. This section gives a brief insight into some of the organizations that form the backbone of venture capital industry in India.

Risk Capital and Technology Finance Corporation Limited

Risk Capital Technology Finance Corporation Ltd. (RCTFC) was set up in January 1988 on reconstitution of the Risk Capital Foundation which was promoted by IFCI in 1975 to cater to the risk capital needs of the first generation entrepreneurs. RCTFC provides both risk capital and venture capital assistance. It has an authorized capital of Rs. 25 crores and a paid-up capital of Rs. 50 crores. RCTFC provides assistance in the form of conventional loans and interest-free conditional loans on a profit and risk sharing basis with the project promoters.

IDBI Venture Capital Fund

The Government of India enacted Research and Development Act 1986 imposing levy and collection of tax of 5% on all payments made for import of technology. The fund is collected to provide financial assistance to those industrial concerns who adopt imported technology to widen domestic applications. The venture capital fund was set up by long term fiscal policy of the Government with an initial capital of Rs. 10 crores to provide equity capital for pilot plants. However, this scheme came into effect from the later half of 1987. Under this scheme, equity fund is disbursed without any interest and voting rights. The minimum and maximum project assistance ranges between Rs. 5–2.5 crores. The promoters' contribution should be at least 10% of the ventures below Rs. 50 lakhs and 15% for those above Rs. 50 lakhs. IDBI venture capital funds provides financial assistance to the ventures which is engaged in the fields of chemicals, computer software, electronics, biotechnology energy, food products, and medical equipments.

Technology Development and Information Company of India Limited (TDICI)

The Technology Development and Information Company of India Limited (TDICI) was established by ICICI and UTI under the Companies Act 1986, in July 1988 as India's first venture finance company. TDICI took over the venture capital operations of ICICI and commenced operation in August 1988. It started with an authorized capital of Rs. 20 crores which was to be increased to Rs. 40–50 crores. TDICI provides assistance to small and medium industries which were set up by technocrat entrepreneurs in the form of equity conditional loans and convertible debenture. It also offers a modern technology information service. TDICI has managed the first venture fund of Rs. 20 crores subscribed equally by ICICI and UTI. This is the first fund floated to provide venture capital to entrepreneurs in the country and is a part of venture capital unit scheme, an innovative scheme of UTI. In January 1990, ICICI and UTI have jointly launched their second venture for Rs. 100 crores. It finances the projects of professional technocrats who take initiative in designing and developing indigenous technology in the country. TDICI's primary focus is on small- and medium-sized unlisted companies with exceptional growth and capital appreciation potential. TDICI favours the firms seeking financial assistance for developing information technology, pharmaceutical, veterinary biological, environmental, engineering, and other innovative services in the country.

Indus Venture Capital Fund

Indus Venture Capital Fund is one of the private venture capital funds which have been established in India. It has been established with a capital of Rs. 2 crores contributed by several Indian and international institutions and companies. The investment of the fund is managed by a separate company, Indus Venture Management Limited. The company is to provide both equity capital as well as management support to entrepreneurs. International Finance Corporation recently invested $1.58 million to help establish privately managed venture capital funds. Indus Venture Management Limited is owned to the extent of 35% by the private sector, 30% by international companies and 35% by the Government of India. However, it cannot invest more than 10% of its fund in one project and will take up to 50% of the project equity. The main aim is to seek long-term capital gains through equity investment, high risk, and high return investments in private companies. It provides financial assistance to the firms operating in the area of health care products, electronics, and computer technology.

Small Industrial Development Bank of India (SIDBI)

SIDBI has set up venture capital fund in July 1993 for support to entrepreneurs in the small sectors. The fund would be augmented in future depending upon requirements.

Gujarat Venture Finance Limited

Gujarat Venture Finance Limited (GVFL) was promoted by the Gujarat Industrial Investment Corporation Limited in July 1990 to provide venture finance. The total size of the funds of the company is Rs. 24 crores which is contributed by GIIC, IDBI, the World Bank, commercial banks, SFCS and private corporate bodies. The extent of financing ranges between Rs. 2 and Rs. 2.5 crores. GVFL provides venture financial assistance in the form of equity and quasi-equity instruments. It provides management support to entrepreneurs. The firms engaged in biotechnology, surgical instruments, conservation of energy, and food processing industries are financed by GVFL.

Credit Capital Venture Fund

Credit Capital Venture Fund is first privately managed venture capital fund set up in April 1989 with Rs. 10 crores to be subscribed by international financial agencies to the extent of Rs. 6.5 crores and the remaining through public subscription.

Andhra Pradesh Industrial Development Corporation (APIDC)

APIDC Venture Capital Ltd. was promoted by APIDC with an authorized capital of Rs. 2 million on 29th August 1989 with an objective to encourage technology-based ventures initiated by first generation technocrat entrepreneurs and ventures involving high risk in the state of Andhra Pradesh.

20th Century Venture Capital Fund

20th century venture capital fund has been established with a corpus of Rs. 20 crores promoted by the 20th Century Finance Ltd. The fund envisages focus on sick industries and first generation entrepreneurs.

State Bank, Canara Bank, and Grindlays Bank Venture Capital Funds

SBI's merchant banking subsidiary, SBI capital market (SBI cap) set up a venture capital fund for brought out deals. SBI cap invests in the equity shares of new and unknown companies. Canara Bank has also set up venture capital fund through Canara Bank financial services. Grindlays bank has started venture capital fund and provides venture capital assistance to high risk projects.

7.6.1 Guidelines for the Venture Capital Companies

The Government of India has issued the following guidelines for various venture capital funds operating in the country:

(1) The financial institutions, State Bank of India, scheduled banks, and foreign banks are eligible to establish venture capital companies or funds subject to the approval as may be required from the Reserve Bank of India.

(2) The venture capital funds have a minimum size of Rs. 10 crores and a debt equity ratio of 1:1.5. If they desire to raise funds from the public, promoters will be required to contribute minimum of 40% of the capital.

(3) The guidelines also provide for NRI investment up to 74% on a non-repatriable basis.

(4) The venture capital funds should be independent of the parent organization.

(5) The venture capital funds will be managed by professionals and can be set up as joint ventures even with non-institutional promoters.

(6) The venture capital funds will not be allowed to undertake activities such as trading, broking, and money market operations but they will be allowed to invest in leasing to the extent of 15% of the total funds deployed. The investment on revival of sick units will be treated as a part of venture capital activity.

(7) A person holding a position of being a full time chairman, chief executive, or managing director of a company will not be allowed to hold the same position simultaneously in the venture capital fund/company.

(8) The venture capital assistance should be extended to the promoters who are new, and are professionally or technically qualified with inadequate resources.

7.6.2 Indian Scenario

The Indian venture capital industry is just about a decade old as compared to that in U.S. and Europe. In the last five years there has been a major shift in the sources of venture capital funds in India. Till 1995, primarily IDBI, ICICI, IFCI, and UTI were the main sources of fund accounting for 60% of the total venture capital corpus. These development agencies which have been instrumental in giving the initial push to the venture capital industry in India slowed down their investment later. In the first half of 2003, Indian private equity funds raised $1.5 billion, as against $1.60 billion in the whole of 2002, showing a pick-up in venture funds activity. More than 20 of the world's leading venture capital players have landed in India scouting for investment opportunities. Table 7.1 indicates the break-up of contribution to venture capital funds in India during 1995–2000.

Table 7.1 Sources of venture funds in India

	1995		1999–2000	
Sources of funds	Rs. in crores	%	Rs. in crores	%
Foreign sources	194.5	22.70	1779.0	59.53
Foreign institutional investors	15.8	1.84	1517.8	50.79
Multilateral development agency	145.4	16.97	229.9	7.69
Non-resident Indians	33.3	3.89	31.3	1.05
Financial institutions	568.8	66.40	1023.6	34.35
All India financial institutions	516.2	59.79	772.7	25.86
State financial institutions	19.5	2.28	36.5	1.22
Nationalized banks	34.7	4.05	43.4	1.45
Other banks	2.4	0.28	171.0	5.72
Corporates	70.8	8.27	106.6	3.57
Public sector	8.7	10.2	44.2	1.48
Private sector	62.1	7.25	62.4	2.09
Others	22.6	2.63	79.2	2.65
Insurance companies	8.3	0.97	6.2	0.21
Mutual funds	0.5	0.05	0.5	0.01
Public	13.8	1.61	72.5	2.43

Source: Indian Venture Capital Association—Venture Activity Reports.

The industry has subsequently witnessed increased activity with a rise in the number as well as the pool of funds for investment. India was the fourth largest active market for venture capital (VC) funding as on December 2002 as depicted in the Table 7.2.

The total investments grew from 1993 to 1998 and the next two years took a beating with the total amount invested decreasing from Rs. 10,000 crores in 1999 to Rs. 4,500 crore in 2001. This is shown in the Fig. 7.1. The decline is due to various factors including the general slow down in the global economy, depressed state of the stock markets, decline in new capital issues, sharp decline in valuation of technology stocks, venture capitalists spending more time with their current portfolio companies, and a decline in interest in e-commerce and Internet related IPOs.

Table 7.2 Investment breakdown from January 1 to December 31, 2002

Country	Amt. invested ($ million)	Number of deals	Number of investees
South Korea	2823.87	30	29
Japan	2067.24	44	44
Australia	1257.01	82	79
India	980.18	53	51
Hong Kong	650.00	17	17
China	423.22	38	37
Singapore	189.03	19	19
Thailand	71.45	12	12
Malaysia	21.18	11	10

Source: ICFAI Reader, January 2004.

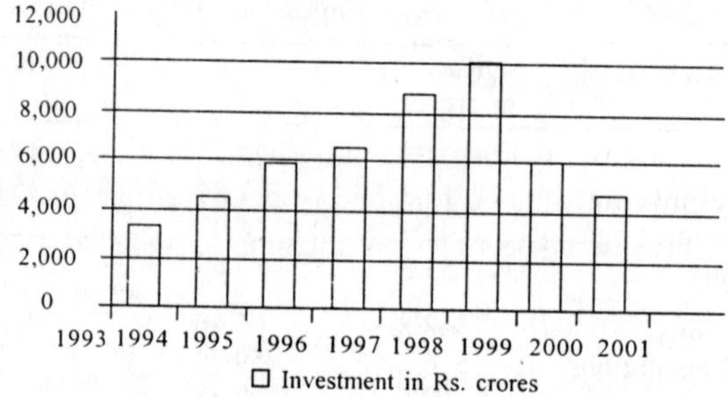

Fig. 7.1 Venture capital investments in India.

Number of VC funds registered with SEBI has also seen an upswing. There has been an increase in the number of funds—from 8 domestic funds till 1998 to 36 domestic funds till 2001, from 24 funds including domestic and foreign funds to around 75 such funds till 2001. During 1988 to 2001, about 11 venture capital institutions came up in India either through reorganizing the businesses or through new entities. Nearly 70% of venture capital investment in India was targetted on to the technology sector and 60% of the investment is in start-ups presented in the Tables 7.3 and 7.4.

Table 7.3 Leading VC/Private equity firms in India

Investor	Amount (US $ million)
CDC Capital partners	117
CDP Capital	154
Citibank Private Equity + Citigroup	125
GE Equity	157
General Atlantic partners LLC	121
ICICI Venture Funds Management Company Ltd.	177
Indocean Chase Capital Advisors Pvt. Ltd.	99
International Finance Corporation (IFC)	164
Government of Singapore Investment Corporation Pvt. Ltd.	322
Warburg Pincus	520

Source: NASSCOM, Strategic Review, 2003.

Table 7.4 VC/Private equity: largest deals in 2002

Investor	Investee	Amount (US $ million)
The Government of Singapore Investment Corporation Pvt. Ltd.	ICICI Bank Ltd.	272.6
CDP Capital	Sony Entertainment	102.4
General Atlantic Partners LLC	Patni Computer Systems	100.0
International Finance Corporation (IFC)	Escotel Telecom	80.0
Texas Pacific Group	Jain Irrigation Systems	38.0
CDC Capital Partners, CLSA Pvt. Equity Management	Jyothy Laboratories	27.6
International Finance Corporation (IFC)	Usha Beltron Ltd.	24.6
General Atlantic Partners LLC	Dakh.com e-services	21.0
Warburg Pincus Asia LLC	Zee Telefilms Ltd.	20.2
Citigroup Investments	Progeon Limited	20.0

Source: ICFAI Reader, January 2004.

Venture capital invest making is a stage-wise process. Venture capitalists in India primarily provide finance for seed, start-up, expansion, and turnaround financing. The investment parttern by business stage is presented in the Table 7.5 and Fig. 7.2.

Table 7.5 Investment pattern by business stage

(Figure in %)

Stage	India	US	Israel	Hong Kong
Seed	5	10	9	27
Start-up	41	11	0	0
Early/First Round	18	32	19	2
Later/Second Round	36	6	27	43
Expansion/Third Round	0	25	36	23
Turnaround	1	16	9	–

Source: IVCA, PWC.

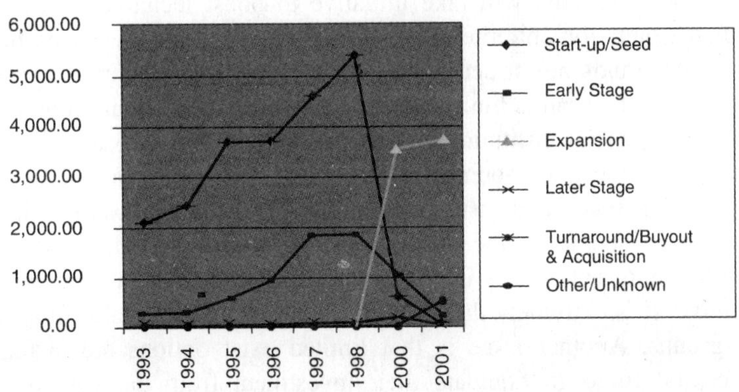

Fig. 7.2 Venture capital investments in India by states (Rs. in crores).

The primary focus of venture capital investors as well as private equity investors in India was in the information technology sector is depicted in the Table 7.6. The venture capital investments in India by other industries are depicted in the Fig. 7.3.

Table 7.6 Investment pattern by different industrial sectors (%)

Sector	India	US	Israel	Asia
Computer related	26	31	44	13
Consumer products	11	8	0	13
Electronics	3	6	12	10
Telecommunication	4	20	29	9
Manufacturing & Others	24	2	15	11

Source: IVCA, PWC.

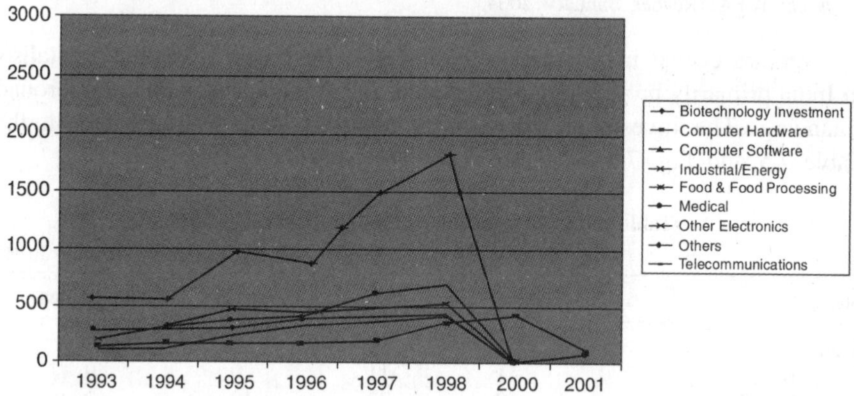

Fig. 7.3 Venture capital investments in India by industries (Rs. in crores).

7.6.3 Issues and Challenges

In the period 1999–2000, the Finance Minister, in his budget, announced that the Government of India will take initiative to boost technology sectors and support first generation entrepreneurs through venture capital activity. In India, venture capital funds are structured in the form of a company. So investors' liability towards the fund is limited to the extent of his contribution in the fund. The domestic financial institutions, multilateral agencies, and state government undertakings are the main sources of funds for venture vapital funds (VCFs). Still the pension funds and insurance companies are not allowed to invest in VCFs. Further, income of the domestic VCFs which provides assistance to small and medium enterprises is not totally exempted from tax. In absence of any incentive, it is extremely difficult for domestic VCFs to raise money from investor groups. Another issue is that limited exist options are available to venture capital funds to liquidate their investment from the venture capital company as there is no market for trading in unlisted securities.

There is shortage of experienced VCs in India who have gone through the complex cycle of fund raising investments and disinvestments. Most fund managers are based in USA, Singapore, Hong Kong due to a variety of reasons related to taxation and their ability to invest outside India. Thus, the government must pass a set of regulations to encourage fund managers to set up their units in India.

7.7 INTERNATIONAL EXPERIENCES IN VENTURE CAPITAL FINANCING

Venture capital is a child of the modern era but has its roots in the oldest of drives in the entrepreneurial skill. The pace of industrial growth has increased because of venture capital activities. Many of the entrepreneurs have shaped their business ideas into a reality. In the UK, venture backed companies have experienced an average rise in sales by 34%. In the U.S., companies such as Digital Equipment Corporation, Apple, Federal Express, Compaq, Sun Microsystems, Intel, Microsoft, and Genetech are famous examples that received venture capital in their early development. The prosperity of many Australian technology concerns can be directly attributed to venture capitalists. The findings show that the sales have risen at an average rate of 12.1%, profits at 34.9% and exports at 15.25%. The Taiwan Hsinchu Park and Industrial Research Institute tell the story of their successful venture capital policy. Buying technology from RCA for IC fabrication in 1970s by the Industrial Research Institute led to the formation of UME and TSMC, the world's largest IC makers. Taiwanese capital is now a significant force in silicon valley. The venture capital pool in Hong Kong is 5.5% of the country's GDP with similar figures in Singapore and South Korea.

In U.S., venture-backed investments decreased from $ 4.3 billion in Q4 of 2002 to $ 3.8 billion for Q1 of 2003, representing a total loss of half billion in investment dollars. In New England, investments grew from $ 551.8 million in Q4 2002 to $ 691.9 million in Q1 2003, comprising an overall increase of $ 140.1 million in funding.

7.7.1 Suggestions

Venture capital finance is an instrument that works hands in hands with technological development stimulating creativity and innovation and nurturing entrepreneurship. Thus, efforts are required by the government, financial institutions, private sector, and other agencies to create environment for the growth of venture capital in India. The following suggestions may help developing venture capital market even further:

(a) To promote and develop venture capital business, the government should give fiscal reliefs in the form of excepting returns from capital gains tax and modifying stock market regulations to provide quick exit routes.

(b) The government should provide long-term finance for venture capital companies through public financial institutions establish an unlisted security market and encourage stock option scheme as an incentive for venture capitalists.

(c) There is poor awareness about the availability of venture capital finance from private and public sector institutions. There is no direct advertisement or publicity. This should be corrected.

(d) Venture capital finance involves risk but high risk involves high returns both for entrepreneur and financers. If this is accepted in reality, there will be better market.

(e) Generally, public sector institutions look for return on capital rather than capital appreciation. There is need for a change in this outlook.

(f) An entrepreneurial tradition must be more broad-based and less family-based. This calls for imparting education and training in entrepreneurship.

(g) Debt/equity gearing of 1:5:1 is unrealistic and it is difficult for the promoters to meet this requirement of the venture capital companies. It should be brought down to at least 3:1.

(h) Tax concessions should be given to banks for setting up venture capital fund through subsidiaries so that the companies can seek venture capital assistance.

(i) Generally the public issues are to be decided on the basis of book value and earning capacity. Stock market provides an excellent disinvestment mechanism for venture funds. But stock market is not so far developed except in few cities.

(j) Orderly and efficient mechanisms must be evolved to facilitate liquidation of investments of venture capital funds.

7.8 CHANGES IN REGULATION

Government of India issued guidelines in September 1995 for overseas venture capital investment in India. There were three sets of regulations dealing with venture capital activity: SEBI Regulations 1996, Guidelines for overseas venture capital investments issued by Department of Economic Affairs in the Ministry of Finance in the year 1995, and CBDT's guidelines for venture capital companies issued in 1995, which were later modified in 1999. Based on the recommendations of K.B. Chandrasekhar Committee, SEBI was made the nodal regulator for VCFs that provide a uniform, single window regulatory framework. SEBI also notified regulations for foreign venture capital investors. SEBI set up an advisory committcc under the chairmanship of Dr. Ashok Lahiri, Chief Economic Advisor, Ministry of Finance, Govt. of India for advising SEBI for the development and regulation of venture capital funds industry in India.

Venture capitals are permitted to invest in real estate, removing lock-in-period for shares of listed venture capital undertakings, and reducing the proportion of funds raised that have to be invested in unlisted companies from 75% to 66.67%. Presently VCFs are allowed to invest in non-bank finance Companies (NBFCs) engaged in equipment leasing and hire–purchase. Also investments can be made in the sectors like gold and jewellry, which were not permitted earlier.

SUMMARY

Venture capital can play a very important role in the growth of the Indian economy, particularly in the sectors where knowledge and ideas can play a catalytic role. The Government of India and SEBI are seriously making attempts to facilitate more and more venture capital funds to flow into the country. India has yet to develop reasonable mechanisms of disinvestments. There is need for separate tax concessions for developing venture capital in India.

REVIEW QUESTIONS

1. Explain the origin and dimensions of venture capital.
2. Discuss the various stages of venture capital financing.
3. Discuss the performance of various venture capital firms in India.
4. What are the problems faced by venture capital in India?

QUIZ

State whether the following are true or false.

1. The venture capital originated in UK. (T/F)
2. Venture capital in India is available in two forms. (T/F)
3. Venture capital is also available for broking firms. (T/F)
4. Venture capital solves the problems of sickness of company. (T/F)
5. Venture capital is providing management support to the company. (T/F)

Fill up the blanks.

6. Technology Development and Information Company of India Limited was set up by .... and ....
7. Indus venture capital is one of the .... venture capital fund.
8. Gujrat Venture Finance Limited was established in the year ....
9. Venture capitals share the .... in the business.
10. Venture capital is regulated by ....

REFERENCES

Bishnoi, N.K. and K.P. Singh, "Future of Venture Capital Financing in India", *The Indian Journal of Commerce*, Vol. 53, No. 3, July–Sept., 2000.

Gupta, Snehlata, "Venture Capital in India", *Business Analyst*, Vol. 14, July–Dec., 1993.

Jalan, B., "*Science, Technology & Development Business Line*", May 5, 1999.

Mishra, A.K., "Venture Capital: Issues, options and strategies", *Productivity*, 39(3), Oct.–Dec.' 1998.

Mishra, A.K., "Indian Venture Capital Industry: Testing times ahead", *ICFAI Reader*, January 2004.

Mishra, R.K., "Venture Capital: Case study of Bio-technology Pharmaceutical Company", *Productivity*, Vol. 40. No. 3, Oct.–Dec., 1999.

Pandey, I.M., "Venture Capital The Adventure", *Chartered Financial Analyst*, July 1994.

Sethi, Sudhir, "Indian Venture Capital Resource Recommendations for 2001, *The Chartered Financing Analyst*, January, 2001.

Sharma, J.P., "Venture Capital Operations and Performance in India", *The Indian Journal of Commerce*, Vol. 55, Nos. 1 & 2, Jan.–June, 2002.

Tripathy, Nalini Prava, "Venture Capital—A New dimension of financial market in India, *The Management Accountant*, December, 1994.

Chapter 8

Credit Rating

8.1 INTRODUCTION

Since lot of companies are raising money in the capital market and each company proposed to raise capital through different types of securities and debt instruments, it is difficult for the investors to judge which investment is safer and more reliable investment opportunity. In order to help the investors make a decision on investments, the need for an independent and reliable agency was felt with the objective of rating debt obligation of companies. In this context, the Industrial Credit and Investment Corporation of India Ltd. (ICICI) and the Unit Trust of India (UTI) promoted the credit rating information service of India in 1988 with the object of rating debt obligation of companies. Now there are three credit rating agencies, i.e., CRISIL, CARE, ICRA that are performing their job.

8.2 CONCEPT

Credit rating reforms the isolated function of credit risk evaluating and reflects borrowers' accountability, expected capability and inclination to pay interest and principal in a timely manner. A credit rating agency acts as an assessor. It provides guidance to the investors in determining the credit risk associated with debt instruments, thus helping the investors to take a decision about their investments. By the dissemination of information, the agency assigns various grades ratings which enable the investors to identify risk levels of the various debt obligations. Ratings have also helped the corporate sector to diversify its credit instruments by evaluating the credit risk associated with the entire range. Credit rating is a qualitative expression of opinions of rating agencies regarding the relative capability of issuer of debt obligations, i.e., financial institution or a manufacturing company to service the debt obligation timely as per the terms of the contract reached with the creditor and safety thereof. In order to understand the concept of credit rating, it is required to know the description of credit rating which is given by well-known rating agencies. According to Moody's Investor Service, 1984, "ratings are designed exclusively for the purpose of grading bonds according to their investment qualities". According to Standard and Poor, 1984, "corporate or municipal debt rating is a current assessment of the credit worthiness of an obligor with respect to specific obligation". A corporate credit rating provides lenders with a simple system of gradation by which the relative capacities of companies that make timely repayment of interest and principal on a particular type of debt can be noted.

The above description analyzes the probability of timely repayment of principal and interest by a borrower company. The rating companies monitor the rating given and modify them suitably.

8.3 OBJECTIVE AND TYPES OF CREDIT RATING

The main objective of these agencies is to restore the confidence in the capital market and to provide unbiased assessment of the credit worthiness of the companies issuing debt instruments. They also provide information about the credit worthiness of corporates to the investors at low cost. In addition to this they provide a sound basis for proper risk-return structure. They also assist to the institutional investment regarding framing of public policy guidelines. Figure 8.1 shows the various types of credit rating.

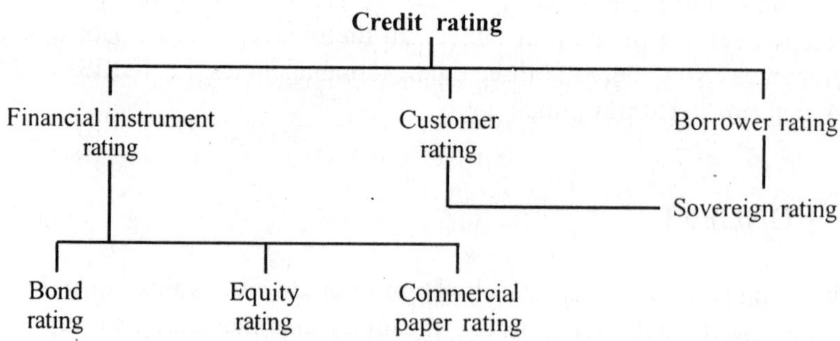

Fig. 8.1 Types of credit rating.

There are three components of credit rating, namely, financial instruments, customer rating, and borrower rating. *Financial instrument rating* comprises bond rating, equity rating, and commercial paper rating. *Sovereign rating* comprises customer rating and borrower rating. Rating of bond or debt securities issued by a company, governmental or quasi-governmental organizations are called bond rating. *Equity rating* refers to the rating of equity shares issued by a company. *Commercial paper rating* refers to the rating of CPs issued by companies. *Customer rating* refers to the assessment of credit worthiness of a customer to whom credit sales are to be made. *Borrower rating* refers to the assessment of the ability of a borrower to repay to whom loan or credit facility is sanctioned. If the customer or the borrower is a country, the evaluation of the credit worthiness of such a country is referred to as sovereign rating.

8.4 CREDIT RATING AGENCIES IN INDIA

Establishment of credit rating agencies forms an important step in the process of financial reforms. This section discusses some such agencies in brief.

CRISIL

The Credit Rating Information Services of India Limited (CRISIL) was promoted in 1987 by the ICICI and UTI. Other shareholders include Asian Development Bank, Life Insurance Corporation of India, State Bank of India, Housing Development Finance Corporation Limited, General Insurance Corporation of India, and its subsidiaries, Standard Chartered Bank, Banque Indosuez, Sakura Bank, Bank of Tokyo, Hong Kong and Shanghai Banking Corporation, Citibank, Grindlays Bank, Bank of India, Bank of Baroda, UCO Bank, Allahabad Bank, Canara Bank, Central Bank of India, Indian Overseas Bank and Bank of Madura Ltd. Its principal objective is to rate debt obligation of Indian companies. Its rating provides guide to the investors as to the degree of certainty of timely payment of interest and principal on a particular debt instrument. CRISIL rates debentures, fixed deposit programmes, and short-term instruments like commercial paper, structural obligations, and formance preference shares. CRISIL is the market leader in India and works as a 'full service' rating agency. It has the most comprehensive range of rating services. Combining its understanding of risk and the science of building risk frameworks with its strong contextual understanding of business, CRISIL ratings provide the most reliable opinions on risk.

The strategic alliance with Standard and Poor's, the world's leading rating agency helps anticipate new market challenges, besides introducing value-added rating methodologies. The Rating Criteria & Product Development Centre, responsible for policy research, new product development, and ratings quality assurance has created new rating methodologies for debt instruments and innovative structures across sectors.

Since its inception till March 31, 1994, CRISIL has rated in all 926 debt instruments issued by 668 companies. It has introduced CRISIL card, CRISIL view, CRISIL ban card, and CRISIL rating digest service. CRISIL has published CRISIL bond yield tables to provide handy reference to investors for determining yield-to-maturity on a debenture, given the price of debenture, its coupon rate, and its maturity period. CRISIL has also published CRISIL RATING Scan containing rating reports on companies whose instruments have been rated by CRISIL during the quarter. CRISIL ratings continue to play a stellar role in the development of the debt markets in India. Till March 31, 2003 it has rated more than 4438 debt instruments worth over Rs. 4,46,329 crores, for more than 2000 companies. Table 8.1 illustrates the rating symbols for CRISIL.

Table 8.1 Rating symbol of CRISIL

Remarks	Debenture	Fixed deposit	Structured obligations	Short-term instruments
Highest safety	AAA	FAAA	AAA(So)	p1 = very strong safety
High safety	AA	FAA	AA (So)	p2 = strong safety
Adequate safety	A	FA	A(So)	p3 = adequate safety
Moderate safety	BBB	—	BBB(So)	p4 = minimal safety
Inadequate safety	BB	FB	BB(So)	P5 = default
High risk	B	FC	B(So)	
Substantial risk	C	—	C(So)	
In default	D	FD	D(So)	

CRISIL may apply + (plus) or – (minus) signs for ratings from p1 to p3 to reflect comparatively higher standing within the category. The contexts within parentheses are guides to the pronunciation of the rating symbols.

The sign (+) or (–) may be used after the rating symbol to indicate the comparative position of the company within the group covered by symbol. A letter 'p' in parentheses after the rating symbol would indicate that the debt instrument is being issued to raise resources by a new company for financing a new project and the rating assumes successful completion of the project.

ICRA

ICRA or the Investment Information and Credit Rating Agencies of India is sponsored by IFCI jointly with the other leading financial institutions and banks and has become operational in September 1991 with the objective of providing guidance to the investors or creditors in determining the credit risk associated with a debt instrument or credit obligation. The ICAR rated debentures, bonds preference shares, fixed deposits, and short-term instruments like commercial paper, etc. of several companies. Since its time of inception till March 1995, ICRA rated 485 debt instruments involving Rs. 17,638 crores. In addition, ICRA provides "general assessment report on different aspects of the company's operations management". ICRA is an independent and professional company providing investment information and credit rating services. As the growth and globalization of Indian Capital Markets have led to an exponential surge in demand for professional credit risk analysis, ICRA has actively responded to this need by executing assignments including credit ratings, equity gradings, and mandated studies spanning diverse industrial sectors. ICRA presently offers its services under three banners, namely, (a) rating services, (b) information services, and (c) advisory services. Table 8.2 depicts various rating symbols of ICRA.

Table 8.2 Rating symbols of ICRA

Remarks	Long-term instruments	Medium-term instruments	Short-term including commercial paper
Highest safety	LAAA	MAAA	A-1
High safety	LAA	MAA	A-2
Adequate safety	LA	MA	—
Moderate safety	LBBB	—	—
Inadequate safety	LBB	MB	—
Risk prone	LB	MC	A-4
Substantial risk	LC	—	—
Default	LD	MD	A-5

CARE

Credit Analysis and Research Limited (CARE) sponsored by the Industrial Development Bank of India jointly with Canara Bank, UTI, private sector banks, and financial service companies to offer credit rating information and equity research services to Indian industry and institutions. CARE was incorporated on April 21, 1993, and commenced its operations in October, 1993. It undertakes rating of all types of debt instruments like commercial paper, fixed deposits, bonds, debentures, and structural obligations, involving an independent and professional assessment of debt servicing capabilities of companies. Since its inception till the end of March 1995, CARE has rated 249 debt instruments covering a total debt volume of Rs. 9,729 crores. Table 8.3 lists the rating symbols of CARE.

ONICRA

A private company, Onida Individual Credit Rating Agency (ONICRA) has been set up by Onida Finance. It undertakes rating for credit cards, leasing, hire/purchase transactions, housing finance, and bank finance. The main objective of these agencies is primarily to restore the confidence in the capital market and to provide unbiased assessment of the credit worthiness of the companies issuing debt instruments. It also provides information about the credit worthiness of corporates to the investors at low cost. In addition to this, it provides a sound basis for proper risk return structure. It also assists the institutional investment regarding framing of public policy guidelines. However ONICRA has been abolished in latter part.

Table 8.3 Rating symbols of CARE

Remarks	Long-term instruments	Medium-term instruments	Short-term instruments
Highest investment grade	CARE AAA	CARE AAA (FD/CD/So)	PR-1, superior capacity for repayment
Upper investment grade	CARE AA	CARE AA (FD/CD/So)	PR-2, strong capacity for repayment
Upper medium investment grade	CARE A	CARE A CFD/CD/So	PR-2, strong capacity
Investment grade	CARE BBB	CARE BB (FD/CD/So)	PR-4, minimal degree of safety
Susceptible to default	CARE B	CAREB (FD/CD/So)	
High investment risk with livelihood of default	CARE C	CARE C (FD/CD/So)	
Lowest category default or likely to be default	CARE D	CARED (FD/CD/So)	PR, default or likely to be default

DPCR

Duff Phelps Credit Rating (DPCR) India Pvt. Ltd. is another private sector credit rating agency set up in 1996. It has already rated a number of companies. But SEBI has started giving guidelines to them with a view to regulate them as one of the capital market institutions.

Fitch Ratings

Fitch Ratings India Ltd. is the latest agency to do credit rating from the foreign sector. It is a 100% subsidiary of its parent company abroad, operating in India.

8.5 RATING METHODOLOGY

A large number of variables affect the quality of rating of a debt instrument of an organization. The rating methodology should include these variables. The variables are: history, quality of management, business fundamentals, accounting quality, liquidity management, quality of the assets, profitability, return on equity and investment, capital structure, past performance, effect of normal business cycle, and interest and debt coverage ratios. This section discusses these variables briefly.

(1) History: The rating agency must understand the ownership, size, geographical spread, product spread, and the organizational structure of the issuer. The size of the issuer can have some access to some sources of funds and to some market segments, and thus impact credit quality. The history of the issuer could establish its export in certain product market and thus have a bearing in credit quality.

(2) Accounting quality: The accounting policies followed should strictly adhere to the concepts, principles, and conventions of accounting theory so as to ascertain a true and fair view of the financial state of affairs of the company. Neither should the accounting methods be manipulated nor should there be any chance of doing so in the accounting practices followed by the issuer company. No controversial accounting practices should be followed by it just to portray a good balance sheet. There are certain areas where the issuer has the freedom to adopt different financial policies but such a policy should not be oriented to distort the financial state of affairs of a company with a motive of influencing the quality of rating.

(3) Business fundamentals: Under this category the issuer company is assessed in the area of its competitive position as compared to the competitors operating in the similar line. Its strategies, policies, strengths, and weaknesses and goals have to be analyzed as they have some sort of bearings in measuring the ratings of the organizations. Its diversification activities having a sound track record of profitability in the industry and future projections of demand for output can have an important bearing in rating the debt instruments issued. If the product is export-oriented or import-substituted, the debt issued for the purpose should obviously influence the rating decision of the rating agency.

(4) Liquidity management: The issuer's sources and uses of funds in terms of cost and availability have to be studied in relation to debt issue. Volatility trends of these parameters are also studied. The issuer's innovativeness and competitive ability to attract cheaper funds is also analyzed. Foreign exchange and interest rate risks associated with each source and management of such risk are scrutinized to estimate the probable impact of credit quality. To understand the liquidity of the issuer, the maturing match between sources and deployment of funds is studied. The rating agency must understand the quantity and quality of liquid assets, past trends, unutilized refinance limit available, and issuer's standing in the financial market to raise resources quickly. A careful study of the liquidity position of the firm in terms of its current ratio and acid test ratio vis-à-vis the debtors turnover and stock turnover has also some bearing on the rating of the debt instruments. Projected income and expenses statement as well as balance sheet and cash flow statements can be computed to have an idea about the liquidity position of the company which has a bearing on credit quality.

(5) Quality of management: This is judged by the team of executives, human resource policies, organizational structure, and the extent of delegation of authority and responsibility. The support of group companies could also be important in determining their success. The management's attitude towards risk is measured as revealed by the track record in the choice of segments, dividend policy, accounting practices, and funding policies. Systems also play an important role in determining the credit quality of the issuer. The statutory audit report can be studied to detect any systematic deficiencies. The status of reconciliation of subsidiary books and inter-bank accounts is analyzed to determine the efficiency of the system.

(6) Quality of assets: Rating agency should analyze the issuer's segment of operation, its competitive environment, and market share in each segment vis-à-vis the risk profile of each segment. The issuer's prudential norms for credit concentration are studied in relation to the past performance to understand their effectiveness. Such credit concentration norms could be fixed for each borrower, each industry, or each geographic area. The extent of non-performing assets in the portfolio and the provisions available to meet any lossess from such assets are considered as important indicators of the quality of the asset.

The quality of the assets in investments is judged by analyzing the type of investment, the internal system for management of investments, policies in respect of disvestment, and charging depreciation in the value of the investments. In this connection, fixed assets turnover and fixed assets to net worth ratio and the rate of return on performing assets must be computed to study the fixed assets components as a portion of net worth or to study the earning power of fixed assets of the firm. The more the earning powers of the fixed assets, the more will be the source of funds generated to the company and more will be the positive impacts felt in assessing the quality of the debt instruments.

(7) Profitability: Since non-fund based income plays an important role in boosting the earnings of the issuer, the rating agency should determine the probability of continuance of such income in relation to sales, component-wise expenses ratios, operating expenses ratio, and operating net profit ratios determined in the past and budgeted figures in the future would also affect the quality of rating.

(8) Return on equity and on investment: Return on equity measures the profitability of equity funds invested in the firm after payment of taxes whereas the return on total investment measures the percentage of earnings remaining after payment of taxes. The total investment comprises creditor's and shareholders' fund, and is a product of net profit ratio and investment turnover ratio. This aspect has an important bearing on credit quality of the company. As a matter of rule of thumb, operating profit as a percentage of total funds employed should not be less than the lending rate of a commercial bank.

(9) Capital structure: The most important indicator in analyzing the capital structure is the capital adequacy ratio. To warrant adequate safety the borrowing of the company as a rule of thumb should not exceed two times its shareholders' funds. This is also an important indicator that determines the quality of rating of debt issues. A lower debt equity ratio indicates a higher degree of protection enjoyed by the creditors and the less is the likelihood of insolvency in future which favourably influence the rating of the debt instruments and vice versa. Then shareholders' equity to fixed assets ratio for the company is analyzed. If assets are more than the shareholders equity, it means that a part of the assets has been financed by the borrowed capital and hence, would deteriorate the quality of ratings of debt issues.

(10) Past performance: The increasing trend of revenues, profit after taxes, net worth, and net asset value of the firm, keeping the total investments, constant indicates the financial strength of the firm. These variables are also useful in judging the assignment of ratings to the issuance of debt instrument. These variables linked with cashflow statements will have a favourable bearing on the ratings of the debt instruments. Therefore a rating agency should carefully analyze these indicators prior to assigning any rating to the instruments issued by a company.

(11) Effect of normal business cycle: The business activities of the firm can be categorized as normal, recovery, boom, recession, and slump. So the rating agency has to consider the state of economic activity facing the company at the time of assigning rating to the debt instruments. This is one of the important factors which the rating agency cannot ignore prior to deciding the worth of the debt instrument. However, once the company decides to use the rating, the rating agency is obliged to monitor the rating over the life of the debt instrument. A rating, unless changed, is valid for the life time of the debt instrument being rated. If the rated non-convertible debenture is redeemed in the 7th, 8th, and 9th years from the date of its issue, the rating would continue till the end of the 9th year. However, depending upon new information, the agency may change the ratings either to be retained, or upgraded, or downgraded and the change so caused is made public for the benefit of the creditors and general public.

(12) Interest and debt coverage ratio including tax considerations: Past trends in connection with interest and debt coverage ratio and payment of taxes are carefully scrutinized to understand the issuer's policy of redemption of debt and payment of taxes in the past and provisions made to do so for the new debt which is proposed to be issued in future. Since profits are estimated for the future, this type of ratio can serve as a good index of long-term solvency of the firm. This is considered a pivotal factor in influencing the judgement on rating assigned by various rating agencies. The rating agency may ignore any of the above factors while assigning the rating of the debt issued but cannot ignore this prominent factor. To warrant adequate safety as a matter of rule of thumb, the firm's operating profit before interest and depreciation should at least be three times the interest commitments.

8.6 RATING PROCESS

The rating of debt instruments differs from company to company and the process begins at the request of the company. Generally, the rating applies to a debt obligation of the company. Thus, it is required to evaluate the ability of the company to meet the financial obligation on the debt instrument in a timely manner. An analytical team consisting of professionally qualified persons well-versed with the working of the industry, which is assigned the task of rating, is required to collect the industry information. Then the findings are reported to a rating committee comprising some directors not connected with any credit agency shareholder. After that the rating which is decided, is communicated to the company. At this stage if the company wishes to present some additional information, it can provide such information and accordingly the rating will be reviewed and revised. During rating process, strict confidential of requisite information should be maintained. Once the company decides to use the rating, the rating agency should monitor the rating over the life of the instrument. The rating agency may change the rating subject to any development concerning the company. The rating process for a new issue is shown in Fig. 8.2.

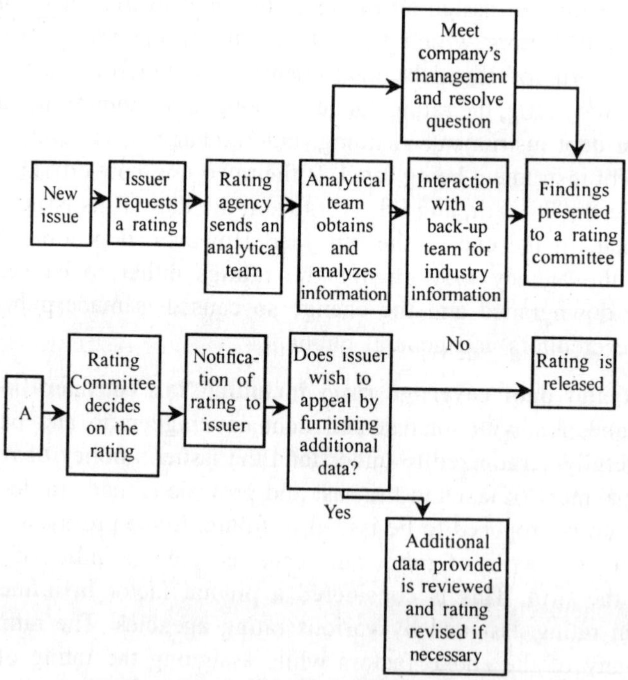

Fig. 8.2 Rating process for a new issue.

8.6.1 Benefit of Ratings

The credit rating is a guidance indicator to the investors and creditors in determining the credit risk associated with debt instruments or credit obligations. By using the credit rating symbol, the borrowing company raises funds in the capital market at cheaper rates. The credit rating also helps the companies in foreign collaborations. It encourages discipline among the borrowing companies. Further, it makes for greater liquidity for the debt instruments in the secondary market. The credit rating very much reduces the burden for the government in safeguarding the interests of the investors. Besides this, credit rating is also beneficial to the investors in the following manner:

(a) It provides superior information at low cost to the investors.

(b) It enables the investors to take calculated risk in their investments.

(c) It encourages the investors to invest in those companies where they will get high returns.

(d) Since the market price is normally be based on the ratings, the price would be more representative.

(e) It deprives the investors of depending on brokers and merchant bankers.

(f) The investors can become able to take quick and comparative decisions can become on the basis of the associated ratings.

(g) It provides liquidity for the debt instruments in secondary market.

(h) The investor gets the benefit of ongoing surveillance.

8.6.2 Limitations of Ratings

The ratings are no doubt important to the investment activity in the capital market. But they have their limitations. Some such limitations are:

(a) They do not give ratings of equity, as equity holders are supposed to take risks.

(b) Ratings of bonds, debentures and other types of instruments of debt are rated, only as indictors of risk.

(c) Ratings become out of date soon and hence they are to be updated at least every six months and any fresh information or developments may change the grade of rating.

(d) Ratings play a useful role to investors when the regulatory authority takes no responsibility for those who raise funds and investors are left to themselves.

(e) Credit rating agencies should maintain expert professional staff with qualifications and competence of lawyers, CAs, CS, M.B.A., finance and bankers, etc. Besides their staff should be permanent and must not change frequently. If these conditions are not satisfied, ratings become undependable.

8.7 THE CHALLENGES

The volume of credit rating business picked up in India only after rating was made compulsory for certain instruments by regulatory agencies. At present, commercial paper, public issues of debentures and bonds with maturities exceeding 18 months, and fixed deposits of large non-banking finance companies registered with the RBI are required to be compulsorily rated. While the range of instruments has been quoted to be wide, the bulk of credit rating so far is confined to CP, fixed deposit, bonds, and debentures. Further, rating of equity has been left out so equity must need to be brought into the preview as it forms a major share in the public borrowing of companies. Again the rating of commercial banks is undertaken by credit rating agencies the world over but the nationalized banks in India have not been very keen on going through a credit rating exercise. Similarly other public sector undertakings also need credit rating services as they have to raise funds through commercial borrowing. Credit rating of individuals is another service which is yet to pick up in India which can offer considerable scope. In addition to this, rating agencies are required to promote multiple rating, under which certain issues are rated by at least two rating agencies. Lastly, the rating methodology adopted must be thorough and transparent.

8.8 SEBI GUIDELINES FOR RATING

(1) The credit rating agencies cannot rate a security issued by its promoters.

(2) If the debt issues is more than Rs. 100 crores, dual rating must compulsorily involve public and rights issue.

(3) The company should provide correct information to the rating agencies.

(4) The net worth of rating agencies has been fixed at Rs. 5 crores.

(5) The rating agencies can choose their own methodology of operation.

(6) No chairman, director, or employee of the promoters shall be a director, chairman, or employee of the rating committee.

SUMMARY

The outlook for the credit rating industry appears positive. But the industry has to continuously strive to improve the professional capabilities and sustain its credibility. No doubt the credit rating agencies today have ample opportunities to play a unique role in strengthening the capital market and building investors' confidence in the financial system.

REVIEW QUESTIONS

1. Explain the meaning, objective, and types of credit rating.
2. Discuss the benefits and limitations of credit rating.
3. Explain the role and functions of CRISIL.
4. Discuss the working of various credit rating agencies in India.

QUIZ

State whether the following are true or false.

1. CARE was established in the year 1990. (T/F)
2. Financial instrument rating comprises bond rating only. (T/F)
3. The rating of debt instrument is differing from company to company. (T/F)
4. Credit rating enables the investors to depend on brokers. (T/F)
5. Rating agency commences rating process at the request of the company. (T/F)

Fill up the blanks.

6. .... and .... promoted the credit rating information service of India in 1988.
7. ICRA was established in the year ....
8. AA refers to ....
9. Credit rating rates .... of the company.
10. DPCR is a private sector agency started in the year ....

REFERENCES

Ali ki lian, Mohd. Akbar, "CRISIL Rating in India—A New financial service in capital market," *Finance India,* Vol. VII, No. 3, Sept. 1993.

CRISIL, "Rating Set—Debentures," Aug. 1993.

Choudhury, P.K., "Credit Rating: A Few simple facts," *The Economic Times,* Calcutta, Aug., 1994.

Dhileepan, P., "Rating of Banks and Financial Companies", *The Economic Times*, Calcutta, Aug., 1994.

Gupta, R.L. and M. Radhaswami, "*Financial Statement Analysis*", Sultan Chand and Sons, New Delhi, 1982, pp. FSA 37–64.

Jhaveri, M.S., "*Premium Investments*", 16th July–22nd July, 1993, p. 11.

IBA Bulletin, Vol. XVI, No.1, January 1993.

Menon, A., "ICRA forms Novel Cashflow Structure for SEBI Raising Funds", *The Economic Times*, Calcutta, Dec., 1994.

Mohansule, "The Importance of being CRISIL", *The Economic Times*, March, 1991.

Punjab National Bank, *Monthly Review*, November, 1992.

Ramchandran, Kalyani, "Critical Factors Influencing Financing Decisions Credit Rating" *Asian. Journal of Management*, Vol. 20, No. 2-3 (Sept.–Dec., 1990).

Rao, B. Ramachandra, "Banking on Credit Rating," *The Banker*, May, 1993.

Shah, Pradip P., "Credit Rating and the Role of CRISIL", *Chartered Secretary*, July, 1993.

Chapter 9

Factoring Services

9.1 INTRODUCTION

The capital market and money market are considered to be the most important segment of the financial system. The capital market has undergone significant transformation and has witnessed an explosive growth in terms of its size, number, and variety of scripts issued and listed on the stock exchange. Similarly the money market has also opened up and witnessed the arrival of new money market instruments like 182 days treasury bills, certificates of deposits, commercial paper, and participation certificates. To encourage bill financing and developing bill culture, the bill discounting rate has been reduced. The bill rediscounting market has been widened by allowing more participants to rediscount bill. As the debts are not collected in time and are handicapped by lack of sufficient working capital, the production and expansion of business is affected. Hence the working group on money market, that is, Vaghul Committee, recommended introduction of factoring services in India to solve the financial problems of the small scale supplies. Reserve Bank of India then appointed a committee under the chairmanship of C.S. Kalyanasundaram, former Managing Director of the State Bank of India and suggested operational modalities of launching such a service. The factoring services have been introduced to ease the problems of collection of debts and delayed payments from the debtors.

9.2 ORIGIN

The origin of factoring can be traced to the 15th and 16th centuries in England and France, which were exporting goods to their colonies and required an agency to distribute the goods, provide funds, and collect the proceeds. In 19th and 20th centuries, such agents only provided funds and collected sale proceeds. Thus, factoring was introduced in the developed countries in UK and USA. At present, USA and European countries account for nearly 90% of global factoring turnover. Factoring is of a recent origin in the Indian context. In 1988, the Reserve Bank of India constituted a high-powered committee to examine the scope for offering factoring services in the country. In 1989, the committee directed that factoring activities could be undertaken by banks through the medium of separate subsidiaries.

9.3 CONCEPT OF FACTORING

The word "factor" has been derived from the Latin word "Facere" which means *to make or do,* i.e., to get things done. The Webster's dictionary states that 'factor' is an agent as a banking or finance company, engaged in financing the operations of certain companies. The Oxford dictionary defines the term 'factor' as a person or an organization acting as a business agent. According to C.S. Kalyanasundaram, "factoring is the outright purchase of credit approved account receivables with the factor assuming bad debt losses". According to Alam Calpin, "factoring is a system designated to eliminate payment risk in overseas sales and ensure that the seller receives prompt settlements". According to Biscoe. "factoring may be defined as a continuing legal relationship between a financial institution (the factor) and a business concern (the client) selling goods or providing services to trade customer's (the customer) open account basis. Whereby the factor purchases the clients books debts (account receivables) either without or with recourse to the client and in relation thereto controls the credit extended to customers and administers the sales ledger". According to Financial Executives Handbook, "the term describes another specialized and important form of credit and collection service. It is essentially the extra service of credit protection that differentiates factoring from accounts receivable financing". In simple words, factoring can be defined as an arrangement under which the factor purchases the account receivables and makes immediate cash payment to the suppliers. The factor undertakes the responsibility of collecting the dues from the buyer hence assumes risk. For this type of services as well as for the interest, the factor changes a fee for intervening period which is technically known as factorage. Figure 9.1 depicts the process of factoring.

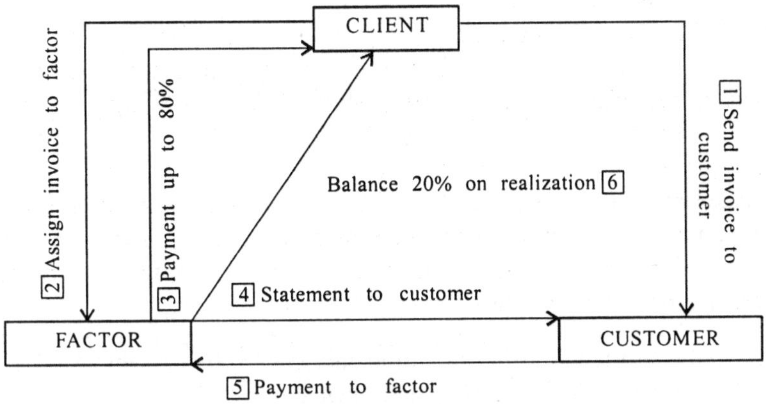

Fig. 9.1 The process of factoring.

Following series of steps are followed in Fig. 9.1.

1. The client sells the goods on credit basis to customer.
2. The client offers the assigned invoice to the factor.
3. The factor makes a pre-payment up to 80% of the value of the assigned invoice.
4. The factor notifies the customer sending a statement of account.
5. Customer remits the amount due to the factor.
6. Factor makes balance 20% of the invoice value to the client when the account is collected or on a guaranteed payment date.

9.4 TYPES OF FACTORING

Factoring can be categorized as follows:

(1) Notified and undisclosed factoring: In case of notified factoring, the customer is informed about the assignment of the debt to the factoring agent and is also asked to pay the dues to the factor instead of to the firm. On the other hand in the undisclosed factoring, the factoring arrangement is not disclosed to the customer but the customer is required to make the payment to the changed address. This is also known as non-notified factoring or confidential factoring.

(2) Recourse and non-recourse factoring: In recourse factoring, the factor purchases the receivables on the condition that the loss arising on account of irrecoverable receivables will be borne by the client, while in non-recourse factoring the bad debts are borne by the factoring agent. Since the factor bears the loss arising on account of irrecoverable debts, the factor charges a higher commission.

(3) Advance and maturity factoring: In case of advance factoring, the factor provides an advance varying between 75–85% of the value of receivables factored and the balance is paid upon collection or on the guaranteed payment date. Whereas in maturity factoring, the factor makes the payment on a guaranteed payment date or on the date of collection.

(4) Bank participation factoring: Under this arrangement, the bank finances against the reserves which is maintained by the factor on which the firm creates a floating charge on the factoring reserves in favour of bank and borrows against these reserves.

(5) Invoice factoring: Strictly speaking, this form of factoring is not considered as an integral part of the present day factoring system because it does not carry the service element of factoring. Under this type of factoring the debts due to the client are purchased by the factor who thus provides improved liquidity under which the supplier's position becomes very comfortable.

(6) Buyer-based, seller-based, and selective factoring: Buyer-based factoring means that the factor would maintain a list of buyers and would be factored without recourse to the seller. Whereas in seller-based factoring, the factor would prefer seller-based factoring with recourse and without recourse. Seller-based factoring is known as selective factoring where the seller is restricted to sell to the approved buyer.

(7) With credit and without credit factoring: The buyer can make a contract in favour of seller that the seller does not assign the credit to any third party. Under such circumstances, the factor is unable to register his power of attorney and has to trust the seller to remit the money to him after realization.

(8) Export factoring: This is also known as *international factoring* or *crossborder factoring*. Export factoring houses deal with export sales and provide financial service, collection service, advisor service, and service for completing legal formalities pertaining to export. Generally, export factoring is quite helpful to small exporters and new entrants to export business in India.

9.5 FUNCTIONS OF FACTORING

The functions of factoring can be listed as follows:

(i) Finance: The factor provides advance money to the client against outstanding debt of about 80% and the balance minus commission on maturity. Hence, the factor acts as a source of short-term funds.

(ii) Debt administration: Under this, the responsibility of the factor is to take care of all the functions relating to the maintenance of the sales leader on open item basis which should clearly show all the outstanding invoices and the unallocated cash. The factor sends monthly statements of accounts and informs the client about the progress of collection of debts from time to time and also informs him/her about the debts collected and overdue accounts. This helps the client to increase his sales with availability of finance.

(iii) Credit risk: One of the important functions of the factoring is credit protection. The factoring organization is required to ascertain the credit worthiness and feasibility position of several buyers and accordingly advice the client. Hence, the client is guided by the factor's advice in this regard, under which the factor reduces the risk of loss through bad debts.

(iv) Advisory services: By virtue of the experience, the factor is also able to provide advisory service on credit and financial dealings and access to extensive credit information. The factor can also advise customers on work-load analysis, replacement programme, on machinery, and other technical problems.

9.6 ADVANTAGES

Factoring offers the following advantages from the point of view of the clients:

1. Through factoring, the client gets immediate cash which reduces the operating cycle and increases the turnover.
2. As the factor takes all the responsibility of maintaining sales ledger administration, credit control, and debt collection, the client is relieved from the administrative burden.
3. As the factor provides instant cash to the client against credit sales, the client can derive benefit from the cash discounts by making prompt payment for this purchases. This will substantially reduce purchase costs and improve profitability.
4. By off-loading the administration, the client has more time for planning, running, and improving the business and exploiting opportunities.
5. Factoring ensures a perfect debtor turnover and improves the profitability of the client by avoiding the risk of bad debts.
6. The factor provides the information like credit standing position of the customer under which the client can avoid poor quality and risky customer.
7. As the factor collects the accounts in time, there is no need for the client to spend his/her valuable time for slow paying customer under which there will be saving in interest payment contributing towards cost savings.

Benefits of factoring

Factoring involves change in the asset-structure of the firm as receivables are converted into cash (advance factoring). This makes the asset-structure of the firm more liquid and enhances its capacity to meet maturing obligations.

The real benefits of factoring get reflected in profit and loss account. A firm has to compare and evaluate financial statements before and after factoring the receivables.

9.7 FACTORING AND BALANCE SHEET

The balance sheet of ABC Co. Ltd. (before and after factoring) is exhibited in Tables 9.2 and 9.3 below to substantiate the relevance of factoring

Table 9.2 Balance sheet of ABC Co. Ltd. (before factoring)

	Rs.		Rs.
Share capital and reserves & surplus	10,00,000	Fixed assets	10,00,000
Long-term debt	6,00,000	Current assets	
Current liabilities	4,00,000	Inventory	4,00,000
		Receivables	4,00,000
		Cash	2,00,000
	20,00,000		20,00,000

Overall working capital position	= Total current assets = Rs. 10,00,000
Net working capital	= Rs. CA – CL = Rs. 10,00,000 – Rs. 4,00,000 = Rs. 6,00,000
Current ratio	= CA/CL = Rs. (10,00,000/4,00,000) = 2.5:1
Liquid ratio	= LA/CL = Rs. (6,00,000/4,00,000) = 1.5:1

Table 9.3 Balance sheet of ABC Co. Ltd. (after factoring 80% of receivables)

	Rs.		Rs.
Share capital and reserves & surplus	10,00,000	Fixed assets	10,00,000
Long-term debt	4,00,000	Current assets	
Current liabilities	6,00,000	Inventory	4,00,000
		Receivables	80,000
		Cash	5,20,000
	20,00,000		20,00,000

(*Cont.*)

Table 9.3 Balance sheet of ABC Co. Ltd. (after factoring 80% of receivables) (*Cont.*)

	Rs.	Rs.
Overall working capital position	= CA – CL = Rs.10,00,000	
Net working capital	= Rs. 10,00,000 – Rs. 4,00,000 = Rs. 6,00,000	
Current ratio	= CA/CL = Rs. (10,00,000/4,00,000) = 2.5:1	
Liquid ratio	= LA/CL = Rs. (6,00,000/4,00,000) = 1.5:1	

The cash position of ABC Co. Ltd. improved from Rs. 2,00,000 to Rs. 5,20,000 without any corresponding increase in any of the liability items or sale of fixed assets. However, there is no change in the overall and net working capital position, and current and liquid ratios as factoring affects only the composition of current assets.

9.8 FACTORING AND PROFIT AND LOSS ACCOUNT

The benefits of factoring in terms of the profit and loss account are analyzed as under:

(1) The factor performs basis functions like administration of seller's sales ledger, credit control, collection of dues, etc. This saves the administration costs.

(2) The factor by providing payment on the purchase of receivables contrasts the length of operating cycle period and reduces the working capital needs. This saves the interest on capital.

(3) The improved liquidity position enables the firm to honour its obligations without any delay. The improved credit standing helps the firm to get the benefits of lower purchase price, longer credit period from suppliers, trade discount on bulk purchases, cash discount on early payment, better market standing, quicker sanction of loans and advances, and better terms and conditions while borrowing, etc.

Cost of factoring

The cost of factoring includes:

(i) Interest on advance extended by the factor.

(ii) Commission/fee for his services. Interest rate ranges between 2–5% over and above the prime rate of interest.

(iii) The commission is usually charged in the range of 2.5% to 3% on the gross value of invoices. In fact, the factoring commission depends on the total volume of receivables, the size of individual receivables, and the quality of receivables.

The following are the important assumptions made in constructing the statement:

(i) The average receivables of the firms are equal to two months' sale.
(ii) All sales are on credit basis.
(iii) Cost of goods sold is equal to 60% of the sales.
(iv) Administration costs (which includes credit department expenses of Rs. 2,00,000) and selling costs are assumed to be Rs. 1,00,000 and Rs. 16,00,000 respectively.
(v) The bad debts loss percentage is 5% of gross value of sales.
(vi) The factor charges 2% commission on gross value of sales.
(vii) The interest charged by the factor as well as by other financial institutions on advances is assumed to be 18% per annum.
(viii) The margin money is 10%.
(ix) Materials cost is saved by 2.5% on account of lower prices, trade discount, cash discount, etc.

The profit and loss account of ABC Co. Ltd. (before and after factoring) is shown in Tables 9.4 and 9.5 respectively.

Table 9.4 Profit and loss account of ABC Co. Ltd. (before factoring)

	Rs.		Rs.
To materials cost	36,00,000	By sales	120,00,000
To labour cost	20,00,000		
To factory expenses	16,00,000		
To gross profit	48,00,000		
	120,00,000		120,00,000
To administrative expenses	6,00,000	By gross profit	48,00,000
To credit dept., expenses	2,00,000		
To selling expenses	16,00,000		
To bad debts	6,00,000		
To interest on loan	3,60,000		
To net profit before tax	14,40,000		
	48,00,000		48,00,000

Notes: Interest on loan = Rs. 120,00,000 × 2/12 × 18/100 = Rs. 3,60,000

Table 9.5 Profit and loss account of ABC Co. Ltd. (after factoring)

	Rs.		Rs.
To materials cost	35,10,000	By sales	120,00,000
To labour cost	20,00,000		
To factory expenses	16,00,000		
To gross profit	48,00,000		
	60,00,000		60,00,000

(*Cont.*)

Table 9.5 Profit and loss account of ABC Co. Ltd. (after factoring) (*Cont.*)

To administrative expenses	6,00,000	By gross profit	48,90,000
To selling expenses	16,00,000		
To factoring commission @2%	2,40,000		
To interest on advance	2,80,800		
To net profit before tax	21,70,200		
	48,90,000		48,90,000

Note: Materials cost = Rs. 36,00,000 – 2.5% of Rs. 36,00,000
Interest on advance: = Rs. 35,10,000

Amount of advance = Average receivables – Commission @2% on sales – 10% reserve
= Rs. 120,00,000 × 2/12 – Rs. 2,40,000 – 10% × Rs. 120,00,000 × 2/12
= Rs. 20,00,000 – Rs. 240,000 – Rs. 20,00,000
= Rs. 15,60,000

Interest on advance = 18% of Rs. 15,60,000
= Rs. 2,80,800

Table 9.6 that follows, gives the summary of costs and benefits of factoring.

Table 9.6 Summary of costs and benefits of factoring for ABC Co. Ltd.

	Rs.	Rs.
Benefits of factoring:		
Savings in material cost	90,000	
Credit dept., expenses	2,00,000	
Bad debt losses avoided	6,00,000	
Interest on loan	3,60,000	12,50,000
Less: costs of factoring:		
Factoring commission	2,40,000	
Interest on advance	2,80,800	5,20,800
Net benefit of factoring	7,29,200	7,29,200

The profit and loss account and its summary clearly indicate that the overall profitability of ABC Co. Ltd. is increased by Rs.7,29,200. This increase the ROI and dividend rate, if the management so desires.

9.9 INTERNATIONAL SCENARIO

Factoring is a global industry with a vast turnover. The annual growth rate of factoring in 2001 was 5.20% in Japan. For Hong Kong, Singapore, China, India and Srilanka, the corresponding rates in 2001 were 12.5%, 18.10% 483.96%, 46.80% and 16.16% respectively. In India and Srilanka, factoring is spreading over time while in south America, financial institutions continue to join the industry. Factoring is growing in significance, especially in the context of the globalization of trade and finance. The total factoring volume generated worldwide in 2001 stood at US $ 634 billion. Table 9.7 reveals that the quantum of international factoring is meagre as compared to its domestic counterport. The share of international factoring ranges only from 4.99% to 7.03% of total world factoring. It reached US $ 42557 million in 2001 as against US $ 3694 in 1983. It is also seen from the Table 9.7 that the world international factoring has gone up by 11.52 times in 19 years which is slightly higher than that of world domestic factoring.

Table 9.7 Global factoring business: domestic and international

(US $ millions)

Year	World domestic factoring			World international factoring			World total	
	Total	Index	Percentage of world total	Total	Index	Percentage of world total	Total	Index
1983	60,888	100.00	94.28	3694	100.0	5.72	64,582	100.00
1984	67,523	110.89	95.01	3544	95.94	4.99	71,067	110.04
1985	80,984	133.00	94.92	4336	117.38	5.08	85,320	132.11
1986	97,782	160.59	94.22	6000	162.42	5.78	1,03,782	160.69
1987	1,31,067	215.26	93.75	8744	236.70	6.25	1,39,811	216.48
1988	1,51,522	248.85	94.49	8844	239.41	5.51	1,60,406	248.37
1989	1,79,198	294.31	94.30	10826	293.07	5.70	1,90,024	294.24
1990	2,30,564	378.67	94.37	13763	372.57	5.63	2,44,327	378.32
1991	2,50,626	411.62	94.09	15744	426.20	5.91	2,66,370	442.45
1992	2,49,414	409.63	94.36	14895	403.22	5.64	2,64,309	409.26
1993	2,46,288	404.49	94.42	14556	394.04	5.58	2,60,844	403.89
1994	2,74,893	451.47	93.21	20033	542.31	6.79	2,94,926	456.67
1995	3,16,729	520.18	93.14	23296	630.64	6.85	3,40,025	526.5
1996	3,68,116	604.58	92.97	27824	753.22	7.03	3,95,940	613.08
1997	4,22,739	694.32	93.55	29130	788.57	6.45	4,51,869	699.68
1998	4,98,175	818.18	94.08	31340	848.40	5.92	5,29,515	819.91
1999	5,40,557	887.79	94.06	34170	925.01	5.94	5,74,727	889.92
2000	5,55,250	911.92	93.01	41725	1129.53	6.99	5,96,975	924.37
2001	5,92,148	972.52	93.29	42557	1152.06	6.71	6,34,705	982.79
Compound growth rate(%)	13.42			15.03			13.54	

Source: Factors Chain International, Amsterdam, the Netherlands, http://www.factors_chain.com

The total world factoring volume was US $ 6,34,705 million in 2001 as against US $ 64,582 million in 1983. The compounded growth rate of world's total volume comes to 13.54%. International factoring survey 1998 states that international factoring is growing considerably faster than international trade.

Table 9.8 presents the ten major countries factoring index and its year-wise growth. It shows that the index number is quite high in 1997 in Italy, Spain, UK, France, and Netherlands. Italy's growth rate in 1997 was 40%

Table 9.8 Index of factoring turnover growth: ten largest factoring markets

Year	World Index	World Growth rate	FCI Index	FCI Growth rate	Finland Index	Finland Growth rate	France Index	France Growth rate	Germany Index	Germany Growth rate	Italy Index	Italy Growth rate	Japan Index	Japan Growth rate	Netherlands Index	Netherlands Growth rate	Spain Index	Spain Growth rate	Sweden Index	Sweden Growth rate	U.K. Index	U.K. Growth rate	U.S.A. Index	U.S.A. Growth rate
1980	100	%	100	%	100	%	100	%	100	%	100	%	100	%	100	%	N.A.	%	100	%	100	%	100	%
1984	120	6	108	2	273	19	240	14	120	4	958	60	213	5	188	21	100	–	120	–7	196	29	132	13
1985	143	19	159	47	316	16	248	3	133	11	1475	54	172	–23	228	21	119	19	121	1	255	30	132	–
1986	175	22	207	30	305	–4	294	19	161	21	1935	31	180	5	262	15	291	144	103	–17	313	23	141	7
1987	135	34	305	47	320	5	379	29	184	14	2920	51	173	–4	278	6	425	46	86	–20	395	26	157	11
1988	270	15	352	15	372	16	480	27	177	–4	4076	40	258	49	346	24	570	34	94	9	522	32	160	2
1989	319	18	448	27	399	7	585	22	191	8	5890	44	259	–	372	8	750	32	81	–16	643	23	165	3
1990	410	28	550	23	348	–13	690	18	235	23	7424	26	404	56	482	30	931	24	107	32	762	19	173	5
1991	448	9	581	6	197	–43	767	11	245	4	7860	6	435	8	534	11	1431	54	68	–18	750	–1	180	4
1992	444	–1	593	2	202	2	888	16	286	17	8100	3	455	5	490	–8	1469	2	81	–8	785	5	187	4
1993	439	–1	617	1	218	8	915	3	295	3	7452	–8	441	–3	598	22	2115	44	75	–8	965	23	200	7
1994	496	13	722	17	209	–4	4180	29	280	–5	6334	–15	481	9	514	14	2348	11	110	46	1370	42	210	5
1995	570	15	895	24	297	42	1664	41	311	11	7347	16	592	23	678	32	2677	14	105	–5	1658	21	214	2
1996	661	16	940	5	404	36	1964	18	407	31	7567	6	805	36	881	30	3453	29	247	135	2130	28	225	5
1997	754	14	1053	12	517	28	2376	21	537	32	10594	40	1006	25	1075	22	4282	24	252	2	2573	18	250	11

Source: Factors Chain International, Amsterdam, the Netherlands, http://www.factors_chain.com

followed by that of Germany and Finland being 32% and 28% respectively, whereas UK, USA, and Sweden have registered 18%, 11%, and 2% growth respectively.

Table 9.9 shows the continent-wise distribution of factoring companies. The total number of factoring companies in the European continent accounts for 427 at the end of 2001. Americas register the second highest expansion with 392 companies. The compound growth rate of the number of continent-wise factoring companies shows an upward trend in all the continents with a compound growth rate of 7.48%. The upward growth rate of factoring business in some major countries namely Finland, France, Germany, Italy Japan, Netherlands, and Spain has also been particularly noticeable.

Table 9.9 Distribution of number of factoring companies in the world continents

	Europe		Americas		Africa		Asia		Australasia		Total	
Year	No.	Index	No.	Index	No.	Index	No.	Index	No.	Index	No.	Index
1983	137	100.00	41	100.00	11	100.00	51	10.00	8	100.00	248	100.00
1984	152	110.95	38	92.68	11	100.00	66	129.41	7	87.50	274	110.48
1985	169	123.36	36	87.80	10	90.91	72	141.17	12	150.00	299	120.56
1986	177	129.19	36	87.80	5	45.45	78	152.94	20	250.00	316	127.42
1987	201	146.72	39	95.12	5	45.45	133	260.78	25	312.5	403	162.50
1988	207	151.09	30	73.17	7	63.63	97	190.19	24	300.00	415	167.34
1989	224	163.50	95	235.70	7	63.63	104	203.92	24	300.00	454	183.06
1990	237	172.99	131	319.51	7	63.63	109	213.73	23	287.50	507	204.44
1991	243	177.37	308	751.22	6	54.54	113	221.57	22	275.00	692	279.03
1992	273	199.27	293	714.63	7	63.63	115	225.50	27	337.50	755	304.43
1993	294	214.60	100	243.90	12	109.09	165	323.53	16	200.00	587	236.69
1994	324	236.50	86	209.75	12	109.09	159	311.76	16	200.00	597	240.73
1995	312	227.73	111	270.73	10	90.91	200	392.16	20	250.00	653	263.31
1996	343	250.37	83	202.44	11	100.00	192	376.47	24	300.00	653	263.31
1997	343	250.37	83	202.44	11	100.00	192	376.47	24	300.00	653	263.31
1998	406	296.35	113	275.61	13	118.18	150	294.11	26	325.00	708	285.48
1999	399	291.24	428	1043.90	13	118.18	114	223.53	25	312.50	979	394.75
2000	435	317.52	411	1002.44	13	118.18	98	192.16	28	350.00	985	397.17
2001	427	311.67	392	956.10	14	127.27	104	203.92	28	350.00	965	389.11
Compound growth rate	6.54		13.09		13.09		4.37		4.91		7.48	

9.10 FACTORING IN INDIA

In Indian context, factoring is being viewed as a source of short-term finance that can offer useful services specially to the supplier. The introduction of factoring services in our country arises not only due to the limitation of the banking industry but on account of managing the receivables of the manufacturers efficiently. Further the professional approach of factors in assessment of credit, debt collection, and management of sales ledger may develop a healthy payment culture. So the factoring organization should be set up as a monolithic institution to handle the entire business in the country. Factoring business has just started in India. The State Bank of India has started its subsidiary known as SBI Factors and Commercial Services Private Limited with effect from 31st August, 1991. It is operating in the western region. As per the first annual report (1991–92) of SBI Factors, it had on its books 25 units that are manufacturers and sellers of goods and 164 customers. Sixty per cent of the units were small scale units which deal in chemicals, packaging plastics and allied products, consumer durables, castings pharma-ceuticals, and light engineering. At present, the Cannt Factors Limited is operating in four southern states and the union territories of Pondicherry and Lakshadweep. Similarly UCO Bank, United Bank of India, and Allahabad Bank are to jointly set a factoring subsidiary in the Eastern part of India. Punjab National Bank is operating in northern India. Thus the introduction of factoring services in India is expected to give a boost to the industrial production, employment, and economic growth.

9.10.1 Challenges

There is no doubt in stating that factoring service is a new dimension in Indian industries in an organized manner. There are many benefits of factoring which a firm can avail. As India is in the process of opening up and liberalizing its economy where the financial service industry including factor has been growing tremendously, it is necessary to implement some of the suggestions from which the factoring service would be able to penetrate and expand their own market. The following are some of the suggestions:

(a) To make factoring economically viable, the government should pass appropriate laws exempting factored debts from payment of stamp duty on assignment.

(b) It is required to regulate prescribed norms for new entrants to factoring business.

(c) Indian legislation does not deal with various aspects involved in factoring business. So it would be necessary to promote special legislation to establish efficient and viable factoring organization.

(d) For communication, computer support is essential for factors for extending their services efficiently and economically.

(e) The civil procedure code should be suitably amended facilitating recovery of factored debts through summary proceedings under order 37 of the code.

(f) There are delinquent debts on account of insufficient budgetary provisions among government departments and large business undertakings of the public and private sectors. In such circumstances, the environment factoring will be more effective.

(g) The saving of financial loss is to be borne by industrial and business concerns on account of employing excess manpower. Hence, credit discipline is needed for the success of factoring system in India.

(h) There is no reliable credit agency in India to provide information like reputation, financial standing, and business prospects of the customer. This is considered to be one of the toughest obstacles for the success of factoring business in India. So though CRISIL has been introduced, the RBI should take immediate measures to set up more agencies in the economy.

SUMMARY

The factoring companies must be allowed to have a debt capacity at par with the other intermediaries like leasing and hire/purchase companies so that the companies can design coefficient capital structure. Factoring service will surely provide new dimensions to achieve the goals of modernizing India and economic prosperity.

REVIEW QUESTIONS

1. Explain the origin, meaning, and characteristics of factoring.
2. Explain the various functions of factoring.
3. Explain the types and advantages of factoring.

QUIZ

State whether the following are true or false.

1. The firm offers the assigned invoice to the factor. (T/F)
2. Advisory services are not the functions of the factor. (T/F)
3. The factor provides credit standing position of the customer. (T/F)
4. The firm offers the assigned invoice to the factor. (T/F)
5. International factoring is also known as cross-border factoring. (T/F)
6. Advisory services are not the functions of factor. (T/F)
7. The factor provides credit standing position of the customer. (T/F)

Fill up the blanks.

8. The first bank in India to start factoring business is ....
9. In .... year, RBI constituted a high-powered committee to examine scope for offering factoring service in the country.
10. The word 'factor' is derived from the word ....

REFERENCES

Bajaj, K.K., "Factoring Service make a doubt in India", *Financial Express*, August 20, 1991.

Bansal, L.K., "Factoring—Another Financing Source", *Chartered Secretary*, January, 1990.

Brandemberg, M., "Why don't they use factoring?", *Accountancy*, January, 1984.

Dendekar, M.N., The Financial System of Factoring—An Approach for introduction in India, *SBI Monthly Review*, March, 1991.

"Factoring Service—A Boon to small scale units", *The Economic Times*, March, 1990.

Hyderabad, R.L., "Factoring: Cost-benefit analysis", *The Management Accountant*, March 1998.

The Economic Times, February 26, 1990.

Srikrishna, P., "Factoring", *SBI Monthly Review*, August, 1988.

Subramanyam, M.J., "Factoring Services—The Long–Awaited Financial Service", *Indian Banking Today and Tomorrow*, November, 1991.

Banerjee, Prasant kumar, "Global Factoring Business: Trend & Performance", *Finance India*, Vol. XVII No. 4, Dec. 2003.

Chapter 10

Forfaiting

10.1 INTRODUCTION

Indian capital market has been experiencing metamorphic changes and these changes have become more pronounced in the last couple of years with the advent of liberalization of industrial policy, licensing policy, financial service industry, interest rates, etc. In most of the developing countries various agencies like commercial banks, Export–import banks, and the export insurance bodies specialize in financing export to importers situated in other countries. But the financial institutions and other agencies are becoming inadequate in terms of providing financial assistance. Further, international banks are compelling to adhere strictly to the capital adequacy norms for which banks find it difficult to put extra funds in the risky line of business. At the same time, letter of credit which was considered at one time the best way of financing exports have the demerit of being transaction-oriented and is not ideal in case of repetitive transaction where fast delivery is required. So exporters receive delayed payment from importers which makes it difficult for them to expand their export business. In consideration of having received the immediate payment, the concept of forfaiting would come as a boon for the Indian exporters as an alternative source of finance to ensure to keep international business expanding. Even though this method of finance is prevailing for more than 30 years in the international market, it is a recent development in India.

10.2 CONCEPT

The concept of "forfaiting" was originally developed in Switzerland in mid 1960s and became important after the end of second world war with the objective of helping to finance the west German exports to eastern block countries. "Forfeit" is a French word which means "to surrender something or give up one's right". Accordingly, the exporters surrender their right to the forfeiter to receive future payment from the buyer to whom goods have been supplied. The exporters offer credit terms to the importer and sell the debt to the forfeiter. Hence, the forfeiter waives recourse to the exporter, if this importer defaults in payments. Generally speaking, forfaiting is a technique to help the exporter sell his goods in credit and yet receive the cash well before the due date. Subsequently with the increased volume of trade between the developed and developing countries, forfaiting provides a suitable channel for grants of some flexible credit to the exporters under situation. So forfaiting has emerged as extremely important tool for offering fixed rate term financing to an importer while retaining the benefit of cash sale.

10.3 SEQUENCE OF OPERATIONS IN FORFAITING

Forfaiting is done without recourse meaning thereby that the forfeiter cannot go back to the exporter for the recovery of the money which the importer may not pay to him. When a forfaiting transaction is to take place between the exporter and forfeiter, it is an essential prerequisite to give detailed information such as the nature of goods, prices, the currency, and the name of the importer and guarantees to the forfeiter. A contract is then made between the exporter and importer specifying the payment would be made by the importer to the forfeiter. As a result, notes are signed by the importer and the local bank is informed. Then the importer's bank guarantees the notes and forwards them to the exporter's bank with instructions to release them to the exporter's bank against shipping documents. The exporter ships the goods and gives the shipping documents to his bank under which the bank releases the notes to the exporter and forwards them to the importer through importer's bank. Eventually the exporter presents the notes to the forfeiter and receives the cash.

10.4 COSTS OF FORFAITING

The cost involved in forfaiting can be classified as:

(i) discount fees towards providing the finance depending upon the risk content of the transactions. However, exporters are willing to pay

15% extra for forfaiting due to additional services provided by the forfeiter. The forfeiter ordinarily charges a commission of about 1% of the face value of the receivable and if the exporter wants an advance against the receivables sold before, then he is required to pay interest to the forfeiter on the amount of advance.

(ii) Front-end management fee to Exim bank for handling the transaction is another type of cost incurred.

(iii) A commitment fee is also charged by the bank normally up to one year of undertaking.

10.5 BENEFITS

Following are the benefits of financial assistance through forfaiting:

(1) Forfaiting provides service in such a manner to meet the needs of the exporters and importers. One of the greatest advantages of forfaiting is its simplicity and flexibility. Forfaiting can be used to finance any export transaction. This technique is highly useful for medium-term fixed rate financing.

(2) Since the transaction does not have a recourse basis, it helps the exporters convert their credit sale into a cash sale.

(3) Where the exporter's bankers are not quick enough to provide additional credit limit for extended period, the forfaiting route, with the advantage of a "fixed interest rate and no currency risk", acts an export facilitator.

(4) The biggest advantage of forfaiting is that exporters do not have to carry the receivables in their balance sheet.

(5) The exporters do not deal with the forfeiter. Instead, the Exim bank does everything for them.

(6) Exporters are saved of all the hassles in collecting dues as once sold to the forfeiter, they are out of the transaction.

(7) Documentation procedure is simple and therefore it provides an opportunity to structure the deal.

(8) Forfaiting is a very good measure of international risk. Therefore, now Indian banks are allowed to discount their overseas customers' bills without adding their name.

(9) Initially, forfaiting was used mainly for capital goods but the situation today has changed and the forfaiting company is now willing to look at smaller export orders.

(10) Forfaiting provides a host of services such as checking the credit worthiness of the foreign buyer, extension of credit lines, advancing money against submission of invoices, sales ledger, administration, etc.

10.6 INDIAN SCENARIO

Indian commercial banks provide concessional finance for export transactions at both the pre- and post-shipment stages. Refinance is provided by the Reserve Bank of India and the Export–Import Bank of India against credit granted by commercial banks. However, inspite of the schemes floated by commercial banks, only the large and well-established exporters are being benefited by this scheme and small exporters are facing difficulties in making arrangement for necessary funds. So forfaiting was introduced in March 1993 as an alternative instrument for export finance, for the first time with the Export–Import Bank of India as the sole authorized intermediary which could help the Indian exporters. A specialist forfaiting company provides exporters and banks with the product of "discount of receivables on a without recourse basis". This instrument is very helpful to the exporters in Indian market and converts their medium to long-term credit for the overseas buyer developing on the extent of risk attached to their individual countries by the forfaiting agency. Previous London-based Banque Indosuez Aval looks for a minimum size for each transaction but now the forfaiting company willing to look at smaller export orders from India. Now about 15–20% of the forfaiting market today is represented by transaction involving commodity exports up to 180–360 days. Recently in November 1993, as per the guidelines of RBI, exporters are also eligible to avail of pre-shipment credit in foreign currency from commercial banks and which both the domestic and imported inputs of the goods exported from India. Therefore, the exporter is able to avail of credit in foreign currency at both pre- and post-shipment levels at internationally competitive rates. This would enable the exporters to quote competitive price for the exported goods which should help them to show better results in the exports in the years ahead.

10.6.1 Challenges Ahead

Forfaiting is an instrument, which facilitates a large number of technological opportunities for the creation and commercialization of new goods and services. Thus, efforts are required to create favourable environments for the growth of forfaiting transactions to tap potentialities of India. The following measures may be taken to ensure effective forfaiting transactions:

(a) There should be a legal framework for the forfaiting transactions.

(b) High potential, sovereign, and commercial risks are involved in such transactions. This should be corrected.

(c) There is a lack of database of importers as well as importing countries. So necessary action should be taken for encouraging forfaiting transactions.

(d) The secondary market is absent. If this is accepted as reality, there will be a better market.

(e) When the exporter deals with a buyer from an overseas, the cost of service involved becomes high. So, there is need for a conducive environment to attract foreign funds.

(f) Exim bank acts as an intermediary between Indian exporter and a forfaiting agency abroad. So this instrument is normally used for difficulties in dealing with other countries. Therefore, specific modifications are required in respect of Exim bank so that it can be involved in direct finance in such cases.

SUMMARY

The exact structure of the financing is determined only by the needs and inventiveness of the exporter, importer, and the forfeiter. As our country is oriented more towards an era of export promotion under liberalized economic system under which forfaiting has a very important role to play, undoubtedly forfaiting would shine in India if these challenges are to be met more effectively.

REVIEW QUESTIONS

1. Critically analyze the role of forfaiting as a source of financing.
2. Distinguish between "factoring" and "forfaiting" and explain their scope in India.

QUIZ

State whether the following are true or false.

1. Forfaiting provides services like checking the credit worthiness of the foreign buyer. (T/F)
2. Exporters are eligible to avail of pre-shipment credit in foreign currency from commercial banks. (T/F)

Fill up the blanks.

3. Forfaiting has originated in ....

4. .... is done without any recourse to the client.

5. Forfaiting is done by .... bank.

REFERENCES

Aruna, M. "Advantage Forfaiting", *Chartered Financial Analyst*, November, 1994.

Batra, D.S. and Narinder Kaur, "An Alternative Source of Trade Financing", *Chartered Secretary*, July, 1993.

Balachandran, P., "PCFC Scheme", *The Journal of the Indian Institute of Bankers*, Oct.–Dec., 1993.

Economic Times, Jan. 21, 1994.

Economic Times, Jan. 15, 1992.

Kochar, M.G., "International Factoring and Forfaiting", *The Journal of the Indian Institute of Bankers*, July–Sept., 1993.

Kaur, Narinder, "*India's Export Performance*", Deep and Deep Publications, Delhi, 1995.

Kaur, Narinder, "*Management Innovations in Trade Financing—Forfaiting*" by D.P. Sinha, (Ed.), *Innovations in Asian Management*, 1996, AMDISA Volume.

Mohanty, A., "Forfaiting Position and Prospects", *State Bank of India Monthly Review,* March, 1993.

Nair, Kishore, "Financing of Long-term Export Receivables—Forfaiting", *The Banker*, April, 1994.

Sankalpa. Jan.–June, 1993.

Trivedi, H.K., "Export Strategy for Indies" in B.S. Gupta, et al. (Eds.), *Export Strategies of 90s*, Anmol Publications, New Delhi.

Verghese, S.K., "Export Assistance Policy and Export Performance of India in the Seventies", *Economic and Political Weekly Annual Number*, Feb., 1978.

11

Chapter

Leasing and Hire/Purchase

11.1 INTRODUCTION

The financial environment in India has changed enormously in recent years and has witnessed an unprecedented growth in stature and size of the NBFCs. Their response had been diversified on an integrated package of diverse financial services. Most of the major companies undertake fund-based and non-funded activities. Among the fund-based activities, leasing has emerged as an important business providing long-term finance to the corporates as well as individuals. The rapid growth in the financial services sector has left every one gasping to breath and the finance companies scouting around for talents to manage the ballooning business. The financial services in general and the NBFCs in particular have witnessed a phenomenal growth. Liberalization, deregulation, delicensing, reforms and restructuring of the economy have opened up, several opportunities for this industry. The industry has flourished immensely and has witnessed an unprecedented growth in stature and size, world over. As a result of these changes, the focus has shifted from the traditional fund-based activities to the non-fund-based activities. Non-fund or fee-based activities include leasing, hire/purchase, bill discounting, venture capital, private placements, etc. Among the fund-based activities, leasing has emerged as an important business that provides long-term finance to the corporates as well as individuals. The boom in the field of leasing erupted when entrepreneur suddenly woke up to the tremendous possibilities offered in an economy chronically affected by the massive paucity of fund availability and a growing realization of enormous resource mobilization opportunities available in capital market.

11.2 CONCEPT

The concept of leasing was initiated in the USA during the late 50s and even today the volume of leasing undertaken on a global scale continues to grow at an impressive 10–12%. The leasing operation started in an organized manner only in the early 80s. In the last 5 to 6 years, leasing has come in a big way to India and it is evident by the mushrooming and growth of leasing. It is estimated that there are over 1200 non-bank financial companies and partnership firms engaged in leasing business of various types with a cumulative gross value of leased assets to the tune of Rs. 1,250 crores by the end of 1988.

Leasing is understood in different ways in different environments. In financing sense, it comes under the general heading of instalment in credit for the acquisition of a wide range of equipment. Leasing, in actual practice, is basically a contractual arrangement whereby the owner (lessor) of assets transfers the right to use the assets to the user (lessee) for a fixed period of time in return of rentals. Once the agreed period lapses, the lease agreement expires and the assets revert back to the owner.

11.2.1 Types of Lease

This section briefly discusses the various types of lease:

Financial lease: A financial lease is also known as *full payout lease*, *capital lease*, *long-term lease*, or *net lease*. In financial lease, the contractual period between the lessee and the lessor is generally equal to the expected full economic life of the equipment. Here, the lessor acts as a financer and the lessee takes the responsibility of maintenance and servicing of the equipment.

Operating lease: Operating lease is generally a short-term and cancellable lease and the contractual period between the lessor and lessee is generally less than the full expected useful economic life of the equipment. The maintenance and other servicing costs are borne by the lessor and consequently the rentals are far higher than in other types of leasing. This type of leasing is not popular in India.

Leveraged lease: In a leveraged lease, there are three parties involved—lessor (leasing company), lessee (user of the equipment), and financer. Leasing company contributes by way of equity capital, financial institution, and/or banks finance by way of term loans towards the purchase of an asset to be leased.

Sale and lease back lease: Under this type of lease, a firm may sell an asset which it already owns to another party and lease it back from the buyer. The lessee receives immediate cash for his assets and repays the lease rentals over the stipulated period.

Primary and secondary lease: Primary and secondary lease is also known as *front-ended lease.* It is split into two parts where first part is known as the primary lease and latter part is a secondary lease. The rentals are generally structured in such a manner that the cost of the assets with profit are recoupled in the primary period of the lease. The secondary lease is a perpetual lease with a nominal rental.

Domestic lease: A lease transaction is said to be a domestic lease if all parties to the transaction are domiciled in the same country. On the other hand, if the parties involved in the leasing transaction are located in two different nations, the transaction is clarified as an international lease transaction.

11.3 MERITS AND DEMERITS

11.3.1 Merits of Leasing

Following are the advantages of leasing:

(1) The major advantage of leasing as available to the lessee is that the funds are not tied up in fixed assets. The company at its discretion can more profitably utilize the available resources. It enables the lessee to acquire and use the most modern equipment rather than waiting to mobilize additional resources or raise funds to purchase the same through the time consuming approval and disbursement process of loans.

(2) Assets can be leased out at today's prices rather than at a high price in future caused by inflationary pressures. Payment of rent makes cash flows regular and thus facilitates budget forecasting. The lessee gets 100% financing of the assets. No margin money is required for raising funds through commercial banks and term lending institutions.

(3) Even though the ownership of the equipment lies with the lessor, the lessee gets all the benefits of ownership of the assets since the leased equipment is not returned to the lessor under a long-term contract and the lessee processes it at a nominal price.

(4) The lessor also gets quality equipment under best terms and conditions on behalf of the lessee to its enterprise.

(5) Through lease finance, the company can maintain improved profitability and liquidity ratios through increased productivity.

(6) Leasing prohibits the company from application of certain asset based on restrictions and thus encourages the growth of the company. It helps to speed up the replacement, expansion, and modernization programmes of the existing company. The company facing the problem of working capital deficit and cash-flow constraints resorts to the system of lease financing.

(7) The lease rentals paid are treated as revenue expenses and derive tax benefits in terms of higher tax saving compared to loans or other methods of financing. Many individual companies raise additional funds through leasing apart from knocking the doors of financial institutions because of the maximum benefit of cash inflows.

(8) Leasing is highly flexible to accommodate almost any category of assets, some of which may not either be eligible for depreciation or may not be eligible for the credit from the conventional source.

(9) Leasing on a short-term basis is more desirable than acquisition of an asset in a rapidly changing field.

(10) Leasing may be suitable when a firm needs assets for a definite period that is substantially less than the useful life of these assets.

(11) Leasing is more flexible than ownership, for it is less permanent and makes adjustments possible when the lease expires.

(12) In some cases, firms which are either small or have very uncertain records of earnings are able to obtain the use of assets through leasing.

(13) Leasing offers certain tax benefits.

(14) It also offers a balance sheet advantage and enhances the company's financial ratios.

11.3.2 Demerits

Following are the drawbacks of the leasing process:

(1) The companies which are not able to borrow from capital market are forced to enter into a leasing arrangements.

(2) Leasing does not shift the title of ownership from lessor to lessee.

(3) Miscellaneous expenses have often to be borne by the lessee.

(4) Certain tax benefits/incentives such as backward area benefits may not be available on leased equipment.

(5) Real estate values may increase during the lease period. In this way, the lessee loses the advantage of a potential capital gain.

(6) The interest cost of lease financing is generally higher than that of debt financing.

(7) Under financial lease, the lessee will not be in a position to terminate the contract except by paying heavy penalties. This may prove to be a handicap for manufacturers when they want to discontinue a particular line of business. In case of owned assets the manufacturers can sell the equipment at the time of winding up.

(8) The limiting industrial base is a hindrance for financing assets of a company on lease basis.

(9) If the lessee is not able to pay rentals regularly, the lessor would suffer a loss.

(10) When lease is long-term and non-cancellable, there is little chance for the lessee to shift the danger of obsolescence to the lessor.

11.4 TAX CONSIDERATION OF LEASING

Recently, the commercial banks and financial institutions have begun acting as leasing intermediaries and dominate the lessor's market to exploit the attractive tax concessions in the form of depreciation and investment allowances.

(a) Accounting treatment of leases

Over the past three decades, the accounting treatment of lease has been changed. At the inception stage, lessee was never disclosed in the financial statements but now it is done by way of footnotes in the financial statements. A statement issued by the Financial Accounting Standards Board (FASB) establishes financial accounting standards for lessees and lessors. The leased asset is shown on the balance sheet of the lessor, and the depreciation and other taxes associated with the leased assets are claimed by the lessor. In addition to this, lessees are allowed to show lease payment as an expense and the lessors are required to show lease receipts as income for income tax purposes.

(b) Sales tax provision for leasing

In a lease transaction, the lessor is not entitled for the concessional rate of central sales tax due to absolute owner of the asset. But the 46th amendment act has brought lease transactions under the purview of sale and has empowered the central and state governments to levy sales tax on lease transactions. Further a new closure 29A as a part of article 366 states that the "tax on purchase or sale of goods" includes a tax on the transfer of the right to use the goods for any purpose for cash deferred payment or other valuable consideration". Following the amendment, several states such as Andhra Pradesh, Tamil Nadu, Maharashtra, Gujarat, Madhya Pradesh, West Bengal, and Uttar Pradesh have amended their sales tax laws to provide for sales tax on all transactions envisaged by clause 29A of Article 366. Except

Andhra Pradesh, it has been notified that the assets purchased locally and the let-out on lease are exempted from lease tax, treating it as a second sale. Only in Maharashtra, the provision has been enacted in the matter of levy of tax on lease transactions.

(c) Break-even lease rental

The lease rentals of leasing vary widely from company to company depending upon the profile of the clients, tax and depreciation planning, cash flows, and cost structure of the leasing companies. The cost structure plays an important role in determining the lease rental quotas of leasing company. The break-even lease rental is the minimum lease rental which the lessee can accept and from lessor's point of view, the net advantage of leasing is equal to zero. To calculate the break-even lease rental, the following parameters are required to be considered:

$$L = \frac{P - \left[M(1-t) + I \cdot P \cdot t + \sum_{i=1}^{n} \frac{di}{(1+k)2} + \frac{S}{(1+k)n} \right]}{\sum_{i=1}^{n} \frac{1-t}{(1+k)i}}$$

where L = break-even lease rent,
P = cost of the asset,
M = management fees for lease agreement,
t = tax rate,
I = invested allowance in percentage,
di = depreciation is the asset in the year i,
k = post tax cost of capital or minimum required rate of return,
S = expected salvage value (after tax) at the end of its life,
n = primary lease period,

and the tax is to be deducted from P at the numerator of the equation implies the tax benefit enjoyed by the lessor.

The comparative study of equipment lease financing by financial institutions and banks vs self finaning is discussed in Table A.

Table A Guideline on equipment finance scheme by IFCI

Period	Rental amount per month per Rs. 1000	Rental amount per month per Rs. 10000	Rental amount per month per Rs. 4 lakhs
1	2	3	4
3rd year	34.85	418.20	1,67,280
4th year	28.03	336.36	1,34,544
5th year	24.00	288.00	1,15,200
6th year	21.85	262.20	1,04,880
7th year	19.50	234.00	93,600
8th year	18.00	216.00	86,400

Source: Guidelines: Equipment Finance Scheme, IFCI.

Table A presents the guidelines on equipment finance scheme by IFCI while Table B presents the determination of the interest and principal components of loan instrument by banks.

Table B Schedule of debt payment.

End of year	Loan payment (principal plus) interest) (in Rs.)	Principal outstanding (in Rs.)	Interest payment (in Rs.)	Principal payment (in Rs.)
1	2	3	4	5
0	0	3,00,000	0	0
1	84,000	2,83,500	67,500	16,500
2	84,000	2,63,288	63,788	20,212
3	84,000	2,38,526	59,238	24,762
4	84,000	2,08,194	53,668	30,332
5	84,000	1,71,038	46,844	37,156
6	84,000	1,25,522	38,484	45,516
7	84,000	69,764	28,242	55,758
8	85,461*	0	15,679	69,764
	6,73,461		**3,73,461**	**3,00,000**

*The excess of Rs. 1461 is due to approximation error.

Table C explains the determination of the interest and principal components of loan instalment by financial institution.

Table C Schedule of debt payment

End of year	Loan payment (principal plus) interest) (in Rs.)	Principal outstanding (in Rs.)	Interest payment (in Rs.)	Principal payment (in Rs.)
1	2	3	4	5
0	0	2,96,000	0	0
1	75,980	2,77,740	57,700	18,260
2	75,980	2,55,919	54,159	21,821
3	75,980	2,29,843	49,904	26,076
4	75,980	1,98,682	44,819	31,161
5	75,980	1,61,445	38,743	37,237
6	75,980	1,16,947	31,482	44,498
7	75,980	63,772	22,805	53,175
8	76,208*	0	12,436	63,772
	6,08,068		**3,12,048**	**2,96,000**

* The excess of Rs. 228 is on account of approximation error.

Now Table D presents the detailed data of equipment on these from IFCI/IDBI.

Table D Equipment on lease from IFCI/IDBI

Year	Cash outflow (Lease payment	Tax saved at 40%	Net outflow	Cash inflow	Tax at 40%	Net inflow	Net factor flow	Net Dis.	NPV
1	2	3	4	5	6	7	8	9	10
1	—	—	—	1,50,000.00	-	150,000.00	1,50,000.00	1.000	1,50,000.00
2	—	—	—	1,50,000.00	60,000.00	90,000.00	90,000.00	0.806	72,540.00
3	1,67,280	—	1,67,280	1,50,000.00	60,000.00	90,000.00	(77,280.00)	0.587	(45,363.00)
4	1,34,544	66,912	0,67,632	1,50,000.00	60,000.00	90,000.00	22,368.00	0.473	10,580.00
5	1,15,200	53,818	0,61,382	1,50,000.00	60,000.00	90,000.00	28,618.00	0.382	10,932.00
6	1,04,880	46,080	0,58,800	1,50,000.00	60,000.00	90,000.00	31,200.00	0.308	9,610.00
7	0,93,600	41,952	0,51,648	1,50,000.00	60,000.00	90,000.00	38,252.00	0.248	9,511.00
8	0,86,400	37,440	0,48,960	1,50,000.00	60,000.00	90,000.00	41,040.00	0.200	8,208.00
9	—	34,560	(0,34,560)	—	60,000.00	60,000.00	(25,440.00)	0.161	(4,096.00)
	7,01,904	2,80,762	4,21,142	1,200,000.00	4,80,000.00	7,20,000.00	2,98,858.00	—	2,21,922.00

Source: Refer Table A.

11.4.1 Methodology and Analysis

As already indicated, the lease rents are treated as revenue expenses for deriving tax benefits. Leasing finance offers higher tax savings as compared to other forms of financing and also warrants the maximum amount of cash inflows. So an analysis has been made to justify the above requirements as to which method has been found out to be the best alternative. For this purpose, the cost of equipment would normally include taxes, duties, transport, and installation. Equipment can be leased depending on the economic life, technological obsolescence, and rate of depreciation of the concerned equipment. The lease rentals quoted as rate per thousand rupees per month by IFCI/IDBI commencing from the first month of third year have been considered in the study (see Table A). For convenience and sake of simplicity of computation, the discount factor for each year has also been averaged. The prevailing interest rate of commercial banks for advancing medium and long-term loans ranging between Rs. 2 lakhs to Rs. 5 lakhs is 22.5%. The cost of capital is assumed to be 24% for alternative investments.

If a firm has decided to acquire an asset costing Rs. 4 lakhs having an economic life of 8 years and no scrap value, requiring 25% margin money, the prevailing market rate of interest being 22.5% through bank financing, we compute the annual payment as under that equates the cost of asset less margin money with the present value of eight instalments of loan payment. The payments include both principal and interest. The proportion of interest in each payment depends on the unpaid balance of the principal amount owing during the year.

$$\text{So,} \qquad \text{Rs. } 3{,}00{,}000 = \sum_{t=1}^{8} (x/1.225)t$$

where x is the loan payment. x = Rs. 84,000 approximately.

The segregation made for payment towards term loan due to commercial banks are as under:

But if the above asset is financed through IFCI/IDBI under the equipment finance scheme, the prevailing market rate of interest would be 19.5% but an amount of 1% of the cost of equipment purchased would be paid as front-end fee. Therefore, the annual payment can be computed in the manner shown in following equation that equates the cost of 8 annual average instalments of the loan payment. The proportion of interest in each payment depends on the unpaid balance of the principal amount owing during the year.

$$\text{So,} \qquad \text{Rs. } 2{,}96{,}000 = \sum_{t=1}^{8} (x/1.195)t$$

where x is the loan payment. x = Rs. 75,980 approximately.

We now discuss the segregation made for payment towards loan due to financial institutions like IFCI/IDBI.

Assuming that the depreciation on the asset discussed is charged at 20% per annum on diminishing balance method, tax rate is 40% and saving in cost resulting from installation of this machinery is Rs. 1,50,000 per annum. The comparative position of finances has been shown in Tables D, E, F, and G. As observed, it was found that when tax rate is 40%, equipment on lease finance gives us the maximum amount of savings followed by term loan finance of commercial banks, term loan financed by financial institution, and purchasing of machinery by own finance in descending order. Thus leasing finance has provided the higher tax saving as compared to other means of financing. When compared with the net cash inflows from various schemes of financing, it can also be concluded that net cash inflows are also maximum under lease financing. Lastly, it was arrived at the decision that the net present value of cash inflows has also been the highest in case of lease financing followed by term loan finance by financial institutions like IDBI/IFCI, term loan finance by commercial banks, and purchase of equipment by self-finance in descending order of their magnitudes. Thus, undoubtedly it can be inferred that equipment leasing is better than other methods of alternative financing.

11.4.2 Comparative Study of Lease versus Buying Outright

Lease is always much cheaper than the conventional borrowing. This has been arrived at based on the parameters of lease buy model.

Value of the asset—10,00,000 repayable in 10 equal instalments. Cost of borrowing—16% per annum. Income tax rate—50%.

Annual lease rental—Rs. 1,47,951.

Table 11.1 Present value (PV) cash outflows under leasing

Year end	Lease payment (Rs.)	Tax shield (Rs.)	Cashout flow after tax (Rs.)	PV factor at 8%	PV (Rs.)
0	1,47,951	—	1,47,951	1.00	1,47,951
1–9	1,47,951	73,976	73,976	6.247	4,62,128
10	—	73,976	73,976	0.463	–34,251
					5,75,828

Table 11.2 Present value (PV) after cash outflow under buying option

Year	Loan instalment (Rs.)	Loan at beginning (Rs.)	Interest (Rs.)	Principal repayment (Rs.)	Principal outstanding (Rs.)
1	2	3	4 (.16)	5 (2–4)	6 (3–5)
1	1,78,348	8,21,652	1,31,464.32	46,883.68	7,74,768.32
2	1,78,348	7,74,768.32	1,23,962.93	54,385.069	7,20,383.25
3	1,78,348	7,20,383.25	1,15,261.32	63,086.68	6,57,296.57
4	1,78,348	65,729.57	1,05,167.45	73,180.549	5,84,116.02
5	1,78,348	5,84,116.02	93,458.563	84,889.437	4,99,226.02
6	1,78,348	4,99,226.02	79,876.253	98,471.747	4,00,754.83
7	1,78,348	4,00,754.83	64,120.773	1,14,227.23	2,86,527.6
8	1,78,348	2,86,527.6	45,844.416	1,32,503.58	1,54,024.02
9	1,78,348	1,54,024.02	23,103.602	1,55,244.40	—

Table 11.3 Present value (PV) of cash outflows under buying option

Year	Loan instalment (Rs.)	Tax shield on interest (Rs.)	on BEP. (Rs.)	Net cash outflow (Rs.)	PV factor (Rs.)	PV (Rs.)
0	1,78,348	—	—	1,78,348	1,000	1,78,348
1	1,78,348	65,732	50,003	62,616	926	57,982
2	1,78,348	61,981	50,000	66,367	851	56,877
3	1,78,348	57,631	50,000	70,718	0.794	56,150
4	1,78,348	52,583	50,000	75,765	0.735	55,687
5	1,78,348	46,729	50,000	81,619	0.681	55,583
6	1,78,348	39,937	50,000	88,411	0.630	55,699
7	1,78,348	32,060	50,000	96,288	0.583	56,136
8	1,78,348	22,921	50,000	1,05,427	0.540	56,930
9	1,78,348	12,167	50,000	1,16,181	0.500	58,091
				–50,000	0.463	–23,150
						6,64,333

As the PV for leasing is less than that for outright purchase, leasing is a financially more viable option.

11.5 PROBLEMS OF LEASING

The leasing companies in India are facing certain problems:

(1) **Resource constraint:** Lack of licensing requirements from the Reserve Bank of India and the Government was responsible for the entry of a large number of companies into leasing business. As a result of cut-throat competition, a considerable fall in the rental was experienced by the leasing companies. Further, the leasing companies are now leasing at rates that do not cover their costs. Since the leasing investment involves huge capital outlay, the companies are finding it very difficult to finance them out to their own funds.

(2) **Risk of obsolescence:** The leasing company will get much trouble since it has to bear the capital loss in case of obsolescence.

(3) **Non-availability of sales-tax consideration:** The implications of sales tax on lease rentals make leasing correspondingly more expensive as the cost of the equipment required under leasing becomes inflated to the extent of sales tax paid by the leasing companies. A combination of higher rate of sales tax on the acquisition of capital equipment and tax on lease rental payments makes the leasing transactions totally uneconomical.

(4) **Cut-throat competition:** Most of the companies doing leasing business come out with maiden dividends. But the companies are paying more interest on loans taken from the financial institutions or commercial banks. In such a situation, the lease rentals have to be increased. But it is not easy to raise the rental payment because the customers are used to lower rates. Thus, lack of finance has become one of the important obstacles to leasing companies on the way of progress.

(4) **Lack of qualified personnel:** The nature of the leasing and hire/purchase business is nothing but financing the capital equipment to the capability of borrowed party, legal matters, recovery of rentals following a special system. But in India it is very difficult to get right man to deal with the problems of this business. On account of this fact, operations of the leasing business are bound to suffer.

(5) **Delay in rental payments:** The late payment of rent has some cost as per the lessor's point of view. But the lessor, while fixing the lease rentals does not take into consideration the delay in recovery of the rentals at the time of lease agreement. Again, there is another type of cost involved in the leasing activity in terms of bad debts. These two types of risks can disturb the future prospects of leasing business.

(6) **Attitude of government:** The Government has not so far come out with well-defined guidelines with regard to sales tax and investment allowances of leasing business.

Table E Term loan financing by commercial banks

Year	Cash flow	Tax at 40%	Cash inflow	Loan payment	Depreciation allowance	Interest paid	Tax saved at 40% of (VI+VII)	Net cash inflow (IV–V+VII) of previous year	Discount factor i.e. $ke = 24\%$	Present value	Remarks
I	II	III	IV	V	VI	VII	VIII	IX	X	XI	XII
0	(1,00,000)	—	(1,00,000)	—	—	—	—	(1,00,000)	1.000	(1,00,000)	3,00,000=
1	1,50,000	—	1,50,000	84,000	80,000	67,500	—	66,000	0.806	53,196	$\sum_{t=1}^{8}[x/1+225)t]$
2	1,50,000	60,000	90,000	84,000	64,000	63,788	59,000	65,000	0.650	42,250	
3	1,50,000	60,000	90,000	84,000	51,200	59,238	51,115	57,115	0.524	29,928	or $x = 84{,}000$
4	1,50,000	60,000	90,000	84,000	40,960	53,668	44,175	50,175	0.423	21,224	Approx. $ki = 22.5\%$,
5	1,50,000	60,000	90,000	84,000	32,768	46,844	37,851	43,851	0.341	14,953	$ke = 24\%$
6	1,50,000	60,000	90,000	84,000	26,214	38,444	31,844	37,844	0.275	10,407	Margin money = 25%
7	1,50,000	60,000	90,000	84,000	20,971	28,242	25,879	31,789	0.222	07,077	
8	1,50,000	60,000	90,000	85,461*	16,777	15,697	19,685	24,224	0.179	04,336	
9	—	60,000	(60,000)	—	67,110	—	12,981	(47,019)	0.144	(06,771)	
10	—	—	—	—	—	—	26,844	26,844	0.144	03,866	
Total					**4,00,000**					**80,466**	

Source: Refer Table B

* Excess is due to approximation.

Table F Term loan financing by financial institutions i.e. IFCI/IDBI

Year	Cash flow	Tax at 40%	Cash inflow	Loan payment	Depreciation allowance	Interest paid	Tax saved at 40% of (VI+VII) of previous year	Net cash inflow (IV–V+VII)	Discount factor i.e. *ke* = 24%	Present value	Remarks
I	II	III	IV	V	VI	VII	VIII	IX	X	XI	XII
0	(104,000)	—	(104,000)	—	—	—	—	(1,04,000)	1.000	(1,04,000)	2,96,000
1	1,50,000	—	1,50,000	75,980	—	57,700	—	74,020	0.806	59,660	
2	1,50,000	60,000	90,000	75,980	64,000	54,159	55,080	69,100	0.650	44,915	
3	1,50,000	60,000	90,000	75,980	51,200	49,904	47,264	61,284	0.524	32,113	$\sum_{t=1}^{8}[x/(1+0.195)t]$
4	1,50,000	60,000	90,000	75,980	40,960	44,819	40,442	54,462	0.423	23,037	
5	1,50,000	60,000	90,000	75,980	32,768	38,743	34,312	48,332	0.341	16,481	or $x = 75{,}980$
6	1,50,000	60,000	90,000	75,980	26,214	31,482	28,604	42,624	0.275	11,722	$ki = 19.5\%$ $ke = 24\%$
7	1,50,000	60,000	90,000	75,980	20,971	22,805	23,078	37,098	0.222	08,236	
8	1,50,000	60,000	90,000	76,208*	16,777	12,436	17,510	31,302	0.179	05,603	Margin money
9	—	60,000	(60,000)	—	67,110	—	11,683	(48,317)	0.144	(06,958)	= 25%
10	—	—	—		—	—	26,842	26,842	0.144	03,865	Front-end fee = 1%
Total					**4,00,000**					**94,674**	

Source: Refer Table C.

* Excess is due to approximation.

Table G Purchase of machinery by self finance

Year	Cash flow	Tax at 40%	Net	Depreciation allowance	Tax saved at 40% of	Net cash	Discount Factor i.e. 24% (*ke* = 0.24)	NPV
I	II	III	IV	V	VI	VII	VIII	IX
0	(4,00,000)	—	(4,00,000)	—	—	(4,00,000)	1.000	(4,00,000)
1	1,50,000	—	1,50,000	80,000	—	1,50,000	0.806	1,20,900
2	1,50,000	60,000	90,000	64,000	32,000	1,22,000	0.650	79,300
3	1,50,000	60,000	90,000	51,200	25,600	1,15,600	0.524	60,574
4	1,50,000	60,000	90,000	40,960	20,480	1,10,480	0.423	46,733
5	1,50,000	60,000	90,000	32,768	16,384	1,06,384	0.341	36,277
6	1,50,000	60,000	90,000	26,214	13,107	1,03,107	0.275	28,354
7	1,50,000	60,000	90,000	20,971	10,486	1,00,486	0.222	22,308
8	1,50,000	60,000	90,000	16,777	8,388	98,388	0.179	17,611
9	—	60,000	(60,000)	67,110	6,711	(53,289)	0.144	(7,673)
10	—	—	—	—	26,844	26,844	0.144	3,866
Total	**8,00,000**	**4,80,000**	**3,20,000**	**4,00,000**	**1,60,000**	**4,00,000**		**8250**

11.6 HIRE/PURCHASE

Hire/purchase is an agreement to the sale of an asset subject to the following conditions: the goods are delivered at the beginning of the agreement on the basis that the hirer will pay an agreed amount in periodical instalments mutually agreed upon; after the last instalment is paid, the title of ownership will pass to the hirer; the hirer can terminate the agreement by paying all the balance instalments and taking the title of the asset. The Hire Purchase Act, 1972 defines a hire purchase agreement as "an agreement under which goods are let on hire and under which the hirer has on option to purchase them in accordance with the terms of the agreement and includes an agreement under which

(1) "Possession of goods is delivered by the owner thereof to a person on condition that such person pays the agreed amount in periodical instalments,

(2) The property in the goods is to pass to such persons on the payment of the last of such instalments, and that such person pays the agreed amount in periodical instalments, and

(3) Such person has a right to terminate the agreement at any time before the property passes."

11.6.1 Salient Features of Hire/Purchase

(a) The hiree purchases the equipment from the equipment supplier and lets it on hire to the hirer.

(b) The hirer is required to pay, hire/purchase instalments over a specified period of time. The hire/purchase instalments are payable monthly in advance.

(c) The ownership of the asset is transferred after the hirer has paid the last instalment.

(d) Each instalment is treated as hire charge so that if default is made in payment of any one instalment, the seller is entitled to take away the goods.

(e) The terms and conditions relating to the usage of the asset, namely its maintenance, insurance, etc. and the rights and obligations of the parties to the agreement are described in the hire/purchase agreement.

11.7 HIRE/PURCHASE IN INDIA

Hire/purchase has been in operation in India for an appreciable period of time. The first hire/purchase companies in India were the Commercial Credit Corporation Ltd. and Motor and General Finance Ltd. which were set up in the beginning of this century to finance the transport sector. Vehicle financing is broadly categorized into motor cars and trucks. Leading truck financers are Ashok Leyland Finance Co., SR Truck Finance, etc. Amongst the motor car finance companies, the leaders are Kotak Mahindra, Escorts Financial Services, and Citi Mobile Finance. Presently, hire/purchase transactions are done on a large scale by finance companies. Certain private banks and foreign banks had also entered this field through establishment of subsidiaries. Hire/purchase is a preferred transaction for banks as it is a superior method than hypothecation. Banks are better placed in recovery of vehicle advances and borrowers would be benefited as more credit would be made available.

11.7.1 Advantages

The main advantages of hire/purchase to a company are:

(1) Higher rate of interest can be charged and as the calculation is on the original advance, higher income would be realized.

(2) As the company is the owner, attachment of the vehicle and subsequent sale even by private auction would keep the NPAs low.

(3) As the borrowers would end up losing the instalments paid as well as the vehicle, defaults would be lower.

(4) The banks can effectively recycle the funds recovered.

11.8 LEASING VERSUS HIRE/PURCHASE

From the hiree's point of view, the following can be cited as differences between leasing and hire/purchase:

Leasing	Hire/Purchase
• Tax shields on depreciation and investment allowance cannot be claimed by the lessee.	• Tax shields on depreciation and investment allowance can be claimed by the hirer.
• The entire lease rental is a tax deductible expense.	• Only the interest component of the hire/purchase instalment is tax deductible.
• The lessee, not being the owner of the asset, does not enjoy the salvage value of the asset.	• The hirer being the owner of the asset enjoys the salvage value of the asset.

11.9 HIRE/PURCHASE AND INSTALMENT SALE

Hire/purchase transaction is different from instalment system. Instalment sale is a credit sale and the legal ownership of the asset passes immediately to the buyer as soon as the agreement is made between the buyer and the seller. Except for the timing of the transfer of ownership, instalment sale and hire/purchase are similar in nature.

11.10 TAX ASPECTS OF HIRE/PURCHASE

The tax aspect of hire/purchase transactions can be divided into three parts—income tax, sales tax, and interest tax aspects.

11.10.1 Income Tax Aspects

The treatment of a hire/purchase transaction from the point of view of income tax is governed by the provisions of a CBDT circular issued way back in 1943. According to this circular, the hirer is entitled to (a) the tax shields on depreciation calculated with reference to the cash purchase price, and (b) the tax shield on the "consideration for hire". The circular defines consideration for hire in the same way is the total charge for credit and requires this amount to be spread evenly over the term of the agreement. From the owner's angle the consideration for hire received by hire is liable to tax.

11.11.2 Sales Tax Aspects

The salient sales tax aspects are as follows:

(a) Hire/purchase transactions per se are liable to sales tax. The 46th amendment act clearly states that the "tax on the sale or purchase of goods includes a tax on the delivery of goods on hire purchase or any other system of payment by instalments".

(b) For the purpose of levying sales tax a sale is deemed to take place only when the hirer exercises the option to purchase.

(c) The amount of sales tax must be determined with reference to the depreciated value of the goods at the time when the hirer exercises the purchase option.

(d) The state in which the goods have been delivered is entitled to levy and collect sales tax.

(e) Sale stax cannot be levied on hire/purchase transaction structured by finance companies provided these companies are not dealers in the class of goods let on hire.

(f) There is no one uniform rate of sales tax applicable to hire/purchase transactions. The rate varies from state to state.

11.10.3 Interest Tax Aspects

The provisions under this act are as follows:

(a) Interest tax is payable on the total amount of interest accruing to a hire/purchase company in the previous year at the rate of 3%.

(b) The amount of interest which is established to have become a bad debt during the previous year can be deducted from the chargeable interest. The interest tax payable by the hire/purchase company is treated as tax-deductible expenses for the purpose of competing the taxable income under the Income Tax Act.

SUMMARY

Despite the initial hic-ups, the future of leasing industry looks to be very bright. The leasing industry has raised funds from the banking system/public deposits, etc. through which approximate Rs. 40,000 million has contributed towards the recreation of jobs and economic opportunities.

In present set-up, finance companies take up leasing activity as one of their diversified activities. Till recently, leasing was the domain of the finance companies and in special cases, of financial institution. To ensure rapid growth in leasing industry, the working environment has to be made more supportive. Also there is need for designing a comprehensive enactment to recognize the professional potential of leasing.

Hire/purchase is a specialized business to be undertaken by experienced financiers only. Today, profitability is the main criterion for evaluating bank performance and banks are saddled with huge investible funds. As a result, both leasing and hire/purchase transactions can well be thought of as a major diversification programme for the future. Leasing and hire/purchase are instruments on which today's treasury managers are relying more than ever before to manage corporate finance. As more and more companies embark on expansion plans, these instruments are going to play a pivotal role. Finance companies have realized the immense potential of these instruments and they are bending their back to hog as much as they can of the growing business.

REVIEW QUESTIONS

1. Define leasing ? Explain the origin of leasing in India?
2. Explain the different types of lease?

3. Explain the advantages and limitation of leasing?
4. Explain the leasing or buying option is better. Give examples.
5. Distinguish between hire purchase and leasing.
6. Explain the advantages of hire/purchase.

QUIZ

State whether the following are true or false.

1. The funds are not tied up in fixed assets in leasing transactions. (T/F)
2. The lessee does not bear the risk of obsolescence in financial lease. (T/F).
3. The lease rentals are treated as revenue expenses. (T/F)
4. In India, commercial banks are engaged in lease business. (T/F)
5. Lessees are not disclosed in the financial statements. (T/F)
6. Leasing finance offers higher tax savings. (T/F)
7. Lease is always much cheaper than the conventional borrowing. (T/F)
8. The hire/purchase instalments are payable monthly in advance. (T/F)
9. The hirer cannot terminate the agreement. (T/F)
10. In hire/purchase, the ownership remains with the seller until last instalment is paid. (T/F).

Fill up the blanks.

11. Financial lease is also known as .... lease.
12. Operating lease is generally .... and .... lease.
13. The leverage lease agreement involves .... parties.
14. The hirer enjoys .... value of the asset.
15. Tax shields on .... and .... can be claimed by the hirer.

REFERENCES

Anabalahan, K., and N.V. Rao "Leasing and Banking: Some Issues", *The Journal of Indian Institute of Bankers*, pp. 13–20.

Bansal, L.K., "Leasing Environment India", *Finance India*, Sept. 1994.

Balakrishnan, S., "Leasing has come to stay", *The Journal of the Indian Institute of Bankers,* pp. 19–196.

Brahmaiah, B., "Leasing and Lease Rentals in India", *The Management Accountant*, Aug. 1991.

Economic Times, Sept. 1994.

Guidelines, Equipment Finance Scheme, IDBI, 1991.

Guidelines, Equipment Finance Scheme, Industrial Finance Corporation of India, 1991.

"Guidelines, Scheme of Equipment Leasing", *IFET*, 1991.

Joshi, Premlal, (Ed.), "*Leasing Comes of Age—Indian Scene*", Amrita Prakashan, 1986.

Karuppiah, K., "*Lease Finance—Origin, Growth, Problems, and Prospects*", Sterling Publishing, New Delhi, 1988.

Kumarasundaram, S., "Equipment Leasing: Complementary Role in Financing of Industry", *Economic and Political Weekly*, Vol. XVII, No.34, Aug. 21, 1982, pp. 1354–1355.

Sandara Subramanian, K., "Leasing, Hire/purchase and Bills Discounting", *The Chartered Accountant*, February, 1994.

Sengupta, Chinta Haran, "Leasing in Competitive Market: Tax Consideration", *The Management Accountant*, Vol. 26, No. 8, Aug. 1991.

Sriram, K., "*Handbook of Leasing, Hire/purchase and Factoring*", Published by ICFAI Hyderabad

Van Horne James, C., "*Financial Management and Policy*", Prentice-Hall of India, New Delhi, 1984.

Wachowicz, Jr., John M., and James Van Horne, "*Fundamentals of Financial Management*", Prentice-Hall of India, New Delhi, 1994.

Chapter

12 Securitization—A New Innovation

12.1 INTRODUCTION

The process of economic liberalization has opened up new vistas for the growth of the financial service sector. Proliferation of innovative financial techniques and new financial instruments in the financial market has started only in recent years in India. Asset securitization is an important financial innovation which stands out not only as important in itself, but also as the springhead of many innovative products and techniques. In India, asset securitization is gaining popularity as a result of expansion of financial market. Securitization packages are now being worked out both by banks and finance companies with the backing of underlying assets such as hire/purchase and properly receivables.

12.2 CONCEPT

Securitization, as a financing technique, originated in the U.S. during the 70s when the Government National Mortgage Association started trading in securities backed by pools of mortgage loans. These securities known as *mortgage pass through securities* facilitated investors in purchasing a fractional undivided interest in a pool of mortgage loans by providing for a share in the income and principal payments generated by the underlying mortgage.

Securitization is a synthetic technique of conversion of assets into securities, securities into liquidity, and subsequently into assets on an ongoing basis, increasing thereby the turnover of business and profit while also providing for flexibility in yield, pricing pattern, issuing risk, and marketability of instruments used to the advantage of both borrowers and lenders. In securitization, generally a financial institutions holds a pool of individual loans and receivables, create securities against them, get them rated, and sell them to investors at large. The most suitable assets for securitization for the banks and financial institutions are housing loans, car and truck loans, credit card receivables, trade receivables, etc. Theoretically, all assets that generate cash flows can be securitized.

12.2.1 Mechanism of Securitization

The crucial link in the securitization chain is the creation of a special purpose vehicle (SPV), which intermediates between the primary market for the underlying asset and the secondary market for the asset backed security. The steps involved in the securitization process are the following:

(1) The originator or lending institution identifies the assets out of its portfolio for securitization. The identification of the assets has to be done in a manner so that an optimum mix of homogeneous assets having almost same maturity forms the portfolio.

(2) The aforementioned pool of identified assets is then "passed through" to another institution, called a special purpose vehicle (SPV) usually by way of a trust. Such trust, which is usually an investment banker, issues the securities to investors. So once the assets are transferred, they are no longer held in the originator's portfolio.

(3) After acquisition of the assets, the SPV splits the pool into individual shares or securities and reimburses itself by selling these to investors. These securities are known as *pay or pass through certificates*. These securities are normally without recourse to the originator. Thus, investor can hold only 'SPV' liable for principal repayment and interest recovery.

(4) In order to make the issue attractive, the SPV enters into credit enhancement procedures either by obtaining an insurance policy to cover the credit losses or by arranging a credit facility from a third party lender to cover the delayed payments. To increase marketability of the securitized assets in the form of securities, these may be rated by some reputed credit rating agencies. Credit rating increases the trading potentials of the certificate thus its liquidity is enhanced. The investor's confidence is heightened owing to the third party objectivity of the rating agencies. The pass through certificates before maturity are tradeable in a secondary market to ensure liquidity for the

investors. Once the end investor gets hold of these instruments created out of securitization, he is to hold it for a specific maturity period which is well defined with all other related terms and conditions. On maturity, the end investors get redemption amount from the issuer along with interest due on the amount. Figure 12.1 gives the diagramatic representation of mechanism of securitization.

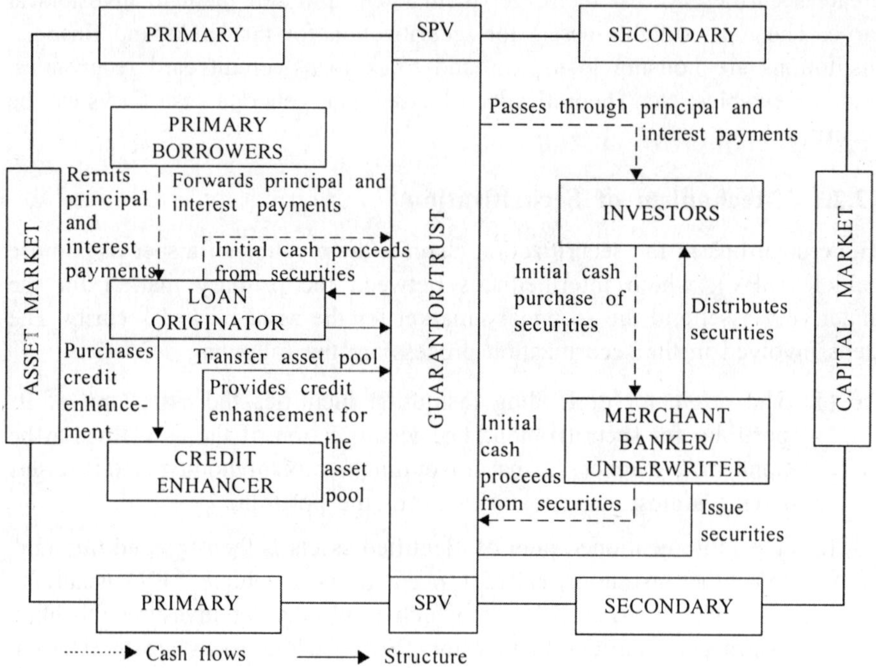

Source: National Housing Bank.

Fig. 12.1 Mechanism of securitization.

12.2.2 Importance and Utility

The phenomenal growth of securitization activities around the globe has only been possible due to the tremendous benefits that have been derived both by the financial institutions and the investors. In the Indian context, the study of securitization assumes great relevance in view of the rapid financial sector reforms, liberalization, and subsequent disintermediation taking place in the banking sector.

12.3 ADVANTAGES OF SECURITIZATION

12.3.1 Gains to Originators

Securitization offers the advantages of off-balance sheet funding as it converts an otherwise liquid asset into ready liquidity, enabling faster recovery of funds, which leads to higher business turnover and profitability. Further, the funding cost is substantially reduced through securitization, compared both to capital as also to conventional fund raising instruments like bonds, debentures, and commercial papers. Structured securitization enables the originators to access securities market at debt ratings higher than their own overall corporate ratings through the novel technique of credit enhancement and diversification of risk. This enables it to secure funds at lower cost. Additionally, securitization facilitates better balance sheet management as the risk weighting of assets now have been transferred to an SPV, under which these are not considered for capital adequacy calculation.

12.3.2 Gains to Investors

Securitization offers many new investment instruments for investors to meet their preferences. But investor will buy only if they are convinced about the risk involved. The unique advantage is that securitization enables the end-investor to look past the issuing entity to the collateral pool that the issue represents. This transparency reduces uncertainty for the investor as to the risk element.

12.3.3 Gains to Borrowers

As the relationship between the borrower and the lender remains unchanged, the process of securitization does not directly affect the borrower. But owing to the greater economy in the use of capital, financial institution passes the benefits to borrowers by providing cheaper funds.

12.3.4 General Gains

Economy as a whole is benefited through securitization. Capital utilization improves in the economy where there are restrictions on lending and recycling of funds.

12.4 GLOBAL SCENARIO

Securitization having originated in the U.S. started with the residential mortgage markets promoted with the support of U.S. Government through Federal National Mortgage Association (FNMA), Government National Mortgage Association (GNMA), and the Federal Home Loan Mortgage Corporation who bought residential mortgage loans, made pools out of them, and then issued mortgage backed securities against guaranteeing payment of principal and interest. It is in March 1985 that non-mortgage collaterals started getting securitized in the USA. The first offering of 192 million of leased backed notes for Sperry Lease Finance Corporation was underwritten by first Boston. Since the concept has grown enormously, today the total value of the asset based securities in USA is estimated at over US $1000 billion. Next to the USA, the only place to have a fairly developed market is the UK. In the UK, it is Bank of England that has issued various guidelines and helped in developing the product. Securitized debt instruments are now popular in Italy, Australia, Canada, France, Spain, Japan, and many other countries and most countries have passed new legislation to assist the process of securitization.

The securitization market has grown much faster than the debt securities market globally. The capital market debt comprises about 25–50% of the overall debt outstanding in the European economies, whereas this figure is closer to 70% in the U.S. economy. Through securitization, an increasing proportion of the bank debt is also getting diverted to the capital markets. The break-up of the U.S. securities market (including government debt), which is world's largest market is provided in the Fig. 12.2.

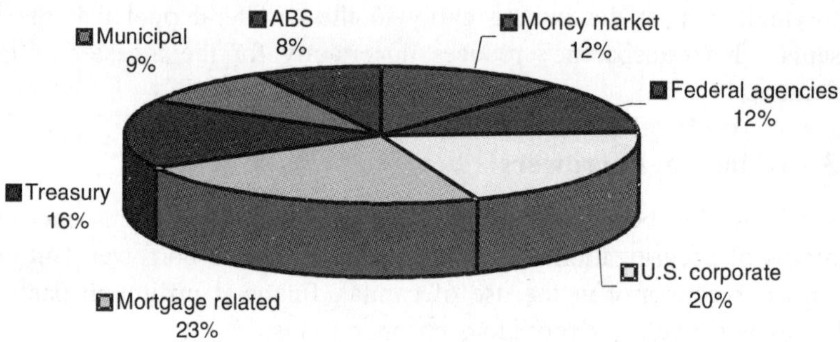

Fig. 12.2 U.S. securities market 2003 Q1.

Securitization comprises a significant proportion of the U.S. securities market. The growth of the ABS/MBS securities in USA relative to other securities over the last decade is shown in Fig. 12.3.

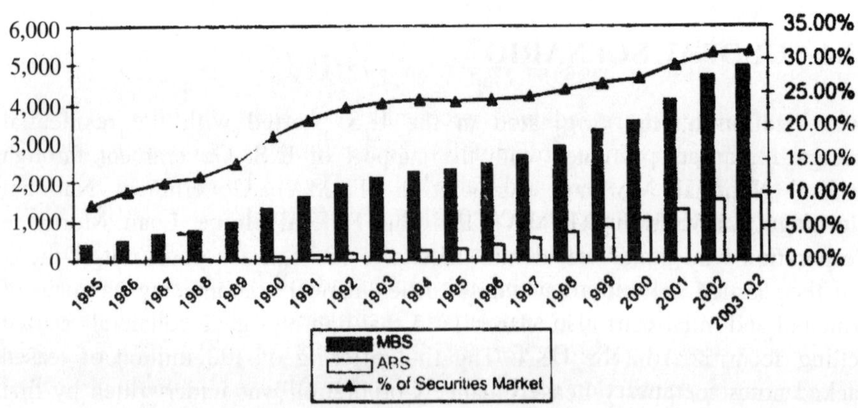

Fig. 12.3 Securitized debt in U.S. dollar (million).

This trend has also been witnessed in other developed countries and in recent times, in the developing countries.

12.5 SECURITIZATION IN INDIA

The technique of securitization is of recent development in India but so far it has been a slow response by the investing public despite the numerous benefits. The first securitization deal in India was made by Citibank, HDFC, and ICICI in February, 1991. Since then Citibank has, with different originators, structured securities in the tune of about Rs. 180 crores. Recently, it was announced that HDFC will securitize housing loans receivable of around Rs. 50 crores through ILFs. The main motive of NBFCs to go for securitization has been to unlock the investment in all liquid assets, recycle cash, and exploit the new business opportunities. In the NBFCs sector, some companies like Sundaram Finance which has access to low cost funding sources did not find securitization attractive. As of 1995, 24 pools of securitized debt have been issued by 10 issuers/originators during the previous four years. Only two of the 24 securitized pools comprised of truck and LCVs receivables while others were all car receivables. Table 12.1 lists some of the originators and the amount securitized.

Table 12.1 Indian originators and their status

Originator	No. of pools	Amount (Rs. in crores)
Citibank	3	50.00
Ashok Leyland Finance	2	43.17
Lease Finance	3	54.45
Tata Finance	3	36.36
SRF Finance	2	29.19
20th Century Finance	2	9.73
Esanda Finance	2	16.26
Overseas Sanmar	3	16.26
CIFCO	1	10.00

Source: CRISIL Rating Scan Various Issues 1993–95.

The assets securitized were receivables from the auto pool. ICICI had securitized assets of the order of Rs. 27.5 billion in its books as on March 1999. Global Tele-Systems Ltd. raised about Rs. 1.3 billion by securitizing its telecom receivables in March 2000. National Housing Bank (NHB) also made an issue of mortgage backed securities during August 2000 involving a deal size of Rs. 19,354 billion comprising 11,106 individual housing loans of HDFC and LICHF. SBI caps also structured a securitization deal for Karnataka State Electricity Board (KSEB) for Rs. 2.94 billion. NHB completed another securitization transaction of Rs. 920 million in May 2001. ICICI has initiated securitization deals worth Rs. 70 billion during 2001–2002 through pass through certificate and other routes.

Some of the major securitization transactions in India in 2002–2003 include ICICI's Rs. 23 billion corporate loan proposal, CitiBank's personal loan deal of Rs. 2.84 billion, HDFC's Rs. 1.56 billion housing loan deal, and KMFL's Rs. 760 million housing loan receivables deal. CRISIL is reported to have rated about Rs. 20 billion over 150 securitized transactions between 1991 and 2002.

The important highlight of the present scenario is that the market for securitization is dominated by a few players.The structured finance market in India has grown in last 3–4 years as shown in Fig. 12.4.

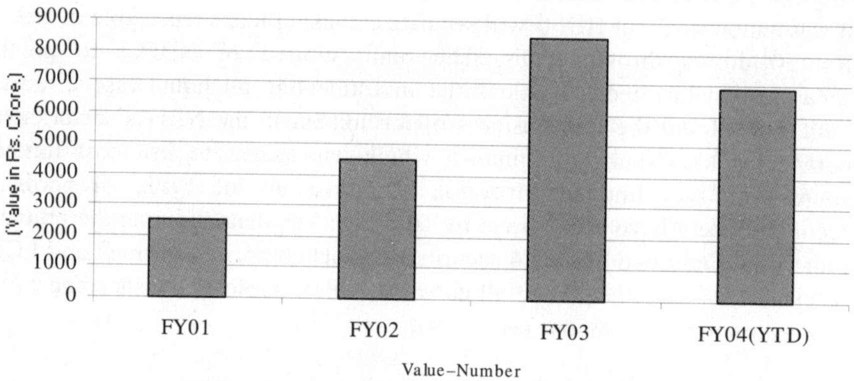

Fig. 12.4 Indian structured finance market.

As can be seen, the market has grown by almost six times in last three years. This growth has been led by Auto loan Backed Securitization (ABS), followed by corporate Loan Sell Offs (LSO), and Mortgage Backed Securities (MBS). Other asset classes including Collateralized Debt Obligations (CDO), Partial Guarantee (PG) structures, and Future Flow Transactions (FFT) have formed a smaller proportion of the issuance and there is significant potential for increase in the market size. The product-wise break-up of issuance in last two and half years is given in Fig. 12.5.

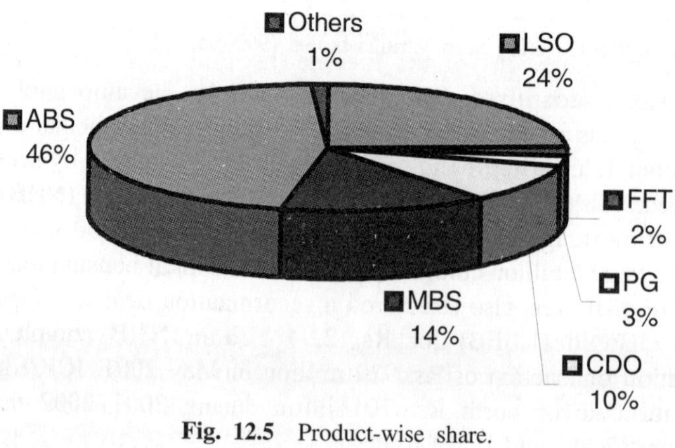

Fig. 12.5 Product-wise share.

However in the present phase of the move towards deregulation and liberalization, securitization has become both opportunities and challenges. It is an opportunity for all commercial organizations, due to its merits as an innovative low cost funding source, ensuring economy in use of capital.

12.5.1 Challenges

In order to make securitization of debt a popular route for raising, resources by banks and finance companies in India, a conducive environment is to be created at the national level by the regulatory authorities, Government, and infrastructural development. In the Indian context, the most important factor which could popularize the market would be credit enhancement. Credit enhancement helps making the transaction attractive on one hand and also get an investment credit rating for the instrument. Since a variety of factors are taken into consideration for rating, it would give a boost to investor confidence in the newly created market of instruments built upon underlying debts which have qualitative differences. The National Stock Exchange has announced that it will allow listing of securitized assets, which help to develop an active secondary market and improve liquidity. So, the requirement of market makers is added to this to improve the secondary market gratuity funds, insurance funds, mutual funds, and provident funds that have restrictions on investing in mortgage foreclosures. When the market driven interest rates come in, investors would like to have the facility of prepayment. Again at the national level, it would be necessary for RBI to frame guidelines addressing various aspects of the securitization process for banks and NBFCs. As the first deal in securitization between HDFC and Infrastructure Leasing and Financial Services Ltd. for securitization of mortgage loans failed because of legal complexities, it would be necessary for the Institute of Chartered Accountants and RBI to lay down the norms for treatment of securitized transactions with a view to maintaining uniformities. Also Companies Act 1956 and Banking Regulation Act 1949, would need amendments to justify the benefits of transfer of assets under securitization of debt. Another major area that needs attention involves issues relating to taxation and legal provisions.

The current provisions of the Income Tax Act 1961 may even impose double taxation and it is not clear whether the originator, as primary recipient of payment of interest and principal, is subject to taxation of interest income. So to encourage the development of the market, the tax authorities could consider tax exemption for securitized paper. A prerequisite for widespread securities action is the development of an extensive and accessible database. So the financial institution should maintain online records of delinquency rates, default history, and repayment performance. Standardized underwriting norms define the guidelines for evaluating the borrower's ability to pay and set standard ratios for loan to cost and instalment to income. Not only such norms smoothen the entire process, it would also reduce information costs to the investor. Another issues is that the secondary market for debt, which offers an easy exit route to investors is still not developed. Public sector banks, which are dealing with a huge pool of debts, have not yet looked at these products seriously. Transactions and provident funds, which are the major sources of huge funds, have limitations on investment in structured products. Though the SARFAESI law has been passed, a number of gray areas still remain to be considered. Stamp duty is one of the major hindrances to the development of securitization in India. Further India sees the lack of effective foreclosure laws. Lastly, securitization of debt also continue to reduce the opportunity cost to capital and act as a versatile mechanism, which facilitates transferring capital from less efficient to more efficient activities.

SUMMARY

Securitization has a lot of potential to satisfy investor preference regarding risk, yield, tenor, reducing the collateral required, giving a face lift to the balance sheet, and enhancing overall liquidity. But there are several legal problems that need to be surmounted before it becomes a reality. So supportive measures like abolition of stamp charges, change in accounting conventions, and development of secondary market need to be undertaken to make asset securitization a smooth process in the coming years.

REVIEW QUESTIONS

1. Explain the meaning of securitization and its modus operandi.
2. Discuss the various advantages of securitization.
3. Discuss the future prospects of securitization in India.

QUIZ

Fill up the blanks.

1. Securitization has originated on ....
2. Securitization offers the advantage of .... sheet funding.
3. The first securitization deal in India was made by ....
4. The pool of identified assets which is passed through to another institution, is called a ....
5. Securitization is mainly associated with the assets of .... companies.

REFERENCES

Chakravarthi, Anand, "Securitization Market: Indian and Global Scenario", *ICFHI Reader*, March 2004.

Bansal, L.K., "Asset Securitization", *Journal of Accounting and Finance*, Vol. IX, No. 2, Feb., 1995.

Gupta, G.D., "Debt Securitization—Making Money from Money", *The Chartered Accountant*, May, 1997, pp. 24–39.

Narender, V., and C.S. Mishra, "Securitization—A New Mode of Financing", *Chartered Secretary,* Feb. 1996, pp. 174–176.

Nair, T.C., and R. Gurcemurthy, "Securitization of Debt: Some Issues", *The Journal of the Indian Institute of Bankers*, July 1995, pp. 135–139.

Rai, Rita, "Securitization: The Concept and its Relevance to Indian Banks", *IBA Bulletin*, Vol. XIV, No. 10, October 1994.

Sen, Abhijit, "Securitization—Plenty of Potential", *Chartered Financial Analyst*, Dec. 1995, pp. 47–48.

Surey, Rajat and Kalpesh Gada, "Securitization in India: Coming of Age", *ICFAI Reader*, January 2004.

Thenmozhi, M., "Critical Issues in Debt Securitization in India", *Accounting in Changing Perspectives*, January, 1997.

The Economic Times, 1994–1996.

The State Bank of India, *Monthly Review*, October, 1992.

Chapter 13
Foreign Direct Investment in India

13.1 INTRODUCTION

The investment scenario has been buoyant and moving upwards since the initiation of economic reforms. This has become inevitable due to radical as well as structural changes which have taken place worldover. So in order to globalize an economy, four vital facets, namely, resources, sophisticated technology, managerial skills, and innovative marketing techniques are required which ultimately ask for liberalization. However, this concept has taken ground very late in India. It was necessary to encourage Indian companies to become global with a view to integrate India with the global market. Since the introduction of economic reforms programme in 1991, India has emerged as a principal host and source in the region. There is a remarkable change in the GDP and GDS. The capital market has become very active and FIIs, foreign investment banks, and asset management companies have shown increasing interest in investing in India.

13.2 TRENDS IN FDI FLOWS

In a globalized financial market, FDI has become an important source of private external finance for those economies where the domestic capital market is either not highly developed or not capable of fulfilling the increasing fund needs of different sectors of the economy. Figure 13.1 depicts the global

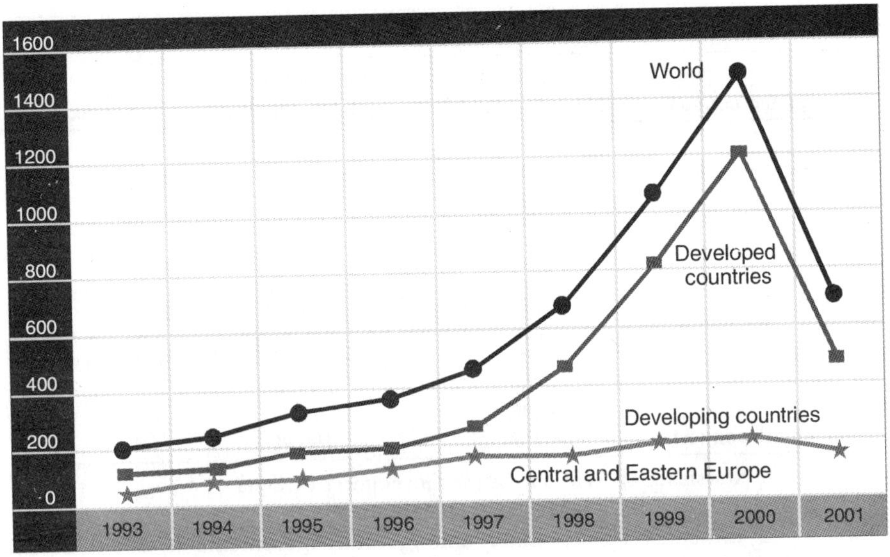

Fig. 13.1 Global inflows of FDI 1993–2001 USD billions, by group of countries.

inflows of FDI in the period 1993–2001. Table 13.1 presents the FDI inflows of major economies of the world in 2002.

Table 13.1 FDI inflows to major economies in 2002

Host region/Economy	Amount (US $ billion)	Host region/Economy	Amount (US $ billion)
World	651.2(100.0%)	Developing countries	162.1(100%)
Developed countries	460.3(70.7%)	Africa	11.0(6.8%)
Developing countries	162.1(24.9%)	Latin America and the Caribbean	56.0(34.6%)
Others	28.8(4.4%)	Central and Eastern Europe	28.7(17.7%)

Source: UNCTAD 2003—The principal destinations of FDI are the developed countries.

Since the initiation of India's new economic liberalization regime, there has been an enormous increase in the FDI inflows from the newly emerged investing nations. Table 13.2 presents the country-wise break-up of approved foreign investments.

Table 13.2 Foreign direct investment approved (country-wise) from 1991 to 2000

Name of the country	No. of approvals	Percentage of total approval	Rank
USA	3882	20.5	1
Germany	2116	11.2	2
UK	1813	9.6	3
Japan	1259	6.7	4
The Netherlands	901	4.8	5
Italy	839	4.4	6
Switzerland	773	4.1	7
France	682	3.6	8
Mauritius	673	3.6	9
Singapore	560	3.0	10
Total	**13,498**	**71.3**	
Total of all countries	**18,919**	**100.00**	

Source: SIA Newsletter of Relevant Issues, Government of India.

Table 13.2 indicates USA's share among total agreements is about 20.5% followed by Germany, UK, Japan, Netherlands, Italy, etc. It is significant to note that some of the new countries are also making investment in India. This may be due to economic reforms in India and the encouragement from the Government through liberalization and globalization policies which attract various foreign countries to invest in India. Table 13.3 presents the FDI inflows to some Asian economies in 2002.

Table 13.3 FDI inflows to Asian economies in 2002

Country	Amount (US $ billions)
Asia	95.1 (100.0%)
China	52.7 (57.2%)
India	5.5 (5.8%)
Korea	2.0 (2.1%)
Malaysia	3.2 (3.4%)
Philippines	1.1 (1.2%)
Thailand	1.1 (1.2%)
Others	29.5 (31.0%)

China and India are the giants of the developing world. In 2002, China was the largest recipient of FDI in the world, surpassing even the U.S. India is ranked first in South Asia. China attracted almost ten times more FDI than India in 2002, accounting for 4.3% of its GDP while India's FDI accounted for 1.1% of its GDP.

Table 13.4 shows the inflows of FDI on year-wise basis. It is very clear that the countries dominating the FDI in India are USA, Japan, Germany, South Korea, and the Netherlands. The annual share of USA in India's total FDI is 20%. Mauritius tops the list of investors with 31% share in total investment inflow.

Table 13.4 Foreign direct investment inflows (country-wise)

(US $ million)

Name of country	92–93	93–94	94–95	95–96	96–97	97–98	98–99	99–2000	Total (annual average) '92–'93 to '99-2000	% share in total
Mauritius	N.A.	N.A.	196.7	507.3	846.4	900.4	590.0	501	442.7	31
USA	21.7	98.8	202.8	194.6	241.6	687.4	452.8	355	218.8	20
Japan	25.7	36.9	94.9	60.9	96.7	163.5	235.1	142	107.0	07
Italy	N.A.	N.A.	N.A.	N.A.	N.A.	27.7	42.9	115.6	38.9	03
Germany	21.4	35.1	34.6	99.7	166.2	151.4	113.5	031	81.6	06
South Korea	N.A.	N.A.	12.0	23.9	6.3	333.1	85.3	008	58.6	04
Netherlands	21.0	46.5	44.7	49.8	123.7	158.9	53.3	082	72.5	02
Singapore	2.8	9.9	24.5	60.1	75.6	N.A.	N.A.	N.A.	21.6	05
UK	6.6	64.1	143.5	70.9	54.2	N.A.	N.A.	N.A.	42.4	03
Switzerland	35.3	22.5	26.2	32.6	N.A.	N.A.	N.A.	N.A.	14.6	01
Others	145.5	55.2	92.1	318.2	418.6	518.4	354.4	337	279.9	20
Total	**1441.6**	**369.0**	**872.0**	**1418.0**	**2057.0**	**2956.0**	**2000**	**1581**	**1441.6**	**100**

Source: RBI—Annual Reports of the Relevant Year.

From the geographical distribution of FDI shown in Table 13.5, it is evident that these investments have been concentrated in a few developed regions of India.

Table 13.5 Foreign direct investment approved in India from April 1991 to Nov. 1999

State	Investment (Rs. in crores)	% share to total investment
Punjab	1,926	0.92
Haryana	2,931	1.41
West Bengal	7,675	3.69
Andhra Pradesh	8,661	4.16
Gujarat	10,902	5.24
Tamil Nadu	13,595	6.53
Karnataka	15,785	7.58
Maharashtra	27,905	13.40
Others	1,18,863	57.08
All India	2,08,243	100

The state of Maharashtra stood as the most dominated destination of FDI followed by Karnataka, Tamil Nadu, and Gujarat during the period April 1991 to Nov. 1999. The reasons for this concentration of FDI could be the FDI-friendly image of the respective state, level of infrastructural developments, as well as investments. Other reasons may be the emergence of IT industry in most of the dominating states.

13.3 SECTOR-WISE ANALYSIS OF FOREIGN INVESTMENT APPROVALS

It has been analyzed sector-wise to determine which sector of the Indian economy has attracted maximum foreign investment proposals and which sector has lost its performance.

Table 13.4 highlights the sectoral composition of FDI inflows since 1992–93 to 2000–2001. The country needs huge sums of FDI for the creation of productive assets and for the development of basic infrastructure in the country. The actual inflows, in many cases are coming either in the form of acquisitions of already created local assets or into the services sectors, which do not involve any huge outlays of capital. And a large proportion of the inflows that are coming into the country are concentrated in some select sectors, leaving the others remain capital-hungry forever. In fact from August 1991 to March 2000, around 80% of the approved FDI went into six sectors, namely fuels, telecom, metallurgical industries, transport, service sector, and electrical equipment. The remaining 20% had to be shared by 30 odd industrials sectors. It is evident from Table 13.6 that engineering, electronics, equipments, and chemical and allied services sector together accounted for

Table 13.6 FDI inflows (industry-wise destination)

(US $ million)

Industry	1992–93	93–94	94–95	95–96	96–97	97–98	98–99	99–2000	2000–2001	Average	C.V.
Finance	3.7	42.2	97.7	270.0	217.0	147.9	184.8	20.0	40.0	113.7	79.21
Engineering	69.8	32.9	131.9	251.9	730.2	579.9	427.6	326.0	273.0	313.7	70.05
Electronics & equipments	32.8	57.1	56.4	129.6	153.6	644.6	228.3	172.0	213.0	187.5	93.08
Chemicals & allied	47.0	37.5	141.2	126.7	303.8	257.3	375.5	120.0	137.0	171.8	63.39
Services	2.4	20.2	93.4	100.5	15.2	321.3	368.5	116.0	226.0	140.4	90.61
Foods & Dairy	27.9	43.5	60.9	85.0	237.5	112.3	18.6	121.0	75.0	86.9	72.15
Pharmaceuticals	3.1	49.5	10.1	54.8	47.6	33.8	28.4	54.0	62.0	38.1	51.29
Computers	8.3	7.6	10.2	52.1	58.7	139.2	106.2	99.0	306.0	87.5	102.0
Others	**69.1**	**76.1**	**162.2**	**347.0**	**278.3**	**659.8**	**262.1**	**553.0**	**578.0**	**331.7**	**62.61**

nearly 54% of the total FDI inflow in 1992–93. On the other hand, finance, services sector, food and dairy, and pharmaceuticals sectors recorded significant improvement in FDI inflows during 1993–94. The erratic fluctuations in inflows of FDI into the different sectors continued in 1998–99. Engineering, chemicals and allied, food and dairy sectors had some positive increase in their inflows of FDI in 2000–2001.

13.4 CATEGORY-WISE FLOW OF FOREIGN INVESTMENT

The response of foreign investment inflows to reforms has been encouraging to a great extent. Since the initiation of economic reforms, the most striking aspect is the change in the hue of the capital inflows from foreign currency borrowings and official assistance to direct and portfolio investments by foreign investors. While bank loans and official development assistance during the period 1975–82 consisted of about 82% of the world's total capital flows, the Foreign Direct Investment and portfolio inflows were just around 11%. Now the FDI and portfolio investments constitute about 55% of the capital flows leaving the rest to bank loans and other forms of assistance. In India too, there has been a steady rise in the inflow of both FDI and portfolio investments since 1991, though the latter has gone down in some recent years.

It can be observed from Table 13.7 that the inflows from SIA/FIBP route accounted for 25.86% followed by RBI 20.8% of total inflows in 2002–03. In the portfolio investment, GDR accounted for 16.89% followed by FIIs 10.61%. The inflow from SIA/FIBP route during 1992–93 accounted for 39.71%, followed by RBI 7.51% and NRI 9.12%. The GDR accounted for 42.93% followed by FIIs 0.17%. So it can be concluded that there has been no consistency of inflows as fluctuated widely during 1992–93 to 2002–03.

13.5 ROLE OF FOREIGN INVESTMENT IN ECONOMIC DEVELOPMENT

The sweeping structural reforms brought in by the government during 1991 were in response to this macroeconomic instability. The reforms were intended to accomplish a fundamental transformation in the Indian economic structure, push up the growth process, and to integrate national economy with the global economic system. In every developing country, the economic development requires investment in certain projects relating to infrastructure development, basic industries etc. which are long gestation projects, low income yielding, but accelerate economic development. So the government has to initiate development activities for which foreign capital is essential. Once the economic engine is activated, in due course, the economic development begin to take place.

Table 13.7 Foreign investment flows

(US $ million)

Item	1990–91	1991–92	1992–93	1993–94	1994–95	1995–96	1996–97	1997–98	1998-99	1999–00	2000–01	2001–02	2002–03
1	2	3	4	5	6	7	8	9	10	11	12	13	14
(A) Direct investment	97	129	315	586	1314	2144	2821	3557	2462	2155	2339	3904	2574
(i) Government (SIA/FIPB)	—	66	222	280	701	1249	1922	2754	1821	1410	1456	2221	919
(ii) RBI	—	—	42	89	171	169	135	202	179	171	454	767	739
(iii) NRIs	—	63	51	217	442	715	639	241	62	84	67	35	—
iv) Acquisition of shares*	—	—	—	—	—	11	125	360	400	490	362	881	916
(B) Portfolio investment	6	4	244	3567	3824	2748	3312	1828	–61	3026	2760	2021	979
(i) GDRs/ADRs	—	—	240	1520	2082	683	1366	645	270	768	831	477	600
(ii) FIIs @	—	—	1	1665	1503	2009	1926	979	–390	2135	1847	1505	377
(iii) Offshare funds and others	6	4	3	382	239	56	20	204	59	123	82	39	2
Total (A + B)	**103**	**133**	**559**	**4153**	**5138**	**4892**	**6133**	**5385**	**2401**	**5181**	**5099**	**5925**	**3553**

Source: RBI Bulletin, April, 2004.

13.6 MAJOR CHALLENGES AND STRATEGY TO PROMOTE FDI

India has failed to attract huge external inflows into the infrastructure sector. The lack of proper business-quality infrastructural facilities in India is cited to be one of the main reasons for India's inability to attract huge FDI inflows. The overall political instability at the centre is another deterrent for FDI. Import substitution acted as a major disincentive for export promotion, which requires a degree of mental openness towards foreign investment and foreign technology. This is also another reason that foreign investment did not develop in the country. FDI companies are basically catering to the domestic markets because of the high protection and profitability of domestic sales. Highly profitable domestic market is also one of the reasons for the lack of competition in the economy and thus results in the inertia on the part of FDI companies to actively formulate an export promoting strategy. So to promote FDI flows to the country and to enhance their export intensity, India needs a consistent, coherent and comprehensive long-term export promotion strategy.

For strengthening competitiveness, it is essential that FDI companies create brand image for the goods produced in India by improving the quality of goods as well as the quality of labelling and packaging. These measures would not only improve the quality of Indian products but also reduce the outflow of foreign exchange from the country. Foreign investors are interested to enter such ventures which have export potential. So the development of proper transport facilities and modernization of ports is paramount. It is essential that India adopts and implements concepts like export processing zones, free trade zones, and special economic zones which provide free market environment to achieve export promotion objective. The Government should identify highly competitive sectors of economy to ascertain export growth areas in the continuously evolving dynamic world.

13.7 WHY INVEST IN INDIA?

Following may be listed as some reasons why India is the right place to invest. It has

(1) One of the largest economies in the world.

(2) Strategic location-access to the vast domestic and South Asian market.

(3) A large and rapidly growing consumer market of up to 300 million people, constitutes the market for branded consumer goods—estimated to be growing at 8% per annum. Demand for several consumer products is growing at over 12% per annum.

(4) Skilled manpower and professional managers are available at competitive cost.

(5) One of the largest manufacturing sectors in the world, spanning almost all areas of manufacturing activities.

(6) One of the largest pools of scientists, engineers, technicians, and managers in the world.

(7) Rich base of mineral and agricultural resource.

(8) Long history of market economy infrastructure.

(9) Sophisticated financial sector.

(10) Vibrant capital market with over 9,000 listed companies and market capitalization of US$ 154 billion (March, 1996).

(11) Well developed R&D infrastructure and technical and marketing services.

(12) Policy environment that provides freedom of entry, investment, location, choice of technology, production, import and export.

(13) Well balanced package of fiscal incentives.

(14) A sophisticated legal and accounting system.

(15) Rupee is convertible on current account at market-determined rate.

(16) Free and full repatriation of capital, technical fee, royalty, and dividends.

(17) A long history of stable parliamentary democracy.

13.8 BARRIERS FOR FDI IN INDIAN MARKET

Tarriffs and tax structure

MNC's are frustrated by the complicated tax and tariff structure followed in India. This is not just a concern for MNC's only, but also for the Indian businessmen. The complicated tax structure contributes to hassles and this makes the image of India bad in terms of foreign investors.

Bureaucracy

The attitude of government personnel and bureaucrats is one of the major hurdles on the path of FDI coming over to India. Many a times, due to this attitude there is delay in decision-making. Many MNCs due to their hassles and not cooperation hosts are not ready to come down to India for setting up their business.

Corruption

One of the major issues in India is corruption. This is one of the biggest drawbacks, as MNCs never favour to carry on business in countries where the entire systems are corrupt.

Infrastructure

This is one of the greatest drawbacks in India. In India, the condition of communication, transportation, and power supply is in a poor state. When the major infrastructure in the country is in a bad shape the operation of business houses are greatly affected.

Due to these reasons, the foreign companies are not attracted to India.

SUMMARY

There has been substantial improvement in the inflows of FDI to India. However, keeping in view the parameters of the global FDI supply position and the need of India in terms of further FDI, there are certain aspects need to be considered for sustaining the flow of FDI to India. The current institutional system does not provide a mechanism for aggressive marketing of India as an FDI location. The Indian investment centre, due to the lack of overseas offices, is not in a position to promote India abroad. It is now desirable to develop a mechanism, which will have the private sector as an integral partner. Several alternative models may be analyzed and develop to identify the best mechanism suited to India needs. Therefore a conducive business environment is required to attract FDI flow by providing better infrastructure, hassle-free government procedures, and most importantly, a degree of autonomy and freedom in various decision-making processes.

REVIEW QUESTIONS

1. Discuss the trends in FDI inflows.
2. What is the role of foreign investment in economic development?
3. Explain the category-wise inflows of foreign investment.

QUIZ

State whether the following are true or false.

1. The country needs huge sums of FDI for the creation of productive assets. (T/F)
2. Import substitution acted as a major disincentive for export promotion. (T/F)
3. FDI companies are basically catering to the domestic market. (T/F)

REFERENCES

Agrawal, H.N., "Foreign Collaborations and Capital Inflows in India: Emerging Trends and Implications", *The Indian Journal of Commerce*, Vol. No. 191, Part II June 1997.

Ambatkar, Sanjay, "Trends in Foreign Investment Interaction between India and Asia in 1990s", *Paradigm*, Vol. 5, No. 1, Jan–June 2001.

CMIE, Monthly Review of the Indian Economy, March 1994.

Economic Times, *Special Issue*, August 13, 1996.

Gangadhar, V., and M. Yadagiri, "Diversities in Foreign Direct Investments in India", *The Management Accountant*, Vol. 31, No. 1, Jan. 1996.

Iqbal, Badar Alam, "FDI Inflows Scenario is Not Bright one", *Monthly Commentary*, 1997.

Jain, S.K, "Indian Euro Issues—Boom or Depression", Financial Services, *The Economic Times*, March 1995.

Pailwar, Veena, "Foreign Direct Investment Flows to India and Export Competitiveness", *Productivity*, Vol. 42, No. 1, April–June 2001.

Patnaik, Umesh Chandra, "The GDR Route to Reach the International Capital Market", *The Utkal Business Review*, Vol. XIV, 1997–98.

Productivity, Vol. 35. No. 2, July–Sept., 1994.

Ray, Alok, "Foreign Capital in Asia and Pacific Region—Trends, Problems and Prospects", *Economic and Political Weekly*, Oct. 22, 1994.

Singh, K.P, and Sunil Kumar, "Foreign Direct Investment Flows and Indian Economy", *The Indian Journal of Commerce*, Vol. XLIX, Part IV, No. 189 Dec. 1996.

Srikanth, C., "Foreign Direct Investment: Prescription for Growth", *Chartered Financial Analyst*, Oct. 2000.

State Bank of India, Monthly Review, Aug. 1995.

RBI Bulletin, April, 2004.

Index